# ROUND-UP 5

## Contents

1. Present Forms ............... 3
2. Past Forms ............... 12
3. Future Forms ............... 25
4. Infinitive / -ing form / Participles ............... 33
- Revision Exercises I ............... 43
5. Modal Verbs ............... 46
6. Passive Voice ............... 57
7. Conditionals - Wishes ............... 66
8. Clauses ............... 76
- Revision Exercises II ............... 92
9. Reported Speech ............... 96
10. Nouns - Articles ............... 108
11. Causative Form (Having something done) ............... 116
12. Adjectives - Adverbs - Comparisons ............... 121
- Revision Exercises III ............... 134
13. Demonstratives - Pronouns - Possessives - Quantifiers ............... 139
14. Prepositions ............... 152
15. Questions and Answers ............... 158
- Revision Exercises IV ............... 167
- Summary of Tenses ............... 171
- Irregular Verbs ............... 173
- Appendix 1 ............... 174
- Appendix 2 ............... 176
- Pre-Tests ............... 177
- Progress Tests ............... 194

## Introduction

Round-Up 5 is aimed at intermediate students of the English language.
The aim of the book is to help students understand and use English grammar structures through exciting, full-colour illustrations and a variety of exercises. All material presented is structurally graded, with revision exercises after every 4 units. Four Pre-Tests are included at the end of the book for students to use as practice before their exam. Eight Progress Tests, each covering two consecutive units, are also included at the end of the book. These may be used to assess students' progress.

There are "Phrasal Verb and Idiom" sections at the end of each unit to help give students a feeling for everyday English language usage. There are also exercises practising prepositions with verbs, adjectives and nouns, along with an appendix which provides a reference for the structures. A regular "Tense Review" is provided to consolidate structures practised in earlier units, and the "In other words" section of each unit gives students the chance to practise the various ways of expressing similar ideas in English.

The oral activities which appear throughout the book help students practise the structures while having fun at the same time. They can be done after the presentation of the appropriate grammar structure or they can be used as revision material throughout the year. The writing activities reinforce students' writing ability.

The author, Virginia Evans, herself a teacher for many years, has written this book on the principle that every structure should first be heard, then practised in oral and finally in written form. The book, based on the use of full-colour visual stimuli, encourages students to speak before writing and allows them to practise English structures through a variety of enjoyable and useful activities.

The Student's Book is accompanied by a Teacher's Guide which contains lesson plans for the presentation of each unit, the answers to the exercises, Pre-Tests and Progress Tests in the Student's Book as well as four tests.

**Pearson Education Limited**,
Edinburgh Gate, Harlow
Essex, CM20 2JE, England
and Associated Companies throughout the world

www.longman.com

© Virginia Evans 1994
*All rights reserved: no part of this publication may be reproduced, stored in a retrieval system, or transmitted in anyform or by any means, electronic, mechanical, photocopying, recording or otherwise without the prior written permission of the copyright holders.*

First published in 1994 by E. Vlachou - "Express Publications".
This edition published by Pearson Education Limited 2003
Tenth impression 2009

Printed in China CTPSC/10

ISBN 978-0-582-82345-7

Illustrated by Philip Vazakas and Terry Wilson

# 1. Present Forms

- What **are** you **doing**, Jenny? You**'ve been sitting** quietly at your desk all morning.
- I**'m drawing** a picture of a cow eating grass, Miss.

- Where's the cow? Where's the grass? I **can't see** anything!
- Well, the cow **has gone** home, Miss, because there **isn't** any more grass!

| Present Simple | Present Cont. | Present Perfect | Present Perf. Cont. |
|---|---|---|---|
| **permanent situations or states**<br>She **works** as a nurse.<br>She **owns** a large shop. | **temporary situations**<br>They**'re staying** at the Park Hotel at present. | **recently completed actions**<br>She **has tidied** her room. (She has finished tidying her room. You can see it is tidy now. - evidence in the present) | **actions started in the past and continuing up to the present**<br>He**'s been writing** a letter for two hours. (He started two hours ago and he's still writing it.) |
| **repeated / habitual actions (especially with frequency adverbs: often, usually etc)**<br>I usually **get up** at 7.30. | **actions happening at or around the moment of speaking**<br>She **is looking** for a better job. | **actions which happened at an unstated past time and are connected with the present**<br>He **has lost** his keys. (He is still looking for them.) | **past actions of certain duration having visible results or effects in the present**<br>She**'s been crying**. (Her eyes are red.) |
| **permanent truths or laws of nature**<br>Money **doesn't buy** happiness.<br>Water **freezes** at 0°C. | **repeated actions with "always" expressing annoyance or criticism**<br>She**'s always interrupting** me! | **personal experiences/ changes which have happened**<br>I**'ve lost** 10 kilos. | **actions expressing anger, irritation, annoyance, explanation or criticism**<br>Who **has been using** my toothbrush? (annoyance) |
| **timetables/programmes (future meaning)**<br>The match **finishes** at 7.45.<br>The plane **leaves** at 6.05. | **fixed arrangements in the near future**<br>The Browns **are visiting** us tonight. (It's all arranged.) | **emphasis on number**<br>She**'s written** three letters since this morning.<br>She **has called on** two clients since 12 o'clock. | **emphasis on duration (usually with for, since or how long)**<br>She**'s been calling on** clients since this morning. |
| **reviews/sports commentaries/ dramatic narrative**<br>Meryl Streep **acts** brilliantly in this film. | **changing or developing situations**<br>His English **is getting** better. | colspan note below | |

**Note**: live, feel and work can be used either in the Present Perfect or the Present Perfect Cont. with no difference in meaning.
I**'ve been living**/I**'ve lived** in Rome for a year.

# 1. Present Forms

| | Time expressions used with: |
|---|---|
| **Present Simple** | every day/week/month/year, usually, often, always, rarely, never, sometimes, in the morning/evening/afternoon, at night, on Mondays etc |
| **Present Cont.** | now, at the moment, at present, nowadays, today, tonight, always, still etc |
| **Present Perfect** | just, ever, never, already, yet (negations & questions), always, how long, so far, recently, since (= from a starting point in the past), for (= over a period of time), today, this week / month etc |
| **Present Perf. Cont.** | how long, for, since |

**1** Put the verbs into the correct column in the 3rd person singular.

watch, play, buy, go, fly, get, drop, kiss, say, cry, write, mix, dry, sneeze, reach, pay, smash, try, drive

| + s | ss, sh, ch, x, o + es | vowel + y + s | consonant + y ➡ ies |
|---|---|---|---|
| gets | watches | plays | flies |

**2** Add -ing to the following verbs and put them into the correct column.

rub, listen, lie, use, bring, run, tie, dive, hope, go, die, cry, come, travel, put

| + ing | - ie ➡ y + ing | - e ➡ ing | double consonant + ing |
|---|---|---|---|
| listening | dying | diving | travelling |

**3** Write the past participle of the following verbs.

1. break ...broken...
2. meet ...............
3. swim ...............
4. finish ...............
5. bring ...............
6. send ...............
7. write ...............
8. read ...............

**4** Match the sentences with the meaning of the tense used in each of them.

1. He drinks a litre of milk every day.
2. Milk contains a lot of vitamins.
3. He is getting stronger.
4. She has just passed her exams.
5. She is having a party at the moment.
6. He has been working all day.
7. She has phoned him three times this morning.
8. He is always borrowing money from me.
9. She has been walking all morning. (Her feet are aching.)
10. They are getting married next week. (They've already sent the invitations.)

a. emphasis on duration
b. temporary situation
c. repeated action expressing annoyance
d. emphasis on number
e. habitual action
f. recently completed action
g. permanent truth
h. changing or developing situation
i. fixed arrangement in the near future
j. past action of certain duration having visible results in the present

1. ...e...  2. ........  3. ........  4. ........  5. ........
6. ........  7. ........  8. ........  9. ........  10. ........

# 1. Present Forms

**5** Fill in with Present Simple or Present Continuous.

June : Hi, Mum!
Mum : Hello, June. Where 1) ..*are you calling*.. (you / call) from?
June : I 2) *am* ............ (be) at work at the moment. My boss 3) *is having* (have) lunch with his wife now. He 4) *often takes* (often/take) her to lunch on Tuesdays.
Mum : Well, why 5) *do you phone* (you/phone)? Is there anything wrong?
June : No, I just want you to know that I 6) *am coming* (come) home next Saturday.
Mum : What time 7) *does your* (your train/arrive) in Leeds?
June : It 8) *leaves* (leave) London at 11 o'clock and 9) *arrives* (arrive) in Leeds at 2 o'clock.
Mum : See you on Saturday then.

## Stative Verbs

Verbs describing a permanent state (stative verbs) do not normally have continuous forms. These are:
**(1) verbs of the senses** : see, hear, smell, feel, taste etc (We often use **can** or **could** with these verbs. eg. *Can you see* that tall boy over there?) The verbs look, watch and listen express deliberate actions and can be used in continuous forms. eg. *Be quiet please! I'm listening* to the news. But: *I can't hear* you. *Can you speak* louder, please? The verbs feel and hurt can be used in either continuous or simple forms, though.
eg. A: *How are you feeling* today? or *How do you feel* today?
    B: *My leg is hurting*. or *My leg hurts*.
**(2) verbs of opinion** : agree, believe, consider etc **(3) verbs of emotions** : feel, forgive, hate, like, love etc
**(4) other verbs** : appear (=seem), be, belong, fit (= be the right shape and size for sth), have (=possess), know, look (= appear), need, prefer, require, want, weigh, wish etc
eg. *He knows* where Peter is. (**not** is knowing)

Some stative verbs (see, smell, taste, feel, think, have etc) have continuous forms but there is a difference in meaning.

| STATE | ACTION |
|---|---|
| I **think** she's rich. (= I believe) | I'm **thinking** about your plan. (= I'm considering) |
| The milk **tastes** awful. (= it has a bad flavour) | He's **tasting** the sauce; it might need some salt. (= he's trying its flavour) |
| He **has** a pet dog. (= he owns) | He's **having** dinner now. (= he's eating) |
| This cloth **feels** like velvet. (= has the texture) | She's **feeling** her way in the dark. (= she's finding her way) |
| I **see** you're in trouble. (= I understand) | I'm **seeing** my lawyer tonight. (= I'm visiting) |
| The kitchen **smells** of burnt meat. (= has the smell) | Why **are you smelling** your food? (= trying the smell of) |
| He **comes** from Spain. (= he was born in) | He's **coming** from Spain. (= he's travelling from) |
| I **love** holidays. (in general) | I'm **loving** this holiday. (= I'm enjoying; specific) |
| Your hair **looks** great. (= it appears) | She's **looking** at some old photographs. (= she's examining) |
| The baby **weighs** 5 kilos. (= it is) | I'm **weighing** myself on my new scales. (= I'm finding out my weight) |
| Ann **is** very tall. | Ann **is being** very kind to me these days. (= she's behaving) |

5

## 1. Present Forms

### 6  Underline the correct item.

1. I <u>see</u> / am seeing that the situation is out of control.
2. The sausages **are tasting**/**taste** delicious.
3. **Do you enjoy**/**Are you enjoying** this party?
4. You haven't said a word all morning. What **are you thinking**/**do you think** about?
5. He **has**/**is having** a Siamese cat.
6. These flowers **are smelling**/**smell** nice.
7. I **don't know**/**am not knowing** where she keeps the keys.
8. Why **are you feeling**/**do you feel** your pockets? Have you lost anything?
9. Why **do you smell**/**are you smelling** the milk? Do you think it has gone off?
10. Anna is Italian. She **is coming**/**comes** from Italy.
11. That dress **looks**/**is looking** nice on you.
12. Paul **listens**/**is listening** to a new record in his room.
13. If you **don't look**/**aren't looking** at that comic book, I'd like to see it.
14. Joan **weighs**/**is weighing** 50 kilos.
15. Mary **is**/**is being** very naughty these days.

### 7  Fill in with Present Simple or Continuous.

Sue : What 1) ...*are you doing*... (you/do) now?
Mark : I 2) ...*'m looking*... (look) through these old film magazines. Look, here's an old picture of Jack Nicholson.
Sue : Oh, I 3) ...*think*... (think) he 4) ...*looks*... (look) awful! And his suit 5) ...*doesn't fit*... (not/fit) him properly.
Mark : Yes, I 6) ...*agree*... (agree). And he 7) ...*appears*... (appear) to be really angry. I wonder what he 8) ...*is thinking*... (think) about.
Sue : He 9) ...*is*... (be) in that new film that's on at the Odeon now, isn't he?
Mark : Yes, I saw it last night. He 10) ...*looks*... (look) very different now. He 11) ...*weighs*... (weigh) a lot more.
Sue : I 12) ...*hope*... (hope) it's a good film. I 13) ...*am seeing*... (see) it tonight. Stuart 14) ...*is taking*... (take) me. Actually, he 15) ...*is being*... (be) very nice to me these days.
Mark : He probably 16) ...*wants*... (want) to borrow some money.
Sue : I 17) ...*see*... (see). That explains it.

### 8  Fill in: yet or already.

Mike : Haven't you cleaned the bathroom 1) ..*yet*..?
Chris : Stop complaining! You've 2) ....*already*.... asked me that three times today. Why is it so important?
Mike : I've 3) ..*already*.. told you. My parents are coming to stay this weekend.
Chris : Well, don't worry! They haven't come 4) ....*yet*...., have they? Anyway, it's not my turn to clean the bathroom. I've 5) ...*already*... done it this month.
Mike : That's not true. You've been living here for nearly a year and I haven't seen you do any cleaning 6) ..*yet*..

### 9  Fill in: since or for.

John and Norma have been married 1) ..*for*... 20 years. They have been living in New York 2) ....*since*.... 1989. John has been working on Wall Street 3) ....*for*.... four years and he has made a lot of money 4) ....*since*.... he started working there. Norma hasn't worked 5) ....*since*.... they moved to New York but she has been writing a book 6) ....*for*.... the past two years. She has had a lot of spare time 7) ....*since*.... their son left home four years ago to work in France.

# 1. Present Forms

## Have gone to / Have been to / Have been in

He **has gone to** Brussels. ( =He's there or on his way to Brussels.)
He **has been to** Brussels once. ( =He's visited Brussels but he's back now.)
He **has been in** Brussels for two months. ( =He's in Brussels now.)

**10** Fill in : has - have been in/to, has - have gone to.

Editor : Where's Stevens? I haven't seen him for days.
Secretary : He 1) ...*has gone to*... Washington to interview Kim Basinger.
Editor : How long 2) ...has... he ...been in... Washington?
Secretary : Three days.
Editor : What about Milton and Knowles?
Secretary : They 3) ...have gone... London. They're going to interview the Royal Family.
Editor : 4) ...has been... anyone ...gone to... Paris to talk to Alain Delon?
Secretary : Smith 5) ...has been to... his country house. He interviewed him there yesterday actually. He's coming back today.

**11** Fill in : yet, since, for, tonight, often or how long.

1. John is flying to Nicosia ....*tonight*................
2. She hasn't met Cathy ........yet...................
3. I haven't seen him ......since........... last week.
4. ....how long...... have you been working here?
5. She ......often............... cooks exotic dishes.
6. Jim has been in Lisbon .....for....... four years.

**12** Match the sentences with the meaning of the tense used in each of them.

1. Vieira passes to Henry ... and Henry scores!
2. Who's been drinking my orange juice?
3. Light travels faster than sound.
4. He's been watching TV since 6 o'clock.
5. Spencer opens the door and sees the murderer.
6. He lives in Tokyo.
7. I've learnt a lot in this class.
8. The film starts at 11 o'clock.
9. My mother is writing a book.
10. He has written to the Prime Minister.

a. action started in the past and continuing up to the present
b. permanent situation
c. past action at an unstated time connected with the present
d. sports commentary
e. personal experience/change which has happened
f. action happening at/around the moment of speaking
g. timetable
h. action expressing irritation
i. dramatic narrative
j. law of nature

1. ...d...  2. ...........  3. ...........  4. ...........  5. ...........
6. ...........  7. ...........  8. ...........  9. ...........  10. ...........

## 1. Present Forms

**13** Put the verbs in brackets into Present Perfect or Present Perfect Continuous.

Dear Linda,
I'm glad to hear that you are enjoying yourself in Australia. Things at home are the same as usual. Your father 1) ...has been working... (work) very hard. Susan 2) ...hasn't... (just/pass) her driving test. Alex 3) ...hasn't... (not/write) for weeks, probably because he 4) ...has been... (study) very hard for his exams. Uncle Tom 5) ...has been... (build) a shed in the garden. I think it will be ready next month. Mr Brown 6) ...hasn't been... (not/feel) well recently. He 7) ...has visited... (visit) the doctor four times this month. The dog 8) ...has had... (have) three puppies. Mrs Smith 9) ...hasn't opened... (not/open) her new shop yet. The decorators 10) ...have been... (paint) it for weeks. I hope you enjoy the rest of your stay in Australia. 11) ...Have you seen... (you/see) the famous Opera House yet? Tina sends her love. Write to me soon.
Love,
Mum

**14** Fill in with Present S., Present Cont., Present Perfect or Present Perfect Cont.

Arthur : I 1) ....'ve been searching...... (search) for a house for a week now but so far I 2) ...haven't found... (not/find) anything suitable.
Sandra : Why 3) ...do you want... (you/want) to move?
Arthur : Well, the people living next to me 4) ...are... (be) the main problem. They 5) ...are always arguing... (always/argue), especially at night.
Sandra : Oh dear! 6) ...have you ever complained... (you/ ever/complain) to them?
Arthur : Yes, but they 7) ...don't stop... (not/stop). They 8) ...keep on... (keep on) making noise. I 9) ...haven't... (not/be able) to sleep well lately, and I 10) ...have been feeling... (feel) sleepy all week.
Sandra : How awful!

**15** Fill in with Present Perfect or Present Perfect Continuous.

**Robinson Crusoe has been stuck on a desert island for the past six months. Here is a letter he wrote and put in a bottle :**

Dear Anybody,
I 1) ...have been... (be) on this island for six months now. It is a miracle that I 2) 've ...survived... (survive) for this long. I 3) 've been eating... (eat) fish and fruit since I got here. Fortunately, I 4) ...haven't seen... (not/see) any dangerous animals yet. When I arrived here the weather was fine, but it 5) ...has been raining... (rain) continuously for the past two weeks, so I 6) 've ...built... (build) a shelter out of sticks and leaves, which is really quite cosy. My main problem is loneliness, as I 7) ...haven't spoken... (not/speak) to anyone for so long. Recently I 8) 've been talking... (talk) to myself, but it isn't very interesting. Please help me.
R. Crusoe

## 1. Present Forms

**16** Fill in with Present S., Present Cont., Present Perfect or Present Perfect Cont.

Tom: 1) ...Have you seen... (you/see) the state of this kitchen? Someone 2) has been washing (wash) clothes in the sink and they're still there!
Fred: Yes, I know. I usually 3) ...use... (use) the bath, but it 4) ...is... (be) too dirty at the moment.
Tom: Why didn't you clean it? You 5) have been living (live) here for two months now, and I 6) have never seen (never/see) you do any housework.
Fred: What do you mean? I 7) have washed (wash) the dishes at least three times and I always 8) make ........... (make) my bed.
Tom: Rubbish! You 9) are always making (always/make) a mess and not cleaning up afterwards.
Fred: What about you? You 10) are always drinking (always/drink) my milk! (annoyance)
Tom: Don't be ridiculous! Where 11) are you going (you/go)?
Fred: Out! I 12) am seeing (see) my girlfriend this evening. = visiting
Tom: What about the kitchen?
Fred: Bye!

### Oral Activity 1

The teacher divides the class into two teams. He/She sets a situation on the board. Then he/she shows the students word flashcards with the time adverbs from page 4. The teams in turn make sentences using the time adverb shown each time. Each correct sentence gets 1 point. The team with the most points is the winner.

**Situations:** she/clean/room, she/iron/clothes, he/wash/dishes, he/write/letter etc

Teacher: (shows **now**)
Team A S1: She's cleaning the room now.

Teacher: (shows **already**)
Team B S1: She has already cleaned the room. etc

### Oral Activity 2

The teacher prepares a list of time expressions and divides the class into two teams. He/She then starts a story. The teams in turn continue the story using the time expression given by the teacher. Each correct sentence gets 1 point. The team with the most points is the winner.

Teacher: **on Sundays**
  We get up late on Sundays.
  **today**
Team A S1: But today we got up early because we are going for a picnic.
Teacher: **yet**

Team B S1: My brother hasn't got up yet.
Teacher: **still**
Team A S2: He's still sleeping.
Teacher: **at the moment**
Team B S2: Mother is trying to wake my brother up at the moment. etc

## 1. Present Forms

### Writing Activity 1

Write the letter in full sentences. Use the present forms.

Dear Ted,
1. I write / you / London.
2. I be / here / a week / and / I enjoy myself / very much.
3. So far / I see / most of / important historic places.
4. I usually / spend / several hours every day / in museums and galleries.
5. The hotel / I stay / be / lovely / but / be very expensive,
6. so I plan / move / cheaper one / rest / my stay.
7. Tomorrow / I take / trip through Kent / which / I look forward to.
8. I hope / you be / OK.

                See you soon,
                Richard

### Writing Activity 2

Use this list of adjectives (happy, pleased, desperate, sad, depressed, angry) to write a letter of 60-80 words to a friend, giving the good/bad news about people you both know.

Dear Paul,
    I'm fine. Everyone here is OK, though we all miss you a lot. Ann is very happy because she has moved to a bigger house. ...

### In Other Words

I've never eaten pizza before.
It's the first time I've ever eaten pizza.

I've never read such a good book.
It's the best book I've ever read.

**17** Rephrase the following sentences.

1. I have never tasted muesli before. It's *the first time I've ever tasted muesli*.
2. I've never seen such a boring film. It's *the most boring film I've ever seen*.
3. He has never been to New York before. It's *the first time he has ever been to NY*.
4. She has never had such a delicious meal. It's *the most delicious meal she has ever had*.
5. She's never flown before. It's *the first time she has ever flown*.

**18** Rephrase the following sentences using the words in bold type.

1. She has never been to the club before.
   **first** ........ *It's the first time she has ever been to the club.*
2. She has never heard such a funny story.
   **funniest** *It's the funniest story she has ever heard.*
3. It's the first time she has ever read Tolstoy.
   **never** *She has never read Tolstoy before.*
4. It's the worst headache she's ever had.
   **bad** *She has never had such a bad headache before.*
5. He's never played cricket before.
   **ever** *It's the first time he has ever played cricket.*

# 1. Present Forms

| Phrasal Verbs 1 | |
|---|---|
| break down : | 1) stop working (of cars, engines, machines etc)<br>2) lose control of feelings (of people) |
| break into (+ object) : | 1) enter by force<br>2) start doing sth suddenly (laughter etc) |
| break out : | 1) begin suddenly (war, fire etc)<br>2) escape from a place |
| break up : | stop for holidays (of schools etc) |

**19 Fill in the correct preposition or adverb.**

1. Our school usually breaks ...*up*... for the summer in July.
2. My car broke ...*down*... on the motorway and I had to walk to a garage.
3. When she fell off the chair, the whole class broke ...*into*... laughter.
4. The prisoner managed to break ...*out*... of prison after murdering the guard.
5. The robber broke ...*into*... the house by smashing a window.
6. The fire broke ...*out*... in the basement and quickly spread upwards.
7. At the funeral, the boy's mother broke ...*down*... and started crying.

**20 Look at Appendix 1 and fill in the correct preposition.**

1. She blamed him ...*for*... the murder.
2. They arrived ............ London at 7:30.
3. I must apologise ........ Mary ........ the delay.
4. I am very annoyed ...*of*... John ...*for*... being so careless.
5. He was accused ...*of*... being a thief.
6. He believes ...*in*... God.
7. She is brilliant ...*at*... gymnastics.
8. I was not aware ...*of*... the problem.
9. I am afraid ............ snakes.
10. He does not associate ...*with*... his colleagues.
11. They were ashamed ...*of*... their children's behaviour.
12. He was astonished ...*by*... the way he spoke to the manager.

| Idioms 1 | |
|---|---|
| be at a loss for words : | be so surprised that one does not know what to say |
| be on good terms (with sb) : | be friendly (with sb) |
| be in sb's shoes : | be in sb's position |
| be in a good mood : | feel happy |
| be broke : | have no money at all |
| do one's best : | try as hard as possible |
| do sb a favour : | do sth to help sb |
| do (sth) for a living : | have a job and earn money |

**21 Fill in the correct idiom.**

1. I was so shocked by the news that I ...*was at a loss for words*... .
2. Look what you've done! I wouldn't like to ............ when Mum gets home.
3. "What do you ............ ?" "I work as a nurse."
4. After the divorce, they didn't talk for months, but now they ............ with each other.
5. I don't get paid till Friday, so now I ............ .
6. Although he ............, he didn't win the race.
7. Could you ............ ? If you're going out, could you get me some milk?
8. Now's a good time to ask for a rise because the boss ............ .

11

## 2. Past Forms

| Past Simple | Past Continuous | Past Perfect | Past Perfect Continuous |
|---|---|---|---|
| past actions which happened one after the other<br>She **sealed** the letter, **put** a stamp on it and **posted** it. | action in the middle of happening at a stated past time<br>He **was playing** tennis at 4.30 yesterday. | past action which occurred before another action or before a stated past time<br>He **had left** by the time I got there. (or by 8.15) | action continuing over a period up to a specific time in the past<br>She **had been working** as a clerk **for 10 years** before she resigned. |
| past habit or state<br>He **used to go/went** to school on foot.<br>complete action or event which happened at a stated past time<br>She **called** an hour **ago**. (When? An hour ago.) | past action in progress interrupted by another past action. The longer action is in the Past Continuous, the shorter action is in the Past Simple. While **I was getting dressed** the bell rang. | complete past action which had visible results in the past<br>She was sad because she **had failed** the test. | past action of certain duration which had visible results in the past<br>They were wet because they **had been walking** in the rain. |
| action which happened at a definite past time although the time is not mentioned. This action is not connected with the present. Shakespeare **wrote** a lot of plays. (Shakespeare is now dead; he won't write again. – period of time now finished) | two or more simultaneous past actions<br>While I **was sunbathing**, Tim **was swimming**.<br>or background description to events in a story<br>She **was flying** to Paris. The sun **was shining** ... | the Past Perfect is the past equivalent of the Present Perfect<br>(He can't find his watch He has lost it.)<br>He couldn't find his watch. He **had lost** it. | the Past Perfect Cont. is the past equivalent of the Present Perfect Continuous<br>(She is going to the doctor. Her leg has been aching for two days.)<br>She went to the doctor. Her leg **had been aching** for two days. |

### Time expressions used with:

| | |
|---|---|
| Past Simple | yesterday, last week etc, (how long) ago, then, just now, when, in 1967 etc |
| Past Continuous | while, when, as etc |
| Past Perfect | for, since, already, after, just, never, yet, before, by, by the time etc |
| Past Perfect Cont. | for, since |

## 2. Past Forms

**22** Add -(e)d to the words, put them in the correct column, then read them out.

like, cry, play, dance, stop, fry, smile, rob, travel, try, pray, stay, live, prefer, empty, destroy

| -e ➡ + d | double consonant + ed | consonant + y ➡ ied | vowel + y + ed |
|---|---|---|---|
| liked, smiled, danced, lived | robbed, travelled, stopped, preferred | tried, fried, cried, emptied | prayed, destroyed, played, stayed |

**23** Add -(e)d to the verbs, put them in the correct column, then read them out.

land, look, watch, smile, correct, start, slip, smash, decorate, cook, offer, collect, dress, prepare, water, iron, suggest, clean

| /ɪd/ after /t/, /d/ | /t/ after /k/, /s/, /ʃ/, /p/, /tʃ/ | /d/ after other sounds |
|---|---|---|
| landed, decorated, corrected, collected, started, suggested | looked, dressed, slipped, smashed, cooked, watched | smiled, cleaned, offered, watered, prepared, ironed |

**24** Complete the correct past form and identify the speech situation.

past action of certain duration with visible results in the past, past habit, simultaneous past actions, complete past action with visible results in the past, past action in progress interrupted by another past action, action continuing over a period up to a specific time in the past

*past habit*

1. When she was young, she ..danced.. (dance) a lot.

*past action in progress interrupted by other action*

2. John ..was driving.. (drive) home when his car ..broke down.. (break down).

*simultaneous past action*

3. Ted ..was reading.. (read) a book while Mary ..was sleeping.. (sleep).

*past action of certain duration with visible results*

4. He was dizzy. He ..had been working.. (work) on the computer all night.

*complete past action with visible results in past*

5. She was upset because she ..had lost.. (lose) her watch.

*action continuing over a period up to specific time in past*

6. She ..had been waiting.. (wait) for an hour before he ..arrived.. (arrive).

## 2. Past Forms

**25** Match the sentences with the correct tense description.

1. It was raining and the wind was blowing.
2. He was exhausted because he had been walking all day.
3. There was no juice left because Jack had drunk it all.
4. She had finished by 8 o'clock.
5. The storm broke out after we had been driving for four hours.
6. He got into the plane, started the engine and flew off into the clouds.
7. The party had already started by the time I arrived.
8. Elvis Presley died in 1977.
9. I was cycling to work when I fell off the bike.
10. My grandfather met Winston Churchill.
11. I was sleeping at 3 o'clock yesterday afternoon.
12. She had been trying to find a job in Hollywood for years.

a. past equivalent of the Present Perfect
b. action in the middle of happening at a stated past time
c. past actions which happened one after the other
d. action which is not connected with the present and happened at a definite past time not mentioned
e. background description to events in a story
f. action continuing over a period up to a specific time in the past
g. past equivalent of the Present Perfect Continuous
h. past action which occurred before another action
i. past action in progress interrupted by another
j. past action which occurred before a stated time in the past
k. event which happened at a stated past time
l. past action of certain duration which had visible results in the past

1. ...e...  2. ...l...  3. ...a...  4. ...j...  5. ...f...  6. ...c...
7. ...h...  8. ...k...  9. ...i...  10. ...d...  11. ...b...  12. ...g...

* W.C. is dead; action not connected with the present.

**26** Fill in with Past Simple or Past Continuous.

Last night I 1) ..was... (be) alone at home. I 2) ...was lying... (lie) on my bed and I 3) ...was watching... (watch) TV when I 4) ...heard... (hear) a strange noise. The noise 5) ...was coming... (come) from the kitchen. I 6) ...went... (go) downstairs, 7) ...picked up... (pick up) a heavy vase from the table and 8) ...headed for... (head for) the kitchen. I 9) ...opened... (open) the door very slowly. Then I 10) ...saw... (see) someone. He 11) ...was searching... (search) in the fridge. I 12) ...was... (be) so frightened that I 13) ...dropped... (drop) the vase I 14) ...was carrying... (carry) and it 15) ...crashed... (crash) onto the floor. The man 16) ...turned... (turn) towards the door and I 17) ...saw... (see) his face. It was my husband!

### Oral Activity 3

The teacher divides the class into two teams and gives them a sentence. The teams in turn ask questions based on the teacher's sentence. Each correct question gets 1 point. The team with the most points is the winner.

**Possible sentences:** They robbed a bank. – He invited her to dinner. – Ann wrote a letter. – She bought a new dress. etc

Team A S1: Who robbed a bank?
Team B S1: Did the police catch the robbers?

Team A S2: How much money did they get?
Team B S2: Did the robbers shoot anyone? etc

## 2. Past Forms

**27** Look at the picture and the list of words, then write what they were doing or did at the time Paul's parents entered the house.

Paul's parents were going away for the weekend. Paul invited some friends to the house. However his parents' car broke down so they had to come back home.

wash - jump out - bark     play cards - stop playing - drop     hold a glass of Cola - spill - stain
sleep - wake up - fall off     dance/listen - not see - continue dancing     smoke - see them - throw

1. Ben ........ *was washing the dog. It jumped out of the bath and started barking.*
2. Jackie *was sleeping on the sofa. She woke up and fell off.*
3. Jim and Peter *were playing cards. They stopped playing and dropped.*
4. Sarah *was dancing and listening music. She didn't see them and continued dancing.*
5. Sindy *was holding a glass of coke. She spilt it on the carpet and stained.*
6. Paul *was smoking. He saw them and threw his cigarette out of the window.*

**28** Fill in with Past Simple or Past Perfect then state which action happened first.

1. When I ...*left*... (leave) the house, I ...*realised*... (realise) that I ..*had forgotten*.... (forget) my keys.
   **First action :** ...*had forgotten*...
2. After I *had finished* (finish) digging the garden I *decided* (decide) to go for a walk.
   **First action :** *had finished*
3. I *lent* (lend) Fiona some money only after she *had promised* (promise) to give it back the next day. **First action :** *had promised*
4. They kept arguing about the money their father *had left* (leave) them in his will when he *died* (die).
   **First action :** *had left*
5. Kate *started* (start) studying after John *had left* (leave). **First action :** *had left*
6. I *bought* (buy) Beckie a plant yesterday because she *had sung* (sing) so well in the concert the night before. **First action :** *had sung*
7. When I *saw* (see) Julie, I *realised* (realise) that I *had met* (meet) her before.
   **First action :** *had met*

## 2. Past Forms

**29** Fill in the appropriate tense, then identify the speech situations.

*recently completed action, past action of certain duration with visible results in the past, past action of certain duration with visible results in the present, personal experience/change, action which occurred before another, past action in progress interrupted by another, past action not connected with the present whose time is not mentioned, past action connected with the present whose time is not mentioned, past action at a stated time, action continuing over a period up to a specific time in the past, simultaneous past actions*

...recently completed action

1. He ..has cleaned.. (clean) the floor but he hasn't cleaned the windows yet.

2. He had a backache. He ........ (dig) the garden.

3. He was angry. He ............ (argue) with his daughter.

4. He was tired. He ............ (swim) for hours.

5. Marilyn Monroe ............ (act) in a lot of films.

6. Michael Jackson ............ (make) a lot of records.

7. He can't find his wallet. He ............ (lose) it.

8. He ............ (not/have) a haircut for ages.

9. She looks exhausted. She ............ (cycle) for two hours.

10. She ............ (wait) for an hour before the bus came.

11. John ............ (already/cook) dinner before Ann came.

12. She had a terrible headache. She ............ (read) all day.

## 2. Past Forms

13. She .................... (clean) the window when she fell off the ladder.

14. Alexander Fleming ............ .................... (discover) penicillin in 1928.

15. She .................... (type) a letter while she ................ (talk) on the phone.

### Oral Activity 4

Students in teams look at the following pictures and give two reasons for each person's accident. What were they doing at the time? What happened to them? Each correct answer gets 1 point. When a team fails to give a reason, it doesn't get a point.

Teacher: picture 1
Team A S1: He was walking across the living room when he tripped over the carpet and hurt his foot.

Team B S1: He was digging in the garden when he hurt his foot.
Teacher: picture 2       etc.

**30) Match the sentences then join them using when, while, and, after or because.**

1. She went to bed
2. Ted was making lunch
3. She went home
4. Jim was reading
5. Sally went to the bank
6. I was washing the dishes
7. Mark went to the butcher's
8. He was very depressed

A. Mary was laying the table.
B. she had finished her work.
C. bought some chops.
D. she was drying them.
E. all her guests had left.
F. he had lost his job.
G. withdrew some money.
H. the doorbell rang.

1. ...E (after)............
2. ....................
3. ....................
4. ....................
5. ....................
6. ....................
7. ....................
8. ....................

17

## 2. Past Forms

**31** Fill in a suitable word or phrase practising present or past forms.

1. As soon as I ......*saw that the house was*...... on fire, I phoned the fire brigade.
2. By the end of 1990 he ........................................ eleven different countries.
3. The river flooded because ........................................ heavily for weeks.
4. Where have you been? I ........................................ for hours.
5. The first time I ........................................ a bicycle, I kept falling off.
6. Steven didn't realise he ........................................ until he put his hand in his pocket.
7. Mark was out of breath. He ........................................ for an hour.
8. He is very strong because ........................................ every day.
9. He ........................................ the park when it started to snow.
10. Don't make too much noise! The baby ........................................ .

**32** Fill in with Past Perfect Continuous or Past Continuous, then identify the speech situation.

*action over a period up to a specific past time, past action in progress interrupted by another, past action of certain duration with visible results in the past*

1. ...*action over a period up to a specific past time*...

He ..*had been cooking*.. (cook) until 12 o'clock.

2. ........................................

She ........................ (fry) fish when the pan caught fire.

3. ........................................

He was tired. He ........................ (drive) all day.

4. ........................................

He ........................ (watch) TV when his wife came home.

5. ........................................

He ........................ (ski) when he fell over and broke his leg.

6. ........................................

He ........................ (ski) all day. He was exhausted.

**33** Put the verbs in brackets into Past Simple or Past Perfect.

Last Monday Angie 1) ..*got up*.... (get up) for work as usual and 2) ........ (go) to the kitchen to have some breakfast. But when she 3) ........ (open) the fridge, she 4) ........ (find) that her flatmate Lucy 5) ........ ........ (drink) all the milk - not a good start to the day! So she 6) ........ (have) a quick cup of black coffee, 7) ........ (get) dressed and 8) ........ (go) out to the car. There she 9) ........ (find) that she 10) ........ (forget) to put the cover on the car the night before and there 11) ........ (be) thick frost all over the windscreen. She 12) ........ (scrape) it all off and 13) ........ (get) into the car. However, when she 14) ........ (turn) the key, nothing 15) ........ (happen)! Someone 16) ........ (leave) the headlights on and the battery 17) ........ (go) flat. She 18) ........ (be) furious as Lucy 19) ........ (use) the car last and it 20) ........ (be) her who 21) ........ (forget) to switch off the lights. Angie 22) ........ (head) for the bus stop to wait in the freezing cold.

## 2. Past Forms

### Used to - Would - Was going to

**Used to** expresses past habits or states. It forms its negative and interrogative with "did" and it is the same in all persons. We can use Past Simple instead of "used to".
She **used to walk/ walked** long distances. She **didn't use to stay** in and watch TV.

**Would** expresses past repeated actions and routine. **Used to** expresses past states or habits.
Grandma **would** always **make** me porridge for breakfast. (also: **used to make**)
When I was young I **used to** live in Leeds. (Not : ~~would~~)

**Was going to** expresses unfulfilled arrangements or unfulfilled plans in the past, or actions one intended to do but did not or could not do.
He **was going to** visit Pam but she wasn't at home.

What did you use to do?
I used to be a tiger hunter in Scotland.
But there aren't any tigers in Scotland.
I know. I shot them all!

**(34)** Mary has found a new job. How is her life different? Use: "used to" or "didn't use to".

| Before | Now |
|---|---|
| She worked in a café. | She works as an air-hostess. |
| She stayed in England. | She travels all the time. |
| She didn't earn much money. | She earns a lot of money. |
| She walked to work. | She drives to work. |
| She didn't get up early. | She gets up early. |

...Mary used to work in a café, but now she works as an air-hostess. She ............................................................
............................................................
............................................................
............................................................

**(35)** Write what was going to happen but didn't happen.

1. He ..was going to drink.. some lemonade but there was none left.
2. She ........................ her red skirt but it was dirty.
3. They ........................ some flowers but the shop was closed.

**(36)** Fill in : used to or would.

I 1) ...used to... live in a small house in the country when I was a little girl. I 2) ................ get up every day at 7 o'clock and get ready for school. My mother 3) ................ get our breakfast ready and then she 4) ................ walk to the bus stop with us and wait for the school bus to pick us up. The bus 5) ................ be on time. We stayed at school until 3.00 pm and then we 6) ................ catch the bus home again. In the afternoon we 7) ................ walk home alone because Mother didn't pick us up. She 8) ................ work in an office, but she stopped working last year and now she stays at home.

## 2. Past Forms

**37** Fill in : was going to, would or used to.

Last week I 1) ..*was going to*... visit an old house where we 2) ................ play as children, but I didn't have the time. We 3) ............. go there every weekend and play cowboys and Indians. We 4) ........... love it! My friend 5) ............. buy it and turn it into a hotel or so he 6) ......... say, but of course he didn't.

**38** Fill in with Past Simple, Present Simple, Present Continuous or Present Perfect.

Jane: Hi, Johnny. I 1) *haven't heard*. (not/hear) from you for a long time. Where 2) ............ (you/be)?
Johnny: I 3) ................ (start) a new job six months ago. I 4) ................ (be) a computer salesman now. I 5) ............ (enjoy) it very much. My company 6) ................ (send) me abroad every few weeks. Last month I 7) .......... (go) to Japan - it 8) ............ (be) fantastic!
Jane: Wow! Japan! How long 9) ........................ (you/stay) there? Tell me all about it.
Johnny: I 10) .......... (stay) there for three weeks in a luxurious hotel. The company always 11) ............. (pay) for everything.
Jane: I'd love a job like yours.
Johnny: Well actually, Jane, that 12) ................ (be) the reason why I 13) ................ (call) you now. I 14) .............. (need) an assistant. Last week, the company 15) ............... (tell) me to choose someone and I immediately 16) ................... (think) of you. What 17) ................ (you/think)?
Jane: When 18) ................ (I/start)?

**39** Put the verbs in brackets into the correct past form.

I remember when I 1) ... *went* ..... (go) on holiday abroad for the first time. I 2) ............................... (just/leave) school. I 3) .................................................. (study) very hard for my final exams and I 4) ................................ (feel) that I needed a holiday. A friend of mine 5) .......................... (want) to come as well so we 6) ................................ (look) at some brochures from the travel agent's. We 7) ............. ........................ (read) for about an hour when my friend 8) ..................... (find) the perfect holiday - two weeks in Hawaii. We 9) .................... (be) very excited about it. Finally the day of our holiday 10) ..................... (arrive). We 11) ...................... (just/leave) the house when the phone 12) ..................... (ring). I 13) ........ ..................... (run) back into the house, but the phone 14) ............... (stop) by the time I 15) .................. (reach) it. When we 16) ...................... (arrive) at the airport we 17) ...................... (sit) in the cafeteria. The airline 18) ................................. (just/make) an announcement. Our flight was delayed for eight hours. We 19) ........................ (get up) very early and rushed to the airport, all for nothing.

**40** Fill in with Past Perfect or Past Perfect Continuous.

When I entered the house something smelt awful. Someone 1) .... *had been cooking* ... (cook) and 2) ..... ............ (burn) the meal. I 3) .................. (visit) the house once before and 4) ....................... (meet) the family but I didn't know what 5) ..................... (happen) since then. The house was a mess. The children 6) ........................ (play) in the living-room and 7) .................... (leave) their toys all over the floor. Someone 8) ..................... (leave) all the windows open. It 9) .................... (rain) for hours and all the curtains 10) .............................. (get) wet and dirty. I asked the children where their parents were. They told me that their mother 11) ................................ (be) in hospital for the past two weeks. Their father 12) ................................ (look after) them since then. Obviously he 13) ........................... (do) his best, but he couldn't do any better since he worked all morning and had to leave them alone most of the day. I had to do something to help them.

## 2. Past Forms

| Past Simple versus Present Perfect | |
|---|---|
| **Past Simple** | **Present Perfect** |
| complete action which happened at a **stated** time in the past<br>She **left** yesterday.<br>(When did she leave? Yesterday.) | complete action which happened at an **unstated** time in the past<br>Don **has left** for Madrid. (We don't know when he left; unstated time; he's now there or on his way there.) |
| past action which is **not connected with the present** and happened at a definite past time not mentioned<br>I **met** John Lennon. (I won't meet him again; he's dead.- period of time finished) | past action which is **connected with the present** and happened at a definite past time not mentioned<br>I**'ve spoken** to Richard Gere. (I may speak to him again; he's alive. - period of time not finished yet) |

**41** Put the verbs in brackets into Past Simple or Present Perfect.

Dear Tom,

Thank you for your letter. It 1) *arrived* (arrive) yesterday and I 2) ............... (decide) to write back immediately. You see, my agent 3) ............... (find) me a part in a new film and I'm going to Hollywood next week! I 4) ............... (speak) to Robert Redford on the phone about the part and I'm meeting him as soon as I arrive. The film is a re-make of a 1956 thriller which I 5) ............... (see) hundreds of times. It starred Marilyn Monroe who, as you know, I 6) ............... (meet) when I was a little girl. Yesterday I 7) ............... (buy) lots of new clothes and I 8) ............... (already/start) packing. Well, I must rush now. There's so much to do!
Love,
Sharon

**42** Fill in with Past Simple or Present Perfect.

1. A: I *Have you been* (you/be) on holiday this year?
   B: No, I *couldn't* (can/not) go, because I *broke* (break) my leg in August and *had* (have) to stay in hospital.
2. A: *Have* (you/visit) the National Museum yet?
   B: Yes, I *have been* (be) there three times, but I *haven't seen* (not/see) everything yet.
3. A: I'm ever so sorry, Jim, but I *have burnt* (burn) your dinner. Maria *phoned* (phone) and I *forgot* (forget) about the food.
   B: That's okay. I *have already eaten* (already/eat).
4. A: I *bought* (buy) a new dress yesterday, but when I *arrived* (arrive) home, I *found* (find) a hole in the seam.
   B: What *did you do* (you/do)? *Have you taken / Did you take* (you/take) it back to the shop?
   A: No, I *haven't been* (not/be) into town yet. I'll do it this afternoon.
5. A: Your hair *has grown* (grow) a lot since I last *saw* (see) you.
   B: Yes. I *wanted* (want) to get it cut yesterday but I *was* (be) too busy.
6. A: I *have never flown* (never/fly) before and I'm very nervous about it.
   B: I *felt* (feel) like that the first time I *flew* (fly), but I thoroughly *enjoyed* (enjoy) it.
7. A: I *have lost* (lose) my glasses. *Have you seen* (you/see) them anywhere?
   B: No. Where *did you put* (you/put) them?
   A: I *put* (put) them on the table a minute ago, but they're not there now.
8. A: *Have you ever met* (you/ever/meet) anyone famous?
   B: Yes, I *'ve spoken* (speak) to Paul McCartney and I *saw* (see) John Lennon before he was killed.

## 2. Past Forms

9. A: Where *did you go* (you/go) on holiday?
   B: To Rhodes. *Have you been* (you/be) there?
   A: Yes, I *went* (go) there last year. We *swam* (swim) every day. It was great!
10. A: How's your job, Mike?
    B: I *have just started* (just/start) a new one. I *left* (leave) the old one because they *didn't pay* (not/pay) me enough money.
11. A: When *did you leave* (you/leave) school?
    B: I *left* (leave) in 1980, I *finished* (finish) university in 1984 and I *have had* (have) three jobs since then.
12. A: *Did you see* (you/see) "Barabas" on TV last night?
    B: No I *have seen* (see) it so many times already that I *didn't want* (not/want) to watch it again.

### Oral Activity 5 (The Alibi Game)

A murder happened at 11 o'clock last night. Two students are the main suspects. They leave the classroom and must create an alibi to prove their innocence (where they were, what they did, what they were wearing etc). In the meantime the rest of the class take the role of detectives and think of questions to ask them. Each "suspect" (student) enters the class and is questioned separately. If their answers are not the same, then they are accused of committing the murder. Students should use Past Continuous and/or Past Simple in their questions.

### Oral Activity 6

The teacher divides the class into two teams and asks students to look at the following situations, giving reasons for each situation. Students should use Present Perfect, Past Perfect Simple or Past Perfect Cont. Each correct reason gets 1 point. The team with the most points is the winner.

Team A S1:  Jo's clothes are dirty because … *she has been playing in the garden*.
Team B S1:  Paul's head ached because … *he had been sitting in the sun*.

3. Mary is furious because …
4. Tom was not hungry because …
5. Sue was hungry because …
6. Mark is excited because …
7. David failed his maths test because …
8. Trevor had ketchup on his tie because …
9. He was out of breath because …
10. Frank's house needed tidying because …
11. Terry felt sick because …
12. Tim had a black eye because …
13. Peter is going to the police station because …
14. Mike's shirt was torn because …
15. Joanne's feet are sore because …
16. Carol is crying because …

### Writing Activity 3

Your house has been robbed. Using the notes from the list below, write a report to the police.
go - return - get out - see men - carry - jump - run after - disappear - not see - go into - realise - steal - clothes lie - take my wife's necklace - my mother give - find glove - drop - call police
**Last night I went to the cinema. I returned home at 10.30. While I was getting out of the car, I saw two men wearing masks coming out of the house. One of them was carrying a big bag…**

## 2. Past Forms

*Tense Review*

**43** Fill in the correct tense.

Sue Thomas is a fashion designer. She 1) ...has been making... (make) clothes ever since she 2) ............ (be) a young girl. She 3) ........................ (get) her first job in a clothes factory when she was sixteen. She 4) ............... (sew) buttons onto a shirt one day when she 5) ................ (have) a brilliant idea for a design. After she 6) ........................ (speak) to her bank manager, she got a loan and she 7) ........................ (open) her own little workshop. Now she 8) ........................ (make) lots of money. Next year she 9) ................ (open) a shop which will sell all her own designs. She 10) ........................ (sell) clothes to a lot of famous people, including film stars and singers, and she 11) ................ (think) she will be very rich soon.

**44** Fill in the correct tense.

Kevin Adams 1) ...loves... trains. He first 2) ................ (see) one when he was four years old and he 3) ................ (think) it was great. He 4) ................ (go) to a different railway station every week and 5) ................ (write down) the engine number of every train he sees. He 6) ................ (do) this since he was eight. By the time he was fifteen he 7) ................ (collect) over ten thousand different engine numbers in various counties. Once, while he 8) ................ (stand) in a station in Cheshire he saw something very unusual. He 9) ................ (wait) for over an hour for a train to go by when suddenly he 10) ................ (see) a very old steam train coming down the track. It 11) ................ (not/stop) at the station and, as it passed, Kevin noticed that all the passengers 12) ................ (wear) old-fashioned clothes. When he told the station guard about this, the poor man turned pale. He said that no steam train 13) ................ (pass) through that station for years, and that the last one 14) ................ (crash), killing everyone on board.

*In Other Words*

| | |
|---|---|
| It's a long time since he called us.<br>He hasn't called us for a long time. | When did he get the job?<br>How long ago did he get the job?<br>How long is it since he got the job? |
| The last time I saw him was a week ago.<br>I haven't seen him for a week. | |

**45** Rephrase the following sentences using the word in bold type.

1. It's months since I saw Jane.
   **for** ....... I haven't seen Jane for months. .................................................
2. When did she come back?
   **since** ........................................................................................
3. I haven't spoken to him for a week.
   **last** .........................................................................................
4. How long is it since he found a new job?
   **when** ........................................................................................
5. It's a month since I saw Chris.
   **seen** ........................................................................................
6. The last time I went to the theatre was a month ago.
   **been** ........................................................................................

23

## 2. Past Forms

### Phrasal Verbs 2

| | |
|---|---|
| bring about : | cause to happen |
| bring out : | publish |
| bring round : | 1) cause to regain consciousness |
| | 2) persuade |
| bring up : | raise a child |

**46** Fill in the correct preposition or adverb.

1. The government's new policies have brought ....*about*..... many changes over the past few months.
2. When Paul fainted, his friends splashed him with cold water to bring him ............................ .
3. As both her parents had died, she was brought ............................ by her grandparents.
4. Susan's first novel will be brought ............... in December.
5. After trying to persuade him for hours, I finally brought him ..................... to my point of view.

**47** Look at Appendix 1 and fill in the correct preposition.

1. Everybody congratulated him ...*on*.. passing his exams.
2. The police have charged him ............. murder.
3. How much did they charge you ...... that haircut?
4. The nurse takes care ................ her patients.
5. The con man was very clever ............. making people believe his stories.
6. The journey was awful because the train was so crowded .............. passengers.
7. I've lost contact ............ Jim since he moved to America.
8. Mr Gibbons is converting his basement ......... a games room.
9. The police questioned him in connection .......... the robbery.
10. If you compare Jim ............ Harry, you'll realise they are very different, even though they are twins.
11. Nothing can compare ..................... a nice hot bath after a hard day's work.
12. The man complained .................... the police .......... his noisy neighbour.
13. This drink consists ............. orange and soda.
14. I don't like people who are cruel ......... animals.
15. Can I change this black pen ........... a blue one, please?
16. While he was driving, he crashed ......... a lamp-post.

### Idioms 2

| | |
|---|---|
| have a good time : | enjoy oneself (**opp:** have a bad time) |
| have the time of one's life : | experience a period of exceptional happiness |
| have an early night : | go to bed early |
| fall in love with : | begin to feel romantic love for sb |
| get along with : | be on friendly terms |
| get into a mess : | get into a difficult situation |
| get on sb's nerves : | irritate sb |
| get rid of : | remove or dispose of |
| give sb one's word : | make a promise |

**48** Fill in the correct idiom.

1. He ..*gave her his word* .... that he would never lie to her again.
2. Did he buy you flowers again? I think he .......... ................................................... you.
3. I ........................ my colleagues in my new job. I really like it there.
4. I'm sure I will .............................................. at the party tonight.
5. I'm so tired. I think I will ............................ .
6. I ............................................... on my honeymoon. We went to Venice.
7. John ............................................ . He never stops talking in class.
8. He spent too much money and ..................... ................ with his credit card payments.
9. I think you should ................................ those old jeans. They're full of holes.

# 3. Future Forms

| Future Simple (Will) | Be Going To | Future Continuous | Future Perfect |
|---|---|---|---|
| decisions taken at the moment of speaking (on-the-spot decisions) *Since it's getting dark, I'll turn on the light.* | actions intended to be performed in the near future *She's going to visit her parents tomorrow.* | actions in progress at a stated future time *He'll be sunbathing in Hawaii this time next week.* | actions which will be finished before a stated future time *She will have come back by the end of July.* **Note:** by or not... until/till are used with Future Perfect. Until/till are normally used with Future Perfect only in negative sentences. *She will have finished by 8 o'clock.* (Not: *until/till*) *She won't have finished until 8 o'clock.* |
| hopes, fears, threats, offers, promises, warnings, predictions, requests, comments etc, esp.with: expect, hope, believe, I'm sure, I'm afraid, probably etc. *I'm afraid I'll be a little late.* | planned actions or intentions *Now that they've settled in their new house, they're going to have a party.* | actions which are the result of a routine (instead of Present Cont.) *I'll be seeing John tomorrow.* (We work in the same office so we'll definitely meet.) | |
| actions or predictions which may (not) happen in the future *She'll probably buy the dress.* (prediction) or actions which we cannot control and will inevitably happen *He will be ten next year.* | evidence that something will definitely happen in the near future *Ann is going to have a baby. Look at the dark clouds in the sky! It's going to rain.* | when we ask politely about people's arrangements to see if they can do sth for us or because we want to offer to do sth for them *Will you be going to the supermarket? Can you buy me some tea?* | **Future Perfect Cont.** duration of an action up to a certain time in the future. *By the end of this year she will have been working here for two years.* |
| things we are not sure about or haven't decided to do yet *She'll probably be promoted.* (not sure yet) | things we are sure about or we have already decided to do in the near future *He's going to be promoted.* (The boss has decided to do it.) | **Present Simple (future meaning)** timetables/programmes *The plane reaches London at 9.45.* | **Present Continuous (future meaning)** fixed arrangement in the near future *Sally is seeing her dentist this week.* (Sally has fixed an appointment). |

## 3. Future Forms

| | Time expressions used with: |
|---|---|
| Will/Be Going To/ Future Cont. | tomorrow, tonight, next week/month, in two/three etc days, the day after tomorrow, soon, in a week/month etc |
| Future Perfect | before, by, by then, by the time, until (is used only in negative sentences with this tense) |
| Fut. Perf. Cont. | by ... for eg. *By* next year he will have been working here *for* two years. |

| Shall is used: | Will is used: |
|---|---|
| with I/we in questions, suggestions, offers or when asking for advice.<br>**Shall** we play tennis?<br>What **shall** I do? | to express offers, threats, promises, predictions, warnings, requests, hopes, fears, on-the-spot decisions, comments (mainly with: think, expect, believe, I'm sure, hope, know, suppose and probably).<br>I hope he**'ll** be on time. |

**Shall** I call you a taxi?

**Will you** call me "madam" like everyone else?

**49** Fill in: will, won't or shall.

Mum : Anna! 1) ..*Will*........ you please stop making so much noise? I
         2) ......................... never finish this work if you don't.
Anna : But Mum, what 3) ......................... I do? If I don't practise, I
         4) ......................... pass my violin exam tomorrow.
Mum : And I 5) ......................... be in trouble at work if I don't finish
         this. Then I 6) ......................... get promoted.
Anna : 7) ......................... I go upstairs then?
Mum : Thanks, Anna. That 8) ......................... help.

**50** Identify the speech situations (sure, not sure yet), then fill in "will" or "be going to".

1. ..*sure*...................   2. *WILL, NOT SURE YET*   3. ........*SURE*...........

They ...*are going to*...... play tennis.

They ......*WILL*.......... go swimming if the weather is nice.

He ...*IS GOING to*... post a letter to his friend Ben.

4. ..*not sure yet*........   5. ........*SURE*...........   6. ..*NOT SURE YET*..

Number 2 ...*WILL*....
....... probably win the race.

They ...*are going to*...
.....................wash the dog.

He ......*WILL*............ go to the cinema if he finishes early.

## 3. Future Forms

**51** Fill in: by or until.

1. What time will you have finished painting your room? I will have finished ......by...... 7 o'clock, I hope.
2. Are you seeing Julie tonight? No, I will have left ......by...... the time she gets here.
3. Have they built their house yet? No, they won't have built it ......until...... the end of May.
4. Will you have done your homework ......by...... tomorrow? No, I won't have done it ......until...... Friday.
5. She'll have saved enough money to buy a car ......by...... Christmas.
6. I'll have worked here for ten years ......by...... the end of this month.
7. We won't have built the shed ......until...... Friday.
8. She'll have finished dressing ......by...... the time the guests arrive.

**52** Match the following sentences with the correct tense description.

1. Look out! That dog is going to bite you.
2. I'll be flying to Morocco this time tomorrow.
3. She is worried that he'll be angry.
4. By 11 o'clock she'll have been waiting for five hours.
5. The London train arrives at 4.45.
6. I'm seeing my bank manager this morning.
7. When I'm older, I'm going to learn to drive.
8. I think I'll make some tea. Do you want some?
9. He'll have finished by tomorrow afternoon.
10. Will you be going into town today?
11. I'm sure he'll pass the test.
12. She'll probably come early.
13. I'm going to buy a new car tomorrow.

a. fixed arrangement in the near future
b. action which will be finished before a stated future time
c. timetable
d. fear about the future
e. evidence that something will definitely happen in the near future
f. future intention
g. action in progress at a stated future time
h. duration of an action up to a certain time in the future
i. action intended to be performed in the near future
j. on-the-spot decision
k. something we are not sure about yet
l. polite enquiry about people's arrangements
m. prediction

1. e   2. g   3. d   4. h   5. c   6. a   7. f   8. j   9. b   10. l   11. m   12. k   13. i

**53** Fill in the correct future form, then identify the speech situations.

1. ...offer...
2. on-the-spot decision
3. deffenctly will happen

...Shall I post... (post) this letter for you?

I'll get (get) a taxi. The bus is late.

Look! He going to (fall).

4. warning
5. planned action
6. fixed arrangements

Don't pull the cat's tail. It will (scratch) you.

We've decided. We are going to (get) married soon.

I am seeing (see) the bank manager tomorrow.

## 3. Future Forms

7. polite ask about arrangements

Will you be using (you/use) your car tonight? Can I borrow it, Dad?

8. action finished before a stated future time

I will have (finish) by 7 o'clock tonight.

9. action in progress

Don't come at 6 o'clock this evening. I will be doing (do) my homework.

### Time words with no Future forms

1. We never use future forms after: **when** (time conjunction), **while, before, until, by the time, if** (conditional), **as soon as, after** etc. However we can use **when** or **if + will** if "when" is a question word and "if" means "whether".
   *She'll send us a letter when she has time.*
   BUT *When will he meet us?*
   *I don't know if he will accept.* (=whether)

2. With **go** and **come** we use Present Continuous rather than "be going to".
   *She's going to London next week.*
   RATHER THAN *She's going to go to London next week.*

What's your son going to be after he passes his exams?

Well, by the time he passes all his exams, he'll be a pensioner.

**54** Put the verbs in brackets into Present Simple or Future.

"You 1) ..'ll meet.... (meet) Agent 205 under the clock at the railway station. When she 2) ...P.S.... (arrive), she 3) 'll give (give) you an envelope. I don't know if you 4) 'll recognise (recognise) her in her disguise, but if she 5) doesn't say (not/say) the secret code word, you 6) will know (know) she is an enemy agent. You 7) 'll take (take) the envelope and head for the train to Waterloo Station. When the train 8) comes (come), you 9) 'll get on (get on) it and go to Waterloo. If you 10) miss (miss) the 9.15 train, you 11) 'll have to (have to) get the next one. As soon as it 12) reaches (reach) Waterloo, leave the train and take a taxi to the Opera House. You 13) 'll meet (meet) Jenny there, although I'm not sure exactly when she 14) 'll get (get) there. Give her the envelope. Wait until she 15) drives (drive) off and then go home. We 16) 'll call (call) you there. Are there any questions?"

**55** Match the sentences and fill in the correct tense.

| | | |
|---|---|---|
| 1. She'll call us | A. until it stops (stop) raining. | 1. D |
| 2. I don't know | B. as soon as I can (can). | 2. G |
| 3. What will you do (you/do) | C. if you (come) home late. | 3. E |
| 4. Turn the lights off | D. as soon as she reaches (reach) London. | 4. H |
| 5. Don't go out | E. if you have an accident? | 5. A |
| 6. I will write (write) to you | F. what (you/buy)? | 6. B |
| 7. He will be angry | G. when he will leave (leave). | 7. C |
| 8. If I give you £5, | H. before you go (go) to bed. | 8. F |

## 3. Future Forms

**56** Fill in : will or be going to.

1. A: I've lost my keys!
   B: I ....'ll.............. help you look for them.
2. A: Watch out! You ................... knock the vase over.
   B: Oh! I didn't see it.
3. A: This ice-cream is delicious!
   B: Don't eat any more. You ............... be sick.
4. A: Here's the waiter! Would you like a drink?
   B: Yes, please. I ........... have a glass of water.
5. A: I'll park the car here.
   B: Be careful, you ................... hit the wall!
6. A: ................ you have a biscuit with your tea?
   B: No, thank you. I'm on a diet.
7. A: Have you decided what to wear tonight?
   B: Yes, I ............. wear my black velvet dress.
8. A: Have you seen John today?
   B: No, but I ............... visit him this afternoon.

**57** Complete the following dialogue using Future Simple or Future Continuous.

Graham : Can I phone you tomorrow, Suzy?
Suzy : What time?
Graham : Well, I'm not working tomorrow so I 1) ...'ll phone (phone) you at 9 o'clock in the morning.
Suzy : Oh no! I 2) ........................ (sleep) then.
Graham : OK. I 3) ........................ (call) you at noon.
Suzy : Well, I 4) ........................ (wash) my hair.
Graham : Perhaps I 5) ........................ (come) and visit you in the afternoon, then. What 6) ........................ (you/do) around 3 o'clock?
Suzy : I 7) ........................ (get) ready for my aerobics class.
Graham : Well, if I phone you at 5, 8) ................ (you/be) at home?
Suzy : No, I'm afraid not. I 9) ........................ (visit) my aunt in hospital.
Graham : When can I see you, Suzy?
Suzy : Phone me tomorrow evening. I 10) ........................ (not/do) anything then.

**58** Put the verbs in brackets into Present Simple, Present Continuous or Future.

Bob : 1) ...*Will you be able*........... (you/be able) to go skiing with us next weekend?
Peter : No, I 2) ........................ (be) in London then.
Bob : Really? Why 3) ........................ (you/go) there?
Peter : There's a very important meeting, and after I 4) ........................ (attend) that I 5) ........................ (visit) a friend in Sussex.
Bob : Before you 6) ........................ (leave), 7) ........................ (you/give) me a ring? There are a few things I'd like you to buy while you 8) ........................ (be) there.
Peter : Yes, of course. I 9) ........................ (ring) you on Friday.

**59** Put the verbs in brackets into Future Perfect or Future Perfect Continuous.

1. By 7.00 pm they ........*will have been playing*................... (play) cricket for eight hours.
2. I ........................ (finish) painting your room by the time you get home.
3. By the end of next month I ........................ (live) in London for exactly three years.
4. Tom ........................ (write) his third novel by the end of this year.
5. By the time he arrives in London, John ........................ (drive) for five hours.
6. This film ........................ (probably/not/finish) until midnight.
7. How long ........................ (you/study) English by the end of this term?

## 3. Future Forms

8. Don't worry! You ................................................... (forget) all about it by this time next year.
9. By Friday I ................................................... (work) on this project for two weeks.
10. Hopefully, he ................................................... (cook) dinner for us by the time we get home.
11. I ................................................... (read) this book by tomorrow night.
12. He hopes he ................................................... (make) a million pounds by the time he is thirty.
13. By 5 o'clock I ................................................... (do) this crossword puzzle for three hours.

**60** Complete the dialogue using the correct future form.

A: What 1) ..are you doing.............. (do) tonight?
B: I 2) m going to try............. (try) to finish my homework because I 3) m going...... (go) to my cousin's wedding on Saturday and I 4) won't be able.... (not/be able) to do it then.
A: What time 5) does............ the wedding ...start......... (start) on Saturday?
B: The ceremony 6) begins........... (begin) at 2 o'clock, then I 7) m going............ (go) to the party in the evening.
A: 8) Will......... any of your friends ...be..... (be) there?
B: Well, my cousin says I can bring a friend. 9) Are you doing................ (you/do) anything on Saturday night?
A: No, but I 10) will feel.......... (feel) shy if I don't know anyone.
B: Never mind. It 11) is going to be...... (be) a big party and I'm sure you 12) will have........... (have) a great time.
A: OK, then. Thanks very much.

**61** Put the verbs in brackets into the correct future form.

Dear Debbie,
Since you want to know what I 1) .....'m doing....... (do) next week, I thought I'd write and let you know. It 2) is going to... (be) a very busy week. On Monday I 3) m going..... (go) to York. I 4) ....will..... (probably/be) there for three days, and by Wednesday I 5) ll have met...... (meet) every important artist in the town. If everything goes well, I 6) will go....... (go) to Newcastle on Thursday morning. There I 7) m meeting........... (meet) the chairman of the Arts Council. Then on Friday and Saturday I 8) m going to....... (visit) several small towns in the area to see what their galleries are like. By Sunday I 9) will have travelling....... (travel) for days and I imagine I 10) ll be........ (be) very tired, so it looks like I 11) won't be coming..... (not/come) to your party on Sunday night. Sorry! I hope you 12) ll invite...... (invite) me to the next one. Give my love to Mike.
Love,
Susan

### Oral Activity 7

The teacher divides the class into two teams and chooses a leader. The teams in turn tell the leader what they are going to do in order to explain why they can't go to the cinema with him/her. Each grammatically correct answer gets 1 point. The team with the most points is the winner.

Leader: Shall we go to the cinema tomorrow, John?
Team A S1: I'm sorry, I can't. I'm going to visit my grandparents tomorrow.
Leader: Shall we go to the cinema tomorrow, Mary?
Team B S1: I'm sorry, I can't. I'm going to paint the kitchen tomorrow. etc

## 3. Future Forms

### Oral Activity 8

The teacher divides the class into two teams and chooses a leader. The teams in turn tell the leader what they will be doing and why he/she can't call them at 6 o'clock today. Each correct sentence gets 1 point. The team with the most points is the winner.

      Leader: Can I phone you at 6 o'clock today, Peter?
Team A S1: Oh, no! I'll be doing my homework then.
      Leader: Can I phone you at 6 o'clock today, Jill?
Team B S1: Oh, no! I'll be cleaning the house then.         etc

### Oral Activity 9

The students have decided to decorate a house they are going to live in. The teacher divides the class into two teams. Team A suggests something but Team B finds a reason to disagree. Then Team A agrees and adds on-the-spot decisions as a compromise for both sides. Students who produce a correct sentence get 1 point. Play the game for some time and then change the roles of the teams.

Here are some ideas:
    **put paintings - buy carpet/furniture/fridge/TV - build a garage - repair the roof - plant trees - fix the doors/windows - paint the walls pink - put up new curtains etc.**

Team A S1: We are going to put paintings on the walls.
Team B S1: We can't put paintings on the walls. They're expensive.
Team A S2: Okay, we'll put posters on the walls then.
Team A S3: We're going to buy new furniture.
Team B S2: We can't buy new furniture. We haven't got enough money. etc

### Oral Activity 10

Each student says two things that he/she will have done in 15 years' time.
e.g. In 15 years' time I will have bought my own house.

### Writing Activity 4

Look at Jim's notes then produce a complete letter using **will** or **be going to**.

**go California - summer holidays - by plane (quickest way) - not alone - friend come - probably brother if decide - stay San Francisco a week - then somewhere else - hope - find - place - sleep - sunbathe a lot - take swimsuit and sunglasses - think - need them - sure - be - good holiday - join us?**

Dear Ted,
I'm going to California for the summer holidays ...

**62** <u>Rephrase the following sentences using the words in bold type.</u>

1. It's years since I spoke to Jenny.
   **for** ...... *I haven't spoken to Jenny for years.* ..................
2. It's the first time I've flown to Mexico.
   **never** ..................
3. How long is it since you moved here?
   **did** ..................
4. We've never been to this museum before.
   **first** ..................

## 3. Future Forms

5. When did you get your diploma?
   how long ....................................................................................
6. I haven't seen such a good film for ages.
   since ....................................................................................

### Phrasal Verbs 3

| | |
|---|---|
| **carry on (with)** : | continue |
| **carry out** : | do, complete sth |
| **hold back** : | control (oneself, crowds etc) |
| **hold on** : | wait (esp on the phone) |
| **hold up** : | 1) delay |
| | 2) rob sth/sb using a weapon |

**63** Fill in the correct preposition or adverb.

1. The police held ...*back*... the fans who were trying to get onto the football pitch.
2. They carried .............. a survey to find out which TV channel was the most popular.
3. We arrived an hour late because we were held .............. in traffic.
4. Could you hold .............., please? Mrs Jones' line is engaged at the moment.
5. Carry .............. that job until I give you something else to do.
6. The gang held .............. a security van and got away with millions.

**64** Look at Appendix 1 and fill in the correct preposition.

1. Her family couldn't decide ..*on*.. the best place to go for their summer holidays.
2. The mountain-climbers died ........ extreme cold.
3. Sally dreams ............ being a famous actress.
4. What's the difference ........ a rabbit and a hare?
5. Sam was so disappointed ............ his birthday present that he burst into tears.
6. The demand ............ new cars is low because they are so expensive.
7. Linda couldn't deal .............. all the typing, so she hired an assistant to help her.
8. Now that he has a good job, Paul doesn't depend .............. his parents for money.
9. Can you explain this .............. me, please?

### Idioms 3

| | |
|---|---|
| **get in touch with** : | communicate with sb one hasn't seen recently |
| **keep in touch with sb** : | maintain contact by visiting, writing etc |
| **keep sth quiet** : | keep sth secret |
| **keep an eye on sth** : | guard sth |
| **keep one's head** : | remain calm |
| **keep one's fingers crossed** : | wish for good luck |
| **make oneself at home** : | act and feel as if one were in one's own house |
| **make room (for sth)** : | allow enough free space |
| **make sure** : | check |

**65** Fill in the correct idiom.

1. Always ..*make sure*.. the cooker is off when you leave the house.
2. She asked Mark to .............. the children while she went to the shops.
3. Peter promised to .............. me after he moved away, but he hasn't written yet.
4. I don't know if they'll give me the job but I .............. that they will.
5. When the fire started, David managed to .............. and get everyone out of the room.
6. I'll tell you what we're planning if you promise to .............. .
7. You can watch TV, get yourself a juice or do whatever you like. Just .............. .
8. We must .............. everyone we invited to the party and tell them it's been cancelled.
9. You can .............. the new sofa by moving that table.

# 4. Infinitive / - ing form / Participles

| | Tenses of the Infinitive | | Tenses of the -ing form | |
|---|---|---|---|---|
| | Active Voice | Passive Voice | Active Voice | Passive Voice |
| Present | (to) offer | (to) be offered | offering | being offered |
| Pres. Cont. | (to) be offering | —— | —— | —— |
| Perfect | (to) have offered | (to) have been offered | having offered | having been offered |
| Perf. Cont. | (to) have been offering | —— | —— | —— |

**The Present Infinitive** refers to the present or future. *I'd like **to go** for a walk.*

**The Present Continuous Infinitive** is used with appear, claim, seem, pretend, must, can't, happen, should, would etc to describe an action happening now. *He must **be working** in the garden now.*

**The Perfect Infinitive** is used with appear, happen, pretend, seem etc to show that the action of the infinitive happened before the action of the verb. *He claims **to have met** the Queen. (First he met the Queen, then he claimed he had met her.)* It is also used with modal verbs should, would etc (see p. 46).

**The Perfect Continuous Infinitive** is used with appear, seem, pretend etc to put emphasis on the duration of the action of the infinitive, which happened before the action of the verb. *She looks tired. She seems **to have been working** all morning.* It is also used with modal verbs (see p. 46).

**The Present Gerund** (-ing form) refers to the present or future. *She enjoys **dancing**.*

**The Perfect Gerund** (-ing form) shows that the action of the gerund has happened before the action of the verb. We can use the Present Gerund instead of the Perfect Gerund without a difference in meaning. *He denied **having stolen** the money.   OR   He denied **stealing** the money.*

## 4. Infinitive / - ing form / Participles

**66  Fill in the correct tense of the infinitive or the -ing form.**

1. We'd better not bother her – she seems ........ *to be studying* ................................... (study).
2. The accused denied ................................................................. (do) anything wrong.
3. Paul pretended ................................. (win) a lot of money but in fact he had won nothing at all.
4. She must ................................. (work) outdoors when we rang. She didn't answer the phone.
5. Jane hoped ................................................. (give) the prize, but someone else won it.
6. He seemed ................................................................. (swim). He was all wet.
7. I should ................................. (give) him some money before I went out, but I forgot.
8. She says she would love ................................................. (come) to dinner with us tonight.
9. He must ................................. (practise) that piece for hours – he plays it very well now.
10. The athlete seemed ............ (be) out of breath – he must ................................. (run) for hours.
11. Peter claims ................................. (choose) as the best-dressed man of the year.
12. They could ................................. (prepare) a meal for us last night instead of making us go out to eat.
13. John must ................................. (be) very busy these days – I never see him.
14. The house looks so clean now. They must ................................. (clean) all day.
15. Jan should ................................. (give) us her new address before she left.
16. The two men appeared ................................. (try) to break into the building when the police arrived.
17. You should ................................. (study) now instead of watching TV.

**67  Fill in the -ing form or the infinitive in the appropriate tense.**

Tom: Do you think Mary would like 1) ...*to go*.. (go) to the theatre with me tonight?
Jo: I don't think so. She seems 2) ................................. (study) very hard at the moment.
Tom: That's a shame! I would have liked 3) ................................. (go) out with her.
Jo: I wouldn't mind 4) ................................. (come) with you.
Tom: OK. But I think you should 5) ................................. (talk) to Mary. The last time I saw her she
claimed 6) ................................. (work) till 2 o'clock every morning for the past month.
It's not good for her, you know.
Jo: I know. I must 7) ................................. (talk) to her about it. But you know how she hates
8) ................................. (tell) what to do.

### Subject of the Infinitive / -ing form

The subject of the infinitive or of the -ing form is omitted when it is the same as the subject of the verb.
**They** want to buy a new house. **She** left without saying goodbye.

When the subject of the infinitive or of the -ing form is different from the subject of the verb then an object pronoun (me, you, him, her, us, you, them) or noun is placed before the infinitive or the -ing form. The subject of the gerund can also be a possessive adjective (my, your etc), the possessive case or a noun.
I want **him to leave** now. (= **He** should leave.)   BUT   I want to leave now. (= **I** should leave.)
I remember **his/him/Tom's/Tom** complaining about the poor service in this hotel.

**68  Rephrase the following as in the example:**

1. I must go to the gym to keep fit.          I want ..... *to go to the gym to keep fit.* ............ .
2. He must eat less.                           I want ................................................. .
3. They must tell her the truth.               I want ................................................. .
4. You must change your clothes. They're wet.  I want ................................................. .
5. She must get up early.                      I want ................................................. .
6. I must learn to type.                       He wants ............................................... .
7. She mustn't speak rudely.                   I don't want .......................................... .
8. She must stay in bed for a week.            The doctor wants ...................................... .
9. They must leave early.                      They want ............................................. .
10. They must apologise.                       I want ................................................. .

# 4. Infinitive / -ing form / Participles

## The to-infinitive is used:

1. **to express purpose**
   She went out **to buy** some milk.

2. **after certain verbs** (advise, agree, appear, decide, expect, hope, promise, refuse etc)
   He promised **to be** back at 10 o'clock.

3. **after certain adjectives** (angry, happy, glad etc) She was glad **to see** him.

4. **after question words** (where, how, what, who, which, but not after "why")
   Has she told you where **to meet** them?
   but: I don't know why he left so early.

5. **after would like/would love/would prefer** (to express specific preference)
   I'd love **to go** for a walk.

6. **after nouns**
   It's a pleasure **to work** with you.

7. **after too/enough constructions**
   He's **too** short **to reach** the top shelf.
   He isn't tall **enough to reach** the top shelf.

8. **with it + be + adjective (+ of + object)**
   It was nice of him **to remember** my birthday.

9. **with "only" to express unsatisfactory result**
   He called me only **to say** that he would be late.

## The infinitive without to is used:

1. **after modal verbs** (must, can, will etc)
   You must **be** back at 12 o'clock.

2. **after had better/would rather**
   I'd rather **have stayed** in last night.

3. **after make/let/see/hear/feel + object**
   Mum **let** me **watch** TV. I **made** him **apologise**.

   BUT: in the passive form: be made/be heard/be seen + to -infinitive
   He **was made to apologise**.

**Note:** help is followed by a to-infinitive or an infinitive without to.
She helped me **(to) wash** the dishes.

## The -ing form is used:

1. **as a noun**
   **Eating** vegetables is good for your health.

2. **after certain verbs** (admit (to), avoid, consider, continue, delay, deny, enjoy, escape, excuse, fancy, finish, forgive, imagine, involve, keep (= continue), look forward to, mention, mind, miss, object to, postpone, practise, prevent, report, resist, risk, save, stand, suggest, understand etc)
   He admitted (to) **stealing** the painting.

3. **after love, like, dislike, hate, enjoy, prefer** (to express general preference)
   He likes **cooking** (in general).
   * Note: like + to - inf = it's a good idea; it's useful
   I like **to eat** a healthy breakfast.(specific preference)

4. **after I'm busy, it's no use, it's (no) good, it's (not) worth, what's the use of, can't help, there's no point (in), can't stand, be/get used to, be/get accustomed to, have difficulty (in)**
   It's no use **complaining**.

5. **after "go" for physical activities**
   They **go skiing** every winter.

6. **after spend/waste time**
   He wasted his time **playing** video games.

7. **after prepositions**
   He entered without **knocking** at the door.

8. **after see, hear, listen, watch** to express an incomplete action, an action in progress or a long action
   I saw Kate **painting** the kitchen. (I saw Kate in the middle of painting. I saw part of the action in progress. I didn't wait until she had finished.)
   BUT: see, hear, listen, watch + infinitive without to to express a complete action, something that one saw or heard from beginning to end
   I watched Kate **paint** the kitchen. It took her two hours. (I saw the whole action from beginning to end.)

**Note:** If two infinitives are joined by "and", the "to" of the second infinitive can be omitted.
I want **to eat** something and **have** a rest.

## 4. Infinitive / - ing form / Participles

**69** Write what each word is followed by: F.I. (full inf.,) B.I. (bare inf.) or -ing (form).

| 1. mind | + ing | 5. decide | + ........ | 9. be seen | + ........ | 13. can | + ........ |
| 2. make | + ........ | 6. suggest | + ........ | 10. it's no use | + ........ | 14. be used to | + ........ |
| 3. what | + ........ | 7. refuse | + ........ | 11. would | + ........ | 15. object to | + ........ |
| 4. used | + ........ | 8. would love | + ........ | 12. risk | + ........ | 16. it's worth | + ........ |

**70** Complete the conversation between a travel agent and a woman, using the infinitive or the -ing form.

A: Good morning, madam. Can I 1) ..help.. (help) you?
W: Yes. I'd like 2) .................. (book) a holiday please.
A: Certainly. I must 3) .................. (ask) you a few questions. Now... where would you like 4) .......... (go)? How long are you going 5) .................. (stay)? Would you prefer 6) .............. (have) a relaxing beach holiday or 7) .......... (go) sightseeing? Which countries are you interested in 8) .............. (visit)? What means of transport do you prefer?
W: Well, young man. I don't know where 9) .............. (go) or how long 10) .................. (stay). I hate 11) .......... (go) to the beach and I don't enjoy sightseeing. I don't want 12) .......... .......... (visit) any foreign countries because foreign food makes me 13) .............. (feel) ill. As for means of transport, I'm too frightened 14) .................. (fly) in an aeroplane. I hate 15) .............. (go) on boats, I don't like 16) .................. (travel) by train and 17) .................. (travel) on a coach makes me 18) .......... (feel) sick.
A: Well madam, I don't know what 19) .................. (suggest). I don't want 20) .................. (appear) rude, but I really think you should 21) .................. (stay) at home!!

**71** Put the verbs in brackets into the -ing form or the infinitive without "to".

Last night I heard car breaks ...screeching.... (screech) and people 2) .................. (shout) in the street. When I looked out of the window I saw a crowd of about twenty people 3) .................. (stand) around a young boy 4) .................. (lie) in the street. Next, I saw the driver of the car 5) .................. (approach) the crowd and 6) .................. (kneel down) by the boy, he was 7) .................. (look) very anxious. 8) .................. (watch) the drama from my window, I began 9) .................. (consider) the boy's family. Then a few minutes later, I saw a young woman 10) .................. (run) towards the scene and 11) .................. (push) her way through the crowd. Soon, I heard an ambulance siren 12) .................. (scream) in the distance 13) .................. (get) closer and closer. Then I saw the ambulance stop in front of my house. I watched the ambulance men 14) .............. (get out) and 15) .................. (run) to the injured boy. Minutes later I saw them 16) .................. (run back) to their ambulance with the boy on a stretcher followed by his mother.

**72** Fill in infinitive with or without "to", or the -ing form.

1. Charlie goes ........swimming........ (swim) every morning in summer.
2. Thompson admitted .................. (murder) his wife.
3. He left England .................. (live) in another country.
4. I think you'd better .................. (go) home.
5. It was kind of you .................. (lend) me your jacket.
6. He ran all the way home without .................. (stop).

## 4. Infinitive / -ing form / Participles

7. The teacher made him ............................................................. (write) the composition again.
8. What's the use of ............................................................................................. (cry)?

### Verbs taking to-infinitive or -ing form without a change in meaning

1. **begin, start, continue** + to-inf. or -ing form. However, we never have two -ing forms together.
   
   She began **dancing/to dance**.
   But: *It's beginning **to get** cold.*
   Not: *It's beginning getting cold.*

2. **advise, allow, permit, recommend, encourage** when followed by an object or in passive form take a to-infinitive. They take the -ing form when not followed by an object.
   
   He **doesn't allow us to smoke** here.
   They **aren't allowed to smoke** here.
   They **don't allow smoking** here.

3. **it needs/it requires/it wants** + -ing form. "It needs" can also be followed by a passive infinitive.
   
   The house **needs/requires/wants painting**.
   The car **needs repairing/to be repaired**.

### Verbs taking to-infinitive or -ing form with a change in meaning

1. **forget + to-inf** = not remember
   *I'm sorry, I **forgot to buy** milk.*
   **forget + ing form** = forget a past event
   *He'll never **forget flying** over the Alps.*

2. **remember + to-inf** = remember to do sth
   ***Remember to turn off** the cooker before leaving.*
   **remember + -ing form** = recall a past event
   *I don't **remember staying** in this hotel before.*

3. **go on + to-inf** = finish doing sth and start doing sth else; then
   *After finishing the report, she **went on to type** some letters.*
   **go on + -ing form** = continue
   *She **went on talking** for hours.*

4. **mean + to-inf** = intend to
   *He **means to find** a job abroad.*
   **mean + -ing form** = involve
   *Finding a job **means attending** many interviews.*

5. **regret + to-inf** = be sorry to
   *I **regret to tell** you that there is no money left in your account.*
   **regret + -ing form** = have second thoughts about sth one has already done
   *I **regret buying/having bought** this dress; it doesn't look nice on me.*

6. **try + to-inf** = do one's best, attempt
   *The firemen are **trying to put out** the fire.*
   **try + -ing form** = do sth as an experiment
   *Why don't you **try adding** some sugar to the sauce? It might taste better.*

7. **want + to-inf** = wish
   *I **want to spend** my holidays in Spain.*
   **want + -ing form** = need sth done
   *This room **wants painting** again.*

8. **stop + to-inf** = pause temporarily
   *She **stopped to get** some petrol before continuing on her journey to Leeds.*
   **stop + -ing form** = finish; end
   ***Stop talking**, please!*

9. **be sorry + to-inf** = regret
   *I'm **sorry to hear** they fired him.*
   **be sorry for + -ing form** = apologise
   *I'm **sorry for being/having been** unfair to you.*

10. **be afraid + to-inf** (the subject is too frightened to do sth)
    *I'm **afraid to climb** up that tree. (I don't want to do it.)*
    **be afraid of + -ing form** (the subject is afraid that what is described by the -ing form may happen)
    *She won't climb up the tree; she **is afraid of falling**. (She is afraid because she might fall.)*

## 4. Infinitive / -ing form / Participles

### 73 Fill in the infinitive or -ing form.

The rules in my new school are very strict. The teachers don't allow 1) ..*talking*.. (talk) in class at all. We are only permitted 2) .............. (speak) if they ask us a question. On the first day, the headmaster advised us all 3) .............. (work) very hard. In fact, he recommended 4) .............. (study) for at least four hours every evening! We are not allowed 5) .......... (leave) the school at lunchtime but we are encouraged 6) .................... (join) one of the school clubs. Next week I'm starting chess.

### 74 Fill in the infinitive or -ing form in the appropriate tense.

My uncle Ted likes 1) ..*to tell/telling*.. (tell) stories. He claims 2) .............. .................... (meet) lots of famous people and 3) .................... (see) many strange things in his life. Many people believe him because he seems 4) .................................... (tell) the truth. Even if they didn't believe him, nobody would risk 5) .............. (say) so, because he's a very big and frightening man. One day he pretended 6) .... .................... (talk) to the President on the phone while my brother and I were in the room. "Hello, Mr President," he said. "You seem 7) ....................(have) some problems running the country and I would like 8) ....................(offer) you some advice." My brother and I started 9) .................................... (laugh) and my uncle Ted slammed down the receiver. "You must 10) .................................... (hear) something amusing," he shouted. "What is it?" We were very frightened. We hated 11) .................................... (think) what he would do to us if he thought we were laughing at him, so we pretended 12) .................... .............. (tell) jokes to each other.

### 75 Fill in the gaps with the verbs in brackets in the infinitive or the -ing form.

1. Remember .................... *to go* .................... (go) to the bank. You've got to pay the bills.
2. I don't remember .................................................... (see) this film before.
3. When he had written his first book he went on .................................... (write) seven more.
4. She went on .................................... (talk) even after her friend had fallen asleep.
5. I regret .................................... (leave) school at the age of 16.
6. I regret .................................... (tell) you that you have failed the test.
7. He means .................................... (build) a boat and travel round the world.
8. Doing well on this course means .................................... (study) very hard.
9. I've been trying .................................... (start) this car for hours.
10. Why don't you try .................................... (put) some petrol in the tank?
11. I don't want to drive a car; I'm afraid of .................................... (have) an accident.
12. He's afraid .................................... (walk) alone at night.
13. She forgot .................................... (invite) her best friend to the party.
14. I'll never forget .................................... (see) snow for the first time.
15. On the way home he stopped .................................... (buy) some chocolate.
16. The baby didn't stop .................................... (cry) all night.
17. These windows are dirty. They need .................................... (wash).
18. I want .................................... (speak) to Sally, please.
19. She's really sorry for .................................... (shout) at you last night.
20. I'm sorry .................................... (tell) you your car has been stolen.

## 4. Infinitive / – ing form / Participles

### Too - Enough

| too + adjective/adverb (negative meaning) | She's **too tired** to go out. (She is so tired that she **can't** go out.) |
|---|---|
| adjective/adverb + enough (positive meaning) | He's **rich enough** to afford a yacht. (He is so rich that he **can** afford a yacht.) |
| enough + noun | He's got **enough patience** to be a teacher. |

**76** Use "too" or "enough" and a word from the list below to complete the sentences.

small, big, fit, early, tall, frightening

1. She can put all her clothes in the case. It is ...*big enough*...

2. He can't put all his clothes in the case. It's ..........................

3. He can't run fast. He isn't ..........................

4. She didn't like the film. It was ..........................

5. He missed the bus. He didn't leave home ..........................

6. Ben can reach the sweets. He is ..........................

## 4. Infinitive / -ing form / Participles

**77** Complete the text using "too" or "enough".

Gary is leaving school this year but he doesn't know what he wants to do. He isn't motivated 1) ..enough... to go to university. He'd quite like to be an engineer but he thinks it would be 2) .............. difficult. His father wants him to work in the family shop but that's not exciting 3) .......................... for Gary. He hasn't got 4) ................... patience to sit in a shop all day. He wants to travel, so the navy seems to be a good idea, although the rules are a bit 5) ...................... strict. Someone suggested driving a taxi but the hours are 6) ....................... long and he wouldn't earn 7) ......................... money. There really is nothing that interests him enough.

### Participles

**Present Participles** (verb + ing) describe what something or somebody is.
Ted is an **interesting** person. (What kind of person? Interesting.)

**Past Participles** (verb + ed) describe how someone feels.
Mary is **interested** in English literature. (How does she feel about English literature? Interested.)

**78** Fill in the correct participle.

Paul: You must be very 1) ........excited........... (excite). Paris is a
2) ........................... (fascinate) city. There are so many
3) ........................... (interest) things to do. You won't
be 4) ........................... (bore).
Jane: Well, I'm a bit 5) ........................... (worry) because I can't
speak French very well.
Paul: You should buy a phrase book and then you won't be
6) ........................... (embarrass) if someone speaks to you.
They won't be 7) ............. (annoy) if you make a mistake, and
most people will be 8) ........................... (please) if you ask for
something in French.
Jane: I'm sure they'll find my accent very 9) ................... (amuse).
Paul: Don't be silly. I'm sure you'll have a very 10) ........................
........................... (stimulate) holiday.

**79** Put the verbs in brackets into the infinitive or -ing form.

Dear Ann,
How are you? We are still busy 1) ...decorating... (decorate) the house. I don't mind
2) ................. (paint) but I can't stand 3) ................. (clean up) afterwards. We started
4) ................. (tile) the kitchen today. We were advised 5) ................. (pay) professional
decorators but I prefer 6) ................. (do) things myself. We need 7) ................. (buy)
some new furniture, of course, and there are still so many things which we have 8) .................
................. (do) but we are not discouraged yet. Anyway, Ted wants me 9) .................
(help) him 10) ................. (move) the sofa so I must 11) ................. (go).
I hope 12) ................. (hear) from you soon. I'm looking forward to your
13) ................. (visit) us in our new house.
Love,
Mary

**80** Underline the correct item.

1. The children were **thrilled** / **thrilling** with the clown's tricks.
2. The adventure was **excited** / **exciting**.

## 4. Infinitive / – ing form / Participles

3. She was **interested** / **interesting** in anything antique.
4. Her experience was **terrified** / **terrifying**.
5. The police were **puzzled** / **puzzling** by the clues.
6. What an **amazing** / **amazed** person he is!
7. He was very **surprised** / **surprising** by her sudden change of attitude.
8. She felt **relaxed** / **relaxing** in the hot sun.
9. He was **disturbed** / **disturbing** by the threatening phone calls.
10. He found the history lesson extremely **bored** / **boring**.

### Oral Activity 11

The teacher divides the class into two teams and starts the story: **Tony denied murdering the old woman.** The teams in turn say one sentence to continue the story using verbs from the list below. Each verb must be used only once. Each correct sentence gets 1 point. The team with the most points is the winner.

**Verb list: suggest, spend, would like, hope, can, advise, continue, keep, agree, delay, get used to, stand, arrange, want, avoid, would rather, admit, be angry, refuse**

Team A S1: He **suggested** contacting his brother Mark who could prove he was innocent.
Team B S1: He said they had **spent** the night listening to records. etc

### Writing Activity 5

Look at the theory on page 35, then write a story using at least 10 words taking an infinitive with or without to, and another 10 words taking the -ing form.

### In Other Words

| | |
|---|---|
| Walking alone at night is dangerous.<br>It is dangerous to walk alone at night. | It took her an hour to do the crossword.<br>She took an hour to do the crossword.<br>Doing the crossword took her an hour.<br>She spent an hour doing the crossword. |
| She is too slow to win the race.<br>She isn't fast enough to win the race. | The policeman made him confess.<br>He was made to confess. |
| Do/Would you mind answering the phone?<br>Could you answer the phone? | The film was fascinating.<br>We were fascinated by the film. |

**81** Rephrase the following sentences using the words in bold type.

1. Could you pass me the salt?
   **mind** ....*Do/Would you mind passing me the salt?*
2. It is dangerous to drive at high speed.
   **driving**
3. The water is too cold to swim in.
   **enough**
4. He took only an hour to learn to play chess.
   **it**
5. Writing the composition took her all night.
   **spent**
6. My mother made me apologise for my behaviour.
   **was**

# 4. Infinitive / – ing form / Participles

7. I found the book boring.
   **bored** ..................................................................................................
8. Do you mind moving over a little?
   **could** ..................................................................................................
9. We were interested in the information.
   **found** ..................................................................................................
10. He isn't old enough to get married.
    **too** ..................................................................................................

### Phrasal Verbs 4

| | |
|---|---|
| **get away** : | escape |
| **get on** : | 1) make progress (also get along) |
| | 2) enter a bus, train etc. (**opp.** get off) |
| **get on with** : | have a friendly relationship with sb; get along with sb |
| **get through** : | 1) reach sb by telephone |
| | 2) manage to finish sth |

**82** Fill in the correct preposition or adverb.

1. Our son is getting .. *on/along* ... well at college.
2. If I can get ........................ all my homework, I'll go to the cinema later.
3. The thief got ........................ by climbing over the garden wall.
4. I really get ........................ my brother. We never argue.
5. I can't get ........................ to Joe. I'll phone again later.
6. Ann got ........................ the train just as it was about to leave and got ................ at Portland.

**83** Look at Appendix 1 and fill in the correct preposition.

1. London is famous ........ *for* ........ its museums.
2. I am fed ........................ this cold weather.
3. My grandmother is very fond ........................ her grandchildren.
4. Don't be frightened ................ the big spider.
5. The teacher was furious ................ the class because they were talking.
6. She will never forgive me ............ lying to her.
7. The boss was generous ................ everyone at Christmas.
8. It was very generous ........................ you to let me use your car.
9. He's good ........................ speaking English.
10. Grandfather is always good ................ me.
11. Sarah was grateful ........................ her friend ........................ babysitting.

### Idioms 4

| | |
|---|---|
| **make a fortune** : | make a lot of money |
| **make a fuss** : | complain loudly |
| **make up one's mind** : | decide |
| **make a living** : | earn money |
| **drop sb a line** : | send sb an informal letter |
| **pull sb's leg** : | make fun of sb by pretending sth is true |
| **break a record** : | make a new record (Olympic, World record etc) |
| **break sb's heart** : | make sb very sad |

**84** Fill in the correct idiom.

1. Bob .. *was pulling my leg* .. when he said there was a snake on my bed. He just wanted to tease me.
2. There's no need to ........................ just because I didn't wash up. I'll do it later.
3. Please ........................ while you're in Germany.
4. I can't ........................ whether to buy a Porsche or a BMW.
5. Her fiancé ........................ when he left her.
6. John Spencer ........................ in business and became a millionaire.
7. The old lady manages to ........................ by selling flowers.
8. The athlete ................ at the last Olympics.

42

# Revision Exercises I

**85** Choose the correct item.

1. How long ..... *C* ..... here?
   A) you live B) do you live
   C) have you lived D) are you living

2. ............................ I help you with the cooking?
   A) Will B) Am
   C) Shall D) Have

3. He denied ......... the money.
   A) to take B) to have taken
   C) take D) having taken

4. She ............. for 12 hours before she finished everything.
   A) had been working B) has been working
   C) is working D) has worked

5. When I was a child I ........... running every day.
   A) have gone B) used to go
   C) was going D) had gone

6. What ................. at 10 o'clock last night?
   A) have you done B) were you doing
   C) have you been doing D) had you done

7. He hasn't left the office ........ .
   A) yet B) before
   C) just D) already

8. They will have finished ............. 8 o'clock.
   A) until B) by the time
   C) since D) by

9. I'm afraid I ................ to come to the party.
   A) don't go B) won't
   C) won't be able D) can't

10. We went into town ............ some new clothes.
    A) to buy B) for buying
    C) to have bought D) buying

11. We'd rather ............... to bed early last night.
    A) to have gone B) to go
    C) going D) have gone

12. Remember ............ the door when you leave.
    A) to lock B) lock
    C) locking D) have locked

13. "You look slimmer." "Yes, I ............ 12 kilos."
    A) had lost B) lost
    C) have been losing D) have lost

14. "I'm having trouble with this exercise."
    "Don't worry. I ............ you."
    A) have helped B) am going to help
    C) helped D) 'll help

15. "Have you ever been to China?"
    "Yes, I ............................ there in 1990."
    A) have gone B) went
    C) have been going D) have been

16. "How long have you worked here?" "By the end of the month I ................ here for three years."
    A) 'll work B) 'm going to work
    C) 'll have been working D) 'll be working

17. "We'll need some cola for the party."
    "I ..................... some."
    A) buy B) will have bought
    C) 've already bought D) had bought

18. "I need to give a message to Susan."
    "I ................ her at the office this afternoon."
    A) see B) have seen
    C) 'll have seen D) 'll be seeing

19. "Have you ever met a famous person?"
    "Yes, I ..................... Maria Callas once."
    A) have met B) met
    C) meet D) have been meeting

20. "These shoes aren't at all comfortable."
    "You shouldn't ..................... them."
    A) have bought B) to buy
    C) bought D) buying

21. "What's wrong with Lynda?"
    "She ................ problems at work lately."
    A) has been having B) will have
    C) was having D) 'll be having

22. "What's Pam doing?" "She seems ............ ."
    A) to be working B) working
    C) to have worked D) to work

23. "How long have you been working here?"
    "................ 6 months."
    A) Since B) For
    C) From D) Ago

24. "I can't stand this any longer!"
    "Calm down. There's no point ............ upset."
    A) to get B) get
    C) in getting D) to getting

25. "How long does it take you to write a novel?"
    "By December I ........ on this one for 3 years."
    A) will work B) will have been working
    C) will be working D) am going to work

## Revision Exercises I

### 86 Choose the correct item.

John Jones is a 45-1) ...*year*... (years/years'/year) -old antique dealer. He studied History of Art 2) .......... (in/at/on) university and 3) ............. (has collected/has been collecting/collected) things since he was a child. He loves 4) ............. (buying/buy/have bought) antiques and 5) ............. (found/had found/has found) some good bargains so far. The only problem is that he finds it 6) ............. (such/too/enough) hard to sell the things he has bought 7) ............. (if/because/while) he likes them all. One day last week he came 8) ..................... (into/across/at) the most beautiful antique wooden trunk he had 9) ..................... (already/ever/never) seen. As he was 10) ............. (in/on/at) a hurry he told his driver to 11) ............. (fetch/bring/take) the trunk to his shop. When the driver 12) ............. (arrived/ reached/got) the shop, he 13) ............. (needn't/couldn't/mustn't) find a place to put the trunk so he left it by the front door. 14) ....... (At/In/By) that moment an old man came 15) ..................... (into/at/by) the shop to 16) ............. (spot/look/search) around. When he saw the trunk, he asked for 17) ............. (it's/each/ its) price. It was just then 18) ..................... (before/that/when) the door opened and a furious lady 19) ..................... (broke into/entered/got) the shop. "Don't touch that trunk!", she screamed. "It belongs 20) ..................... (in/to/at) me."

### 87 Rephrase the following sentences using the words in bold type.

1. I've never heard this group before.
   **first** ............ *It's the first time I've (ever) heard this group.* ............
2. She hasn't written to me for a long time.
   **since** ................................................................
3. This is the worst food I've ever eaten.
   **never** ................................................................
4. I haven't been to the cinema for months.
   **last** ................................................................
5. When did you leave school?
   **how** ................................................................
6. They took only one day to paint the house.
   **it** ................................................................
7. It's exciting to climb mountains.
   **climbing** ................................................................

### 88 Fill in the correct preposition or adverb.

1. When do schools break .... *up* ... for Christmas?
2. The detective came ............. an important clue quite by chance.
3. War broke ..................... between Britain and Germany in 1939.
4. She ignored the ringing telephone and carried ..................... her work.
5. After leaving London we headed ......... Oxford.
6. Someone broke ..................... the school and stole the computers.
7. There was so much noise that I couldn't concentrate ..................... my work.
8. Can I borrow some money ..................... you until tomorrow?
9. Although I'm bad ..................... crosswords, I love doing them.
10. Have you heard ......... the earthquake in Italy?

### 89 Put the verbs in brackets into the correct tense.

Sammy Milton 1) ...*is not*.. (not/be) very clever. He 2) ..................... (walk) along the beach one day when he 3) ..................... (trip) over something and 4) ..................... (fall) on the sand. He 5) ..................... (not/look) where he was going. "What 6) ..................... (be) this?" he said, picking up the object he 7) ..................... (trip) over. "I 8) ..................... (never/see) anything like it before." It was, in fact, a very old oil lamp, and as he 9) ..................... (rub) it, a genie suddenly 10) ..................... (fly) out of it. "You 11) ..................... (just/release) me from the lamp!" said the genie. "Now you may have three wishes." "Great" said Sammy who 12) ..................... (feel) very thirsty. "I 13) ............. (want) a bottle of lemonade that never 14) ..................... (run out)."

"No problem," said the genie, and 15) .......................... (produce) one instantly. Sammy picked up the bottle and 16) ................. (drink) all the lemonade in one go. Magically, the bottle 17) ............... (fill) itself up again. Sammy drank all that, and exactly the same thing 18) ........................ (happen) again. "That's amazing!" he said. "Thanks very much!" "You still 19) .......... (have) two more wishes young man." "That's easy," said Sammy. "I 20) ............................ (have) two more of these bottles of lemonade!"

**90** Put the verbs in brackets into Past S., Past Perf., Past Cont. or Past Perf. Cont.

Sally Deedes 1) ...*was walking*... (walk) home late one night. She 2) ........................ (be) to a dinner party at her friend's house. The city streets 3) ..................... (be) empty and it 4) ............ ............ (rain) slightly. She 5) ................. (look forward) to getting safely home to bed because at dinner her friends 6) .......... ............ (talk) about a dangerous murderer who 7) ............ ............ (escape) from prison the week before. Her friend Mark 8) ............................ (offer) to walk home with her but, as she 9) ............. (live) only a mile away, she 10) ............... (tell) him that she would be OK. She was about halfway home when she 11) ............ (hear) footsteps behind her. She 12) .................. (stop) and 13) .................... (turn) around, but she couldn't see anyone and the footsteps 14) ............. (stop) as well. When she continued on her way the footsteps 15) ................ (start) again. She 16) ............... (begin) to feel afraid. She started to run. The footsteps 17) .................. (get) closer. Suddenly she 18) ................ (feel) a hand on her shoulder and she 19) ......................... (scream) in terror. "Sally! Sally! It's me, Mark." He tried to explain that he 20) ................ (be) worried about her and 21) ........................ (decide) to follow her home. But Sally 22) ........................ (can/not) hear a word because she 23) ........................ (already/faint).

**91** Read the numbered lines and correct the mistakes in the spaces provided. Some lines are correct. Indicate these lines with a tick ( ✓ ).

1. James Tibbs was travelling on a train i̶n̶ his way to a job          ......*on*........
2. interview in the city centre when he realise with horror that    ....................
3. he was on the wrong train. He was knowing he would be late       ....................
4. for the interview and wouldn't get the job. He has thought how   ....................
5. silly he had been when suddenly the train screeched to a halt.   ....................
6. A lady which was sitting opposite him fell off her seat onto the ....................
7. floor. James helped her get up and picked up her things which lie ....................
8. on the carriage floor. The train set off again. The women        ....................
9. thanked him and they began talk. James was telling her about his ....................
10. job interview after she suddenly burst into laughter. James     ....................
11. was very confusing. The lady explained that her husband was    ....................
12. the boss of the company where his interview is to have been.   ....................
13. James was relaxing at home the other day when the telephone   ....................
14. rang. It was the lady husband. He was calling to offer him the job. ....................

**92** Put the verbs in brackets into the correct tense.

One day a little Indian boy 1) ... *was sitting*... (sit) outside his wigwam. He 2) ..................... (wonder) how the Indians 3) ............................ (choose) their children's names. He 4) ................. (decide) to go and ask the Indian Chief. "Well," 5) ....................... (explain) the Chief, "we 6) ..................... (love) nature and when a new baby 7) ................ (be) born, we 8) ..................... (look) around and we 9) ........................ (choose) a name from what we 10) ............................. (see), like Flowing Waterfall, Bright Star, Running Bull and so on. 11) ..................... (you/understand)?" "Yes, chief," the little Indian boy said. "Why 12) ............................ (you/be) so interested in this, Two Dogs Fighting?", the Chief asked.

## 5. Modal Verbs

The modal verbs are: **can**, **could**, **may**, **might**, **must**, **ought to**, **will**, **would**, **shall**, **should**, **have to**, **need**. They take no **-s** in the third person singular except for **have to** and **need**. They come before the subject in questions and take "not" after them in negations. Except for **ought to** and **have to**, modal verbs are followed by an **infinitive without to**. eg. Sorry, I **can't** come. I **have to** meet Pam.

Modal verbs are used to express : ability, possibility, probability, logical assumptions, permission, requests, offers, suggestions, advice, criticism, obligation, prohibition or necessity.

### Ability

| | |
|---|---|
| **Can/be able to** (ability in the present/future) "Can" is more usual and less formal than "be able to" when talking about the present or future. | Ann **can** run fast. I **can** pay you next week. (usual) I **will be able to** pay you next week. (less usual) |
| **Was able to** (= managed to - ability in the past) is used for either repeated or single actions. | I **was able to** go on a trip round the city last week. (single action) |
| **Could** (ability in the past). "Could" is more usual than "was able to"; it is used in statements for repeated actions. However, with the verbs see, hear, smell, understand etc, we normally use "could" for single actions. | She **could/was able to** play the violin when she was six. (repeated action) I **could** smell something burning. (single action) (not : I was able to smell ...) |
| **Could/was able to** can both be used in negations and questions for either repeated or single actions. | She **couldn't/wasn't able to** pass her driving test. (single action) **Were you able to/Could you** get to work yesterday? (single action) |

**Can** is the Present Simple and **could** is the Past Simple. **Can** borrows the rest of its tenses from **be able to**. eg. He **hasn't been able to** call them yet but he **can** call them tomorrow.

**93)** Fill in **can** or **be able to** in the appropriate tense and form.

1. I've been looking for your glasses but I ......... *haven't been able to* ..................... find them yet.
2. By the time Phillis was ten, she ............................................................ speak three languages.
3. If you don't tell me what your problem is, I ............................................................ help you.

# 5. Modal Verbs

4. I got home early last night, so I ........................................ watch my favourite programme on TV.
5. I ........................................ eat anything when I was younger, but now I have to be more careful.
6. He ........................................ pass the exam because he had studied hard.

## Possibility - Probability - Logical assumptions

### Possibility

**may/might/could + present infinitive** (perhaps; it's possible that something will happen in the future or perhaps it is true at the moment)
**may/might/could + perfect infinitive** (perhaps something happened in the past)
**Could + perfect infinitive** is also used for something which was possible but didn't actually happen.

Sam **may/might/could** pass his test this time. (It's possible that he will pass his test.)
Where's Jean? She **could** be at school.
She looks miserable. She **may/might/could have lost** her job. (Perhaps she has lost her job.)
Don't drive so fast! You **could have killed** that boy. (Luckily, you didn't kill the boy.)

### Probability

**ought to/should + present infinitive** show that something is probable now or in the future
**ought to/should + perfect infinitive** show that we expected something to happen but we don't know if it happened or not

Tom **ought to/should** pass his exams. (He will probably pass.)
Has Nancy phoned yet? She **ought to/should have phoned** an hour ago. (We don't know whether she phoned or not.)

### Logical assumptions

**can't/couldn't + present infinitive** (I don't think; it's logically improbable)
**must + present infinitive** (I think, I'm fairly sure; it's logically probable)
**can't** is the opposite of **must**
**can't/couldn't + perfect infinitive** (It's impossible that something happened in the past.)
**must + perfect infinitive** (It's very probable that something happened in the past.)

She **can't** be rich. Her house is too small. (I don't think she's rich.)
His face is red. He **must** be very angry. (I think he's very angry.)
It **can't** be true. It **must** be a lie.
She **can't/couldn't have lost** her way; she **must have missed** the train. (= I don't think she's lost her way; I think she has missed the train.)

To express possibility in questions we don't use **may**. We use : **Can he? Could he? Is he likely to? Is it likely that? Might he? Can he** succeed? **Could he** succeed? **Is he likely to** succeed? **Is it likely that** he will succeed? (= Is it possible that he will succeed?) **Can/Could he have** finished? (= Is it possible that he has finished?) **Might he** succeed?

## 5. Modal Verbs

**94** Fill in: can't, might, must or could.

I wonder where Paul is. He 1) ......*can't*............ be at work because he never works on a Sunday. He 2) ........................... be at Sally's, but I doubt it because they haven't been speaking lately. I wonder if he 3) ....................... be at his cottage in the country. No, he 4) ........................... be because he told me they've rented it to someone else for the summer. He 5) ................... have gone bowling, but I'm almost sure he told me he'd got tired of it. I know! He 6) ................... have gone swimming, because I remember him asking me if I wanted to go with him.

**95** How else can you express the following?

1) You may be wrong. 2) It's likely that she will lend you the money. 3) I'm sure they have invited her too. 4) I don't think he will forget your birthday. 5) They may have hurt her feelings.

### Permission

Could I try on that dress in the window, please?

I'm afraid you can't, madam. You'll have to try it on in the changing room like everyone else.

| Asking for permission | |
|---|---|
| **can** (informal) / **could** (more polite) <br> **may** (formal) / **might** (more formal) | **Can/Could** I interrupt you for a second? <br> **May/Might** I speak to the bank manager, please? |
| **Giving or refusing permission** | |
| **can** (informal; giving permission) <br> \* could is not used in the present to give permission <br> **may** (formal; giving permission - also used in written notices or formal announcements) <br> **mustn't/can't** (informal - refusing permission) <br> **may not** (formal - refusing permission) | **Can** I use your phone? Of course you **can**. (informal) <br> **Could** I use your phone? Of course you **can**. (not : ~~of course you could~~) <br> **May** I use your phone? Certainly you **may**. (formal) <br> Luggage **may** be left here. (written notice) <br> I'm afraid you **can't/mustn't** enter the room. <br> Rubbish **may not** be left here. (written notice) |
| **Talking about permission** | |
| **can/be allowed to** (to talk about the future or present) <br> **could** (to talk about the past - used for repeated actions) <br> **was/were allowed to** (to talk about the past - used for repeated or single actions) <br> **couldn't/wasn't allowed to** (in negations or questions for either repeated or single actions) | Pupils **are allowed to/can** use the school swimming pool free of charge. <br> She **was** always **allowed to/could** always play with her friends after school. (repeated action) <br> The reporter **was allowed to** (not: ~~could~~) take a photo of the pop singer. (single action) <br> The foreigner **wasn't allowed to/couldn't** enter the country without a visa. (single action) |

## 5. Modal Verbs

**96** Fill in: can, couldn't, may, mustn't, can't or (not) be allowed to.

David : 1) ..Can... I go to the cinema tonight?
Mrs Stone : You know you 2) .................... go out during the week.
David : But I 3) .................... go out last Saturday either. I think Dad is too strict.
Mrs Stone : You 4) ............................ speak about your father like that. He's doing what he thinks is best.
David : 5) .................... I have some friends over, then?
Mrs Stone : I'm afraid you 6) .................... . We're having some friends to dinner.
David : 7) .................... I at least watch TV for a while?
Mrs Stone : Yes, you 8) ...................., but only after you've done your homework.
David : But I haven't got any homework!
Mrs Stone : Oh! Well, in that case, you 9) .................... go out, but you 10) .................... be home late.
David : I'll be home by 11, I promise.

### Requests - Offers - Suggestions

**Requests (asking someone to do something)**

| | |
|---|---|
| Can you? (informal request) | Can you help me, please? |
| Will you? (familiar) | Will you get me my glasses please? |
| Could you? (polite request) | Could you make me some tea? |
| May I? (formal request) | May I have a glass of water? (request) |
| | compare : May I open the window? (asking for permission) |
| Would you/Would you mind? (more polite and formal than "could you") | Would you post this letter for me? |
| | Would you mind typing these letters for me? |

**Offers (offering to do something)**

| | |
|---|---|
| I'll (I'm willing to do sth - informal) | I'll do the shopping if you like. |
| Shall I/we/Can I/we (Do you want me/us to...? – informal) | Shall I help you with your luggage? |
| Would you like/Would you like me to ...? | Would you like some more tea? |

**Suggestions (making suggestions)**

| | |
|---|---|
| Shall I/we? | Shall we go to the theatre? |
| I/We can/could | We can/could go to the pub if you like. |
| We also express suggestions with : | |
| Let's/How about/Why don't we?/ | Let's go to the park. How about going to the park? |
| What about? | Why don't we go to the park? What about going to the park? |

49

## 5. Modal Verbs

**97** Fill in : would you, I'll, shall, could, why don't you or how about.

Husband : I've got a splitting headache.
    Wife : 1) ...*Why don't you*... go and lie down?
Husband : Yes, I think I will. 2) ............................. you bring me some aspirin?
    Wife : Yes, of course I will. 3) ............................. I call the doctor?
Husband : No. 4) ............................. wait and see how I feel later.
    Wife : 5) ............................. like a glass of water?
Husband : Yes, please. 6) ............................. you also telephone the office to say I'm ill?
    Wife : Yes. 7) ............................. you tell me where to find the number?
Husband : 8) ............................. looking in the address book by the phone?
    Wife : 9) ............................. I say you'll be in the office this afternoon?
Husband : Yes, you 10) ............................. say I'll be in about 2 – I should be all right by then.

### Advice - Criticism

| Advice (saying what the best thing to do is) | |
|---|---|
| **should/ought to + present infinitive**<br>(it is the best thing to do; I advise you to)<br>* (ought to is sometimes used for advice based on laws, rules or generally accepted ideas)<br>**Shall I?** (asking for advice)<br>**had better** (it's a good idea - advice for a specific situation) | You **should** stop smoking. (general advice; I advise you)<br>You **ought to** treat animals kindly. (Most people believe this.)<br>**Shall** I tell him the truth? (Is it the right thing to do?)<br>You**'d better** call your parents or they'll worry. (It's a good idea; specific situation) |
| **Criticism (saying what the best thing to do in the past was)** | |
| **should/ought to + perfect infinitive** | You **shouldn't have been** rude to her yesterday. (but you were)<br>You **should have locked** the car before leaving. (but you didn't) |

**98** Fill in: should, shouldn't, ought to or had better.

David : You 1) ...*should*... really do something about your car.
 Sally : What do you mean?
David : It's in terrible condition. You 2) ................ get a new one before the police stop you.
 Sally : But I can't afford a new one!
David : Well, you 3) ................ at least have the exhaust seen to. And you 4) ................ have the brakes repaired before you kill somebody.
 Sally : I suppose I 5) ............. . But you 6) ................ lend me some money to pay for the repairs.
David : Sally, have you spent the money I lent you last week? You 7) ................ have spent it all!

## 5. Modal Verbs

**99** Fill in: should, had better or ought to.

Dear Pete,
I am sorry to hear your sister is being so horrible to you. I think you 1) ..should/.. ..ought to.. continue being pleasant to her. You 2) ................ try at least. If she is still nasty to you, you 3) ........................ tell your parents what has been happening. Your sister 4) .... ........................ be punished for what she has been doing to you. You 5) ........................ have told your parents straight away, but you seemed determined to solve the problem yourself.

Good Luck,
Auntie Marge.

**100** Fill in the correct modal verb and form of the infinitive.

There was a bank robbery in town this morning and PC Jones was sent to investigate. He's reporting his findings to the Chief of Police. Complete what he says.

"Well sir, it 1) ....*must have been*... (be) a professional gang because it was a very clever job. They 2) ............................. (know) exactly what they were doing because they didn't leave even one clue behind them. It definitely 3) ....... ........................ (be) Freddy Fingers and his gang because they are in prison. I thought it 4) ........................ (be) Harry but he was in hospital at the time of the robbery, so it 5) ................... (be) him either. I 6) .............................. (be) sure, but it 7) ...................... (be) Sly Steve's gang, because they are the only suspects who don't have an alibi; they 8) ............................. (commit) the robbery. 9) ................... (I/ bring) them in for questioning, sir?"

**101** How else can you express the following?

1. Shall we invite them? ..*How about inviting them?* ... *Let's invite them. We could invite them.*......
2. May I go out for a minute? ........................
3. I'll baby-sit if you like. ............................
4. Let's go for a swim. ............................

5. You can't use the photocopier. ....................
6. He might move to Brazil. ............................
7. Would you mind carrying my luggage? ...........
8. I couldn't swim when I was five. ....................

**102** Write the functions of the modal verbs according to register.

|  | informal | polite | formal | more formal |
|---|---|---|---|---|
| 1. May I borrow your car? |  |  | permission |  |
| 2. Can I borrow your car? |  |  |  |  |
| 3. Could I borrow your car? |  |  |  |  |
| 4. Might I borrow your car? |  |  |  |  |
| 5. Shall I drive you home? |  |  |  |  |
| 6. Would you like me to drive you home? |  |  |  |  |
| 7. Would you bring me some water? |  |  |  |  |
| 8. Can you bring me some water? |  |  |  |  |
| 9. Could you bring me some water? |  |  |  |  |

## 5. Modal Verbs

### Necessity - Obligation - Prohibition

#### Obligation – Necessity

| | |
|---|---|
| **must/have to** (it is necessary, I'm obliged to) <br> **Must** is used only in the present and future when the speaker decides. <br> **Have to** is used when the necessity comes from outside the speaker or when others decide for him. <br> **Have got to** (more informal and usual than "have to") is used for obligation on a single occasion. <br> **Ought to** (duty; it's the right thing to do but people don't always do it.) <br> **Need** (it's necessary) is followed by a passive full infinitive or an -ing form and takes -s in the 3rd person singular in statements. | I **must** lose some weight. (I say so.) <br> I **had to** go to work early yesterday. ("Must" is not possible here as it is used only in the present.) <br> I **have to** lose some weight. (The doctor says so; the doctor decides for me.) <br> I'**ve got to** tidy my room; Mother is angry. <br> I'**ve got to** phone her; she will be worried. <br> We **ought to** respect the environment. (But we don't always do it.) <br> Your hair **needs** to be cut. **or** <br> Your hair **needs** cutting. |

**Must** is used only for present and future situations. It borrows the rest of its tenses from **have to**. **Have to** forms its questions and negations with **do/does** (Present Simple) and **did** (Past Simple).
**Did you have to** stay late at work yesterday? Yes, I **had to** type some urgent letters. ("Must" is not possible in the past tense.)

#### Absence of Necessity

| | |
|---|---|
| **needn't + bare present infinitive / don't have to/ don't need to** (it is not necessary in the present or future) | You **needn't** take a jacket. It's rather warm. <br> You **don't have to/don't need to** take a jacket. It's rather warm. |
| **didn't need to/didn't have to** (It wasn't necessary in the past and we may not know if the action happened or not.) | He **didn't need/have to** buy any milk. There was a lot in the fridge. (I don't know if he bought any.) |
| **needn't + bare perfect infinitive** (We know that something happened in the past although it was not necessary.) | She **needn't have bought** any milk. There was a lot in the fridge. (I know she bought some milk but there was no need.) |

#### Prohibition

| | |
|---|---|
| **mustn't** (it's forbidden) <br> **can't** (you aren't allowed to) | You **mustn't** enter the room. (it's forbidden) <br> You **can't** wait here. (you are not allowed to) |

## 5. Modal Verbs

**103** Fill in: must(n't), (not) have to, ought to or need(n't) in the correct form.

Yesterday when I was at the museum a fire broke out. We 1) ...*had to*... leave the building. We were told that we 2) ..................... panic as it was a small fire, but that we should all go outside. In the end, they were able to put out the fire and they 3) ........................... call the fire brigade. Unfortunately, one of the rooms 4) ................ painting again as the smoke damaged it. The police said that the museum 5) ................. have better security and that all visitors 6) ..................... make sure they know where the fire exits are.

**104** State who decides, the speaker or others, then fill in: must or have to.

1. I .....*must*..... cut the grass.

2. I ................. cut the grass.

3. I ....... wear a uniform at work.

4. I ................. repair the roof.

5. I ................. repair the roof.

6. I ......... find a way to escape.

**105** Fill in: mustn't, needn't or can't.

In this school students 1) ..*can't/mustn't*... smoke. Students 2) ............. wear school uniforms, but they 3) ....................... wear dirty clothes. Students 4) ..................... leave school until 3 pm. They 5) ................ forget to do their homework. They 6) ..................... bring a doctor's note if they are sick. Older students 7) ................. park their cars in the teachers' car park. Students 8) ................ walk or ride their bikes across the grass. Students 9) ............... be late for class or talk loudly in lessons. Students 10) ................ forget these rules, but teachers 11) ................ obey them as they have a separate set of rules to follow.

**106** Fill in: can't, must(n't), need(n't), ought to, have (got) to or don't have to.

Jo : Hello, Mum. Are you still awake? You 1) ...*needn't*.. have waited up for me.
Mum : Do you know what time it is? It's after midnight and you 2) ................. go to school in the morning.
Jo : I'm sorry, but I missed the last bus.
Mum : Well, you 3) ......................... have phoned me then. You 4) ......................... come in at any time you want. I was worried.
Jo : Oh Mum, you 5) ..................... worry about me. Anyway, you 6) ................... walk miles to find a telephone that works.
Mum : Then next time you 7) ..................... be sure to catch the bus. You 8) ................ walk in the dark alone.
Jo : Yes, Mum. I'm going to bed now – I 9) ........................... to get some sleep. And by the way, I 10) ................ go to school in the morning – tomorrow's Saturday.

## 5. Modal Verbs

**107** Fill in the correct modal verb.

1. ...May/Might I... come in? — Certainly you may.
2. ............ smoke in here? — No, you can't.
3. ............ hold these books for me? — Yes, I will.
4. ............ go to the cinema? — Sorry, I don't feel like it.
5. ............ some more water? — Yes, please!
6. ............ book a room? — Yes, of course you can.

**108** First write a synonym, then write the meaning of the verbs in bold type.

ability (present/future) - ability (past) - possibility - deduction - permission - request - offer - suggestion - advice - criticism - absence of obligation/necessity - prohibition

1. He **can't** speak German. ....... *He is not able to (ability - present)* ...
2. He **might** be in his office. ..........................
3. You **may** go home now. ..........................
4. **Could** you lend me £5? ..........................
5. **Shall** we dance? ..........................
6. You **ought to** take more exercise. ..........................
7. She **shouldn't** have told you that. ..........................
8. You **don't have to** apologise. ..........................
9. I **couldn't** find my socks. ..........................
10. She **must** have left her bag on the train. ..........................
11. You **had better** ask your mother. ..........................
12. I'**ll** carry your bag if you like. ..........................
13. You **mustn't** make any noise. ..........................
14. His car **needs** washing. ..........................
15. We **can** go to the beach if you like. ..........................

### In Other Words

**109** Rephrase the following situations using an appropriate modal verb as in the example:

1. It's not possible that he's finished already. He ....... *can't have finished already.* ..........................
2. It wasn't necessary for you to give him a present. You ..........................
3. I advise you to stop eating chocolate. You ..........................
4. I insist that you do your homework. You ..........................
5. It was wrong of him to kick that dog. He ..........................

## 5. Modal Verbs

6. It's possible that she's already phoned him. She ..................
7. I'll take the dog out if you like. Would ..................
8. Will you let me speak to George, please? May ..................
9. Let's go to a disco. What ..................
10. It's possible that he is lying. He ..................
11. He wasn't able to write until he was eight. He ..................
12. Talking is not permitted during the test. You ..................
13. It would be a good idea for me to give up smoking. I had ..................
14. I'm sure that he has gone home. He ..................
15. It isn't right to speak to your mother like that. You ..................
16. It isn't possible for me to come to the party tonight. I ..................
17. He is obliged to go to the police station twice a week. He ..................

### Oral Activity 12

The teacher divides the class into two teams. The teams in turn make comments and speculations about each picture using modals. Each correct answer gets 1 point. The team with the most points is the winner.

Picture 1:  Team A S1: He may have stolen some money. or He may have murdered someone.
Team B S1: He shouldn't have stolen it. or He shouldn't have murdered him.
Team A S2: He could stay in prison for a long time. or He may regret it. etc

### Writing Activity 6

Your friend has lost his job and is very upset. Write a letter to him using the appropriate modal verbs.
Include : **should, shouldn't, could, couldn't, may, might, mustn't, can't** etc
**Dear Stewart,**
Thank you for your letter. Well, what can I say? I can't believe you've lost your job. ...

### Tense Review

**110 Fill in Past Simple, Past Continuous, Present Perfect, Past Perfect or will.**

My cat, Thomas, 1) .....*loves*..... (love) playing in the garden. I 2) ..................... (sit) in the kitchen one day when I 3) ..................... (hear) him scratching at the back door. When I 4) ..................... (open)

## 5. Modal Verbs

the door I was horrified to see him sitting there with a live bird in his mouth. The bird 5) ................ (try) to escape but Thomas 6) ................ (hold) it by its neck. What 7) ................ (can) I do? Thomas 8) ................ (never/do) anything like this before. "The poor bird 9) ................ (die) if I don't act fast," I thought, so I 10) ................ (run) into the kitchen, 11) ................ (fill) a bucket with water and 12) ................ (throw) it over my naughty cat. He 13) ................ (drop) the bird and it 14) ................ (fly) off into the trees. Thomas 15) ................ (not/bring) any more birds to my doorstep since that day.

### Phrasal Verbs 5

| | |
|---|---|
| give sth/sb away : | 1) reveal sth/betray sb |
| | 2) give sth free of charge |
| give back : | return |
| give off : | emit (a smell etc) |
| give out : | come to an end |
| give up : | abandon a habit; quit |
| give oneself up : | surrender; give in |

**111** Fill in the correct preposition or adverb.

1. This chemical gives ....*off*...... a strange smell.
2. Can I borrow that book? I'll give it *back* to you tomorrow.
3. After the operation David had to give *up* smoking.
4. Their food supplies gave ..*out*.... sooner than they had planned, so they had to return home.
5. The hijackers finally gave themselves ..*up*.... to the police.
6. You'd better not give ......*away*...... this secret to anyone, or I'll be very angry with you.
7. They are giving ......*away*...... free glasses with every box of washing powder they sell.

**112** Look at Appendix 1 and fill in the correct preposition.

1. Have you heard ..*about*...... what happened at school yesterday?
2. Have you heard ................ Phyllis lately? She hasn't written to me for ages.
3. Who is this writer? I've never heard ......... her.
4. Tom is jealous ................ his brother because he has a much better job.
5. I know I've made some mistakes, but there's no need to be impatient ................ me.
6. The escaped prisoners headed ................ the woods.
7. He introduced me ................ his parents.
8. Although I can't play an instrument, I'm very interested ................ music.
9. Our teacher insists ................ everyone doing their compositions on time.
10. I have no problem with Biology, but I'm hopeless ................ Physics.

### Idioms 5

| | |
|---|---|
| throw a party : | have a party |
| hit the roof : | get very angry |
| fight like cat and dog : | disagree violently |
| rain cats and dogs : | rain heavily |
| swim like a fish : | swim very well |
| cut a long story short : | tell sb sth briefly |
| have a memory like an elephant : | never forget |
| eat like a horse : | eat a lot of food |

**113** Fill in the correct idiom.

1. If you go out, be sure you take your umbrella because it *'s raining cats and dogs.* ............
2. She never forgets a name or a date – she ................ .
3. It's Sharon's birthday on Friday. Why don't we ................ for her?
4. My brother and sister ................ ; they never agree about anything.
5. There's no point going into the details. To ................ , he simply isn't right for the job.
6. You'd better prepare some extra food for Bob – you know he ................ .
7. Paula, who spent her childhood by the sea, can ................ .
8. My father will ................ when he finds out I've crashed the car.

56

# 6. Passive Voice

The Passive is formed by using the appropriate tense of the verb **to be + past participle**.

| | Active Voice | Passive Voice |
|---|---|---|
| Present Simple | They **repair** cars. | Cars **are repaired**. |
| Present Continuous | They **are repairing** the car. | The car **is being repaired**. |
| Past Simple | They **repaired** the car. | The car **was repaired**. |
| Past Continuous | They **were repairing** the car. | The car **was being repaired**. |
| Future Simple | They **will repair** the car. | The car **will be repaired**. |
| Present Perfect | They **have repaired** the car. | The car **has been repaired**. |
| Past Perfect | They **had repaired** the car. | The car **had been repaired**. |
| Future Perfect | They **will have repaired** the car. | The car **will have been repaired**. |
| Present Infinitive | They will have **to repair** the car. | The car will have **to be repaired**. |
| Perfect Infinitive | She ought **to have repaired** the car. | The car ought to **have been repaired**. |
| Gerund | He likes people **admiring** his new car. | He likes his new car **being admired**. |
| Perfect Gerund | **Having repaired** the car, ... | The car, **having been repaired**, ... |
| Modals + be + p.p. | You **must repair** this car. | This car **must be repaired**. |

**The passive is used:**

1. **when the agent (the person who does the action) is unknown, unimportant or obvious from the context.**
   My car **was stolen** yesterday. (unknown agent)
   The road repairs **were completed** last week. (unimportant agent)
   The kidnappers **have been arrested**. (by the police - obvious agent)

2. **to make statements more polite or formal.**
   My new suit **has been burnt**. (It's more polite than saying "You've burnt my new suit".)

3. **when the action is more important than the agent - as in news reports, formal notices, instructions, processes, headlines, advertisements etc.**
   Taking pictures **is not allowed**. (written notice)
   The local bank **was robbed** this morning. (news report)
   Bread **is baked** in an oven for about 45 minutes. (process)

4. **to put emphasis on the agent.**
   The Tower of London was built by **William the Conqueror**.

# 6. Passive Voice

> **Note :** We use the Passive only with transitive verbs (verbs which take an object).
> They built **that castle** in 1600. That castle was built in 1600.
>
> In colloquial English **get** can be used instead of **be** to express something happening by accident. She **got** sunburnt last week. (more usual than "She **was** sunburnt last week.")

**114) Put the verbs in brackets into the correct passive form.**

There is an old castle in Norwich which 1) ...is believed... (believe) to 2) ...be haunted... (haunt). It 3) ...is called... (call) North Castle and it 4) ...is said... (say) that ghosts can 5) ...be seen... (see) there at night. The castle 6) .................. (build) 400 years ago and 7) .................. (own) by two old ladies who 8) .................. (believe) to be witches. One day, long ago, they both disappeared and they 9) .................. (never/see) again. In 1985 the castle 10) .................. (buy) by a businessman and 11) .................. (convert) into a luxurious hotel. The castle 12) .................. (visit) by quite a few guests every year and special groups 13) .................. (organise) to watch for ghosts. It has been a long time since any ghosts 14) .................. (see), but one night a trick 15) .................. (play) on some visitors by a local couple, who dressed up as the two "witches". They 16) .................. (see) by a guest, who said she 17) .................. (frighten) almost to death. The couple apologised the next day, and 18) .................. (tell) never to visit the castle again, certainly not in the middle of the night dressed up as witches.

**115) Rewrite the newspaper headlines as complete sentences.**

| 1. RARE BIRD FOUND IN REMOTE COUNTRYSIDE | 2. QUEEN WELCOMED TO AUSTRALIA YESTERDAY | 3. NEW JERSEY TO BE HIT BY BAD WEATHER TOMORROW |
| --- | --- | --- |
| 4. FIVE PEOPLE INJURED IN CAR ACCIDENT | 5. EXPERIMENTS BEING CARRIED OUT ON MOON ROCKS | 6. POP CONCERT CALLED OFF YESTERDAY BECAUSE OF RAIN |

1. ...A rare bird has been found in the remote countryside.
2. ..............................................................
3. ..............................................................
4. ..............................................................
5. ..............................................................
6. ..............................................................

**116) Put the verbs in brackets into the correct passive form.**

Professor Higgins, who 1) ...was awarded... (award) a major science prize last month, 2) .................. (invite) to take part in a conference which 3) .................. (hold) in London last week. He 4) .................. (meet) at the airport by a driver who, unfortunately, 5) .................. (give) the name of the wrong hotel to take the professor to. A large reception 6) .................. (organise) for the professor, and at least 200 eminent scientists 7) .................. (invite) to meet him that evening. The poor professor, however, 8) .................. (leave) at a small hotel in a rather bad area, and when he asked to speak to the Head of the Conference Committee he 9) .................. (tell) to try somewhere else because he 10) .................. (not/hear of) there. Luckily, later that evening, the driver 11) .................. (send) to the hotel where the reception 12) .................. (hold), and when he 13) .................. (ask) what he had done with the professor, everyone realised that a mistake 14) .................. (make). The professor says that if he 15) .................. (ever/send) another invitation to a conference, he hopes it 16) .................. (organise) more efficiently.

# 6. Passive Voice

**117** Fill in the Passive in the appropriate tense, then justify its use.

*unknown agent, unimportant/obvious agent, polite statement, emphasis on the agent, action more important than the agent, process, news report*

1. ...polite statement...
(animals/shouldn't/feed)
..Animals shouldn't be fed..

2. ..........
(Hamlet/write/Shakespeare)

3. ..........
(just/tell/the bad news)

4. ..........
(dinner/serve)

5. ..........
(the building/destroy/fire)

6. ..........
(juice/make/from orange)

7. ..........
(the room/not tidy/yet)

8. ..........
(a bomb/place/station yesterday)

9. ..........
(the jewellery/steal)

 **118** Fill in the correct passive form.

A new wing 1) ..is being built.. (build). The walls 2) .......... (paint). Some trees 3) .......... (plant). The roof 4) .......... (repair). The school 5) .......... (change) from a primary school to a secondary school. A library 6) .......... (open) next week. Computers 7) .......... (deliver) at the moment. New desks 8) .......... (already/buy).

## 6. Passive Voice

### Changing from Active into Passive

The object of the active verb becomes the subject in the new sentence. The active verb changes into a passive form and the subject of the active verb

|  | Subject | Verb | Object | Agent |
|---|---|---|---|---|
| Active | Bell | invented | the telephone. |  |
| Passive | The telephone | was invented |  | by Bell. |

becomes the agent. The agent (= person who does the action) is introduced with "by" or it is omitted.

We use **by + agent** to say who or what did the action. We use **with + instrument** or **material** to say what instrument or material the agent used.
He was knocked down **by a lorry**. (The lorry did the action.)
The door was locked **by** a man **with** a key. (The key is the instrument the agent used.)
The cake was made **with flour, sugar** and **eggs**. (Flour, sugar and eggs are the materials the agent used.)

We put the agent (=person who performs the action) into the passive only if it adds information. When the agent is unknown, unimportant or obvious from the context, it is omitted. Agents such as: someone, people, I, you etc are omitted.
Macbeth was written **by Shakespeare**. (The agent is not omitted; it adds information.)
Somebody took my pen. ⇒ My pen was taken (by somebody). (unknown agent; it is omitted.)

After modal verbs (will, can, may etc) we use **be + past participle** or **have been + past participle**.
They may close down the supermarket. ⇒ The supermarket **may be closed down**.
They may have reported the bank robbery. ⇒ The bank robbery **may have been reported**.

With verbs that take two objects it is more usual to begin the passive sentence with the person.
They sent a letter to him. ⇒ **He** was sent a letter. (more usual) / **A letter** was sent to him. (less usual)

Make, hear, see, help are followed by a **to-infinitive** in the passive.
They made me apologise. ⇒ I was made to apologise.

The verbs believe, expect, feel, hope, know, report, say, think etc can be used in the following passive patterns:

a) **It + passive + that - clause** (impersonal construction)
b) **subject (person) + passive + to-infinitive** (personal construction)

People say she is rich.
**It is said that** she is rich.
**She is said to be** rich.

### 119) Turn from Active into Passive.

1. An expert is restoring the antique car. *The antique car is being restored by an expert.*
2. Steven Spielberg has directed a lot of successful films.
3. The judge has fined him £300.
4. A number of reporters will meet the professor at the airport.
5. A famous designer is going to redecorate the President's house.
6. The Romans founded Bath in the first century A.D.
7. A nightmare woke Mary up.
8. Muslims celebrate Ramadan.
9. Van Gogh painted "Sunflowers".
10. Astronauts are exploring space.

### 120) Turn from Active into Passive. Omit the agent where it can be omitted.

1. They kill elephants for ivory. *Elephants are killed for ivory. (omitted)*
2. Homer wrote the "Iliad".
3. People chop down a lot of trees every year.

# 6. Passive Voice

4. The government will introduce new measures against crime. ..................
5. Someone has burgled Ann's house. ..................
6. She offered me a cup of tea. ..................
7. They check passports at Passport Control. ..................
8. A million people visit the cathedral every year. ..................
9. Someone has stolen Mike's bicycle. ..................

### 121) Rewrite the following passage in the Passive.

Somebody gave me a goat for my birthday last year. They had bought it from a farm down the road. We keep it tied to a tree in our garden. My father normally looks after it, but last week his company sent him abroad on business. A few days later, our neighbour called me to the window. I hadn't tied the goat up properly. The goat was eating her washing!

........................................................................
........................................................................
........................................................................
........................................................................
........................................................................
........................................................................

### 122) Fill in "by" or "with".

1. The window was broken ..*with*.. a hammer.
2. He was knocked down .............. a car.
3. The lion was shot .............. a rifle.
4. That novel was written .......... D. H. Lawrence.
5. The garden was dug .............. a spade.
6. The city was attacked .............. the enemy.
7. The pudding was made ....... fruit and chocolate.
8. He was hit .............. a handbag.
9. The picture was painted ....... Jackson Pollack.
10. The house was built .......... wood and bricks.

### 123) Fill in the correct form of the verbs.

**A florist is taking a telephone order from a customer.**

Customer : Hello, I'd like to order some flowers, please.
Florist : Certainly, sir. When would you like them 1) .*to be delivered*... (deliver)?
Customer : Can they 2) .................. (deliver) on Monday?
Florist : Oh, I'm sorry, sir. No flowers can 3) .................. (send) on Monday because it's a bank holiday. The shop will be closed.
Customer : Oh, can they 4) .................. (send) on Friday then?
Florist : Certainly, sir. Where should they 5) .................. (take) to?
Customer : 47, Hanson Road, Croydon.
Florist : Okay, and who should they 6) .................. (address) to?

### 124) Turn the following sentences into the Passive.

1. Scientists might discover a cure for cancer. ...*A cure for cancer might be discovered.*..................
2. Someone should help the old woman across the street. ..................
3. They might have arrested the escaped prisoner. ..................
4. They should have provided more food at the reception. ..................
5. They ought to warn the public about him. ..................

## 6. Passive Voice

6. They should build more bus lanes. ...............
7. They could have written the answers more clearly. ...............

**125** Rewrite the following passage in the Passive.

Our apartment-block is starting a new scheme. We will collect all the old newspapers and tin cans. We will put them in a special container. When the container is full, the council will collect it. They will take it to a factory. The factory will recycle the newspapers and cans into something new.

**126** Turn the following into the Passive in two ways.

1. They gave him a watch when he retired.
   He ...*was given a watch when he retired.*......
   A watch ..*was given to him when he retired.*..
2. They have offered him the job.
   He ...............
   The job ...............
3. She will send you a fax.
   You ...............
   A fax ...............
4. They are going to show me a new technique.
   I ...............
   A new technique ...............
5. Someone gave her a book.
   She ...............
   A book ...............
6. They give the students extra lessons.
   The students ...............
   Extra lessons ...............
7. They have shown her the plans for the house.
   She ...............
   The plans for the house ...............
8. They should have sent you a receipt.
   You ...............
   A receipt ...............

**127** Turn the following into the Passive as in the example:

1. People expect him to win.
   He .....*is expected to win.* / It *is expected that he will win.*...............
2. Journalists have reported that the President is ill.
   The President ...............
   It ...............
3. Everyone knows that the statement was untrue.
   The statement ...............
   It ...............
4. Many people believe that the climate is changing.
   The climate ...............
   It ...............
5. Everyone knows that he has been in prison.
   He ...............
   It ...............
6. Many people say that the new prices are too high.
   The new prices ...............
   It ...............
7. They claim that this diamond is the largest in the world.
   This diamond ...............
   It ...............

## 6. Passive Voice

**128** Turn the following into the Passive.

1. I don't like people shouting at me. ...... *I don't like being shouted at.* ...................
2. I hate people staring at me. ..................................................................
3. I don't like people talking about me. ..........................................................
4. I hate people asking me questions. ...........................................................

**129** Fill in the Past Continuous Passive or the Past Perfect Passive.

1. They didn't leave the restaurant until the bill .................. *had been paid.* .................. (pay).
2. I couldn't go to my favourite café for a drink. It ........................................................ (redecorate).
3. He .................................................... (take) to the hospital when the ambulance crashed.
4. The search was called off. The escaped criminal .......................................................... (find).
5. When I looked for my television set I couldn't find it. I had forgotten it .............................. (repair).
6. By the time I returned from work, my new washing machine .................................... (deliver).
7. I didn't go to her party because I ............................................................... (not/invite).

**130** Rewrite the following passage in the Passive.

Somebody left a box on the No. 53 bus last night. A woman found it under her seat. She gave it to the bus driver. No one knows where it came from. The police are making enquiries now. The police are searching for the owner of the box because they have found a bomb in it. They hope they will arrest the person soon.

..................................................................................................
..................................................................................................
..................................................................................................
..................................................................................................
..................................................................................................
..................................................................................................

**131** Turn from Active into Passive.

1. The ancient Greeks built the Acropolis. ..... *The Acropolis was built by the ancient Greeks.* ...........
2. Martin is writing the company report this year. ..................................................
3. Somebody will clean the room tomorrow. ........................................................
4. They put fresh flowers in the hotel rooms every day. ............................................
5. Bad weather may delay your flight. .............................................................
6. They gave Sandy a present. ...................................................................
7. They think the President is dying. .............................................................
8. They made her cry. ............................................................................
9. The mechanic has repaired the car. ............................................................
10. The bomb destroyed the building. .............................................................

**132** Turn from Passive into Active.

1. He was hit by a falling brick. ...... *A falling brick hit him.* ....................................
2. She was employed by an international company. ................................................
3. This essay was written by Sandra. ............................................................
4. The burglar might have been arrested. ........................................................
5. He has been sent a parcel. ...................................................................
6. Roger was seen to leave. .....................................................................
7. The kidnappers are known to have left the country. ............................................
8. The exhibition will be opened by the mayor. ...................................................
9. It is hoped that the economy will improve. ....................................................

# 6. Passive Voice

## Oral Activity 13

The teacher sets the situation first : **Sarah Ford, the well-known millionaire's daughter, was kidnapped yesterday.** Then he/she asks the students to look at the cues below and, working in groups of three, to prepare the story in 2 minutes using the passive. Each group then reports its story to the class. Students decide which group's story is the best and has the fewest mistakes.

Cues : Sarah Ford kidnapped/yesterday. threatening calls made/before. Sarah seen/last/park. same day/letter sent. Sarah released/as soon as/kidnappers given £300,000. police informed/immediately. all areas searched/since yesterday. nothing found/so far.

## Writing Activity 7

**Look at the notes and write a news report using the Passive.**

Lives - lose - in a major sea tragedy in the Pacific Ocean. The disaster happened when the ship - hit - something unknown. Women and children - put - into lifeboats first while the men - tell - to stay on the ship. A nearby ship - bring - into action as a rescue vessel. The men who - leave - on the ship - rescue. Unfortunately some of the men - frighten - and jump into the water. It - believe - they are now dead. Survivors - take - to hospital - by helicopter and maximum effort now - make - to find the missing men.

**Many lives have been lost in a major sea tragedy in the Pacific Ocean. …**

## Tense Review

**133) Fill in the correct tense. Use Passive or Active according to the context.**

1. When she heard that her dog ..............*had been killed*.............. (kill), she burst into tears.
2. We hope that the missing money .............................................. (find) soon.
3. A new bridge .............................................. (build) at the moment.
4. When she discovered that Tom .............................................. (eat) all the biscuits she got very angry.
5. It's no use trying – you .............................................. (waste) your time.
6. A lot of money .............................................. (spend) on weapons nowadays.
7. Too many offices .............................................. (build) in London over the last ten years.
8. The President .............................................. (give) a speech next Monday.
9. The driver .............................................. (go) too fast when he hit the child.

## In Other Words

| He is expected to come tonight. | Our lawyer will contact you. |
| It is expected that he will come tonight. | You will be contacted by our lawyer. |

**134) Rephrase the following sentences.**

1. People say that the company is having problems. The company …*is said to be having problems.*……
2. Everyone thought that he was lying. It ..............................................
3. People believe that a spy revealed the secret. A spy ..............................................
4. Journalists report that the war is over. The war ..............................................
5. People expect that she will win an Oscar. It ..............................................
6. Someone should clean up this mess. This mess ..............................................
7. The crew had not checked the plane before we boarded. The plane ..............................................

# 6. Passive Voice

8. Everyone expects that it will rain this weekend. It ..................................................
9. They will execute the prisoner tomorrow. The prisoner ..................................................
10. They sold the car factory to a German company. The car factory ..................................................
11. People believe he is the richest man in the world. He ..................................................

## Phrasal verbs 6

| | |
|---|---|
| go away : | leave |
| go in for : | enter a competition, exam etc |
| go on : | 1) continue, 2) happen |
| go round : | be enough for everyone to have a share |
| go through : | examine in detail |
| call for : | require; demand |
| call in : | visit briefly |
| call off : | cancel |
| call out : | 1) shout, 2) send for sb in an emergency |

**135** Fill in the correct preposition or adverb.

1. Ben went *in for* the competition and won first prize.
2. Ssh! There's a meeting going .............. next door.
3. The teacher went .............. my homework to check for mistakes.
4. Will you go .............. working after the baby's born?
5. We're going .............. on holiday tomorrow morning.
6. I don't think there's enough coffee to go .............. . Does anyone want tea?
7. When I got stuck in the lift I called .......... for help.
8. The football match was called .............. because it was snowing.
9. The fire brigade was called .............. when a bomb exploded in the city centre.
10. I'll call .............. to see Ted on my way to work. He isn't feeling well.
11. Looking after very small children calls .............. a lot of patience.

**136** Look at Appendix 1 and fill in the correct preposition.

1. Tim is not particularly keen *on* golf, but he loves tennis.
2. My grandmother has been married .............. my grandfather for nearly sixty years.
3. It must be very difficult to live .............. the amount of money he makes.
4. There is a great need .............. extra water in countries where there is very little rain.
5. It never occurred .............. me to look under the bed for my lost watch.
6. I don't know much .............. Peter, but he seems to be a nice person.
7. I looked .............. the picture for a while, trying to understand it.
8. Lois is very nice .............. her elderly neighbours - she always takes them meals.
9. Everyone laughed .............. his new haircut.
10. Don is often mean .............. his little sister.
11. It was mean .............. you not to help your friend.
12. You should always be kind .............. animals.

## Idioms 6

| | |
|---|---|
| take sth into account : | regard, consider |
| take part in : | participate |
| take place : | occur, happen |
| take a look : | look at sth quickly |
| give sb a hand : | help sb |
| give sb a ring : | telephone sb |

**137** Fill in the correct idiom.

1. During the war, most of the fighting ... *took* ...... *place* ...... in the mountains.
2. If you can't come to my house tonight, can you at least .......... so we can decide about tomorrow?
3. When you buy a house, you should always take the location .............................. .
4. Susan ............................... in the garden, so I didn't have to do it all myself after all.
5. If you want to ..................... the competition, you have to sign up at least three weeks in advance.
6. Can you ..................... at my composition and see if there are any mistakes?

# 7. Conditionals - Wishes

|  | If - clause | Main clause | Use |
|---|---|---|---|
| **Type 1 real present** | If + any present form (Present S., Present Cont. or Present Perf.) | Future/Imperative can/may/might/must/should + bare inf. Present Simple (for general truths) | real - likely to happen in the present or future |
|  | If he **leaves** early, he**'ll be** on time for the meeting.   If you**'re tired, go** to bed! If you **have finished** your work, we **can go** for a walk.   If you **heat** water, it **boils**. |||
| **Type 2 unreal present** | If + Past Simple or Past Continuous | would/could/might + bare infinitive | unreal-unlikely to happen in the present or future; also used to give advice |
|  | If I **saw** a ghost, I **would run** away. (not likely to happen) If I **were** you, I **wouldn't go** out with him. (advice) |||
| **Type 3 unreal past** | If + Past Perfect or Past Perfect Continuous | would/could/might + have + past participle | unreal situation in the past; also used to express regrets and criticism |
|  | If I **had locked** the car, it **wouldn't have been** stolen. (regret; It's a pity I didn't lock it.) If he **had behaved** well, the teacher **wouldn't have punished** him. (criticism) |||

When the if-clause is before the main clause, we separate the two clauses with a comma.
If you **come** early, we **can go** for a walk. But : We **can go** for a walk if you **come** early.

We do not normally use will, would or should in an if-clause.
If you **hurry**, you **will catch** the train. (not : ~~If you will hurry, you will ...~~)
However, we can use will/would in Type 1 Conditionals to make a request or to express insistence or annoyance, and should when we are less sure about a possibility. (slight possibility)
If you **will** give me a hand with the dishes, we can go out together. (Please, give me a hand with the dishes.)
If you **would** give me a hand with the dishes, we could go out together. (Please, give me a hand with ...)
If you **will continue** to go out every night, you'll fail your exams. (insistence; if you insist on going out)
If I **meet** her, I'll ask her. (I may meet her.) If I **should meet** her, I'll ask her. (I may meet her, but I doubt it.)

After if, we can use were instead of was in all persons. If I **was / were** you, I would try harder.

## 7. Conditionals – Wishes

**Unless** means **if not**.
**Unless** she **studies**, she **won't pass** her test. (If she doesn't study, she won't pass her test.)

**As long as, providing/provided that**, can be used instead of **if**.
**As long as** he's on time, we won't be late for the meeting. (If he's on time, we won't be late for the meeting.)
We'll come by car **provided/providing that** Father lends us his. (We'll come by car if Father lends us his.)

**138** Write real present, unreal present or unreal past conditionals.
Then state the types of conditionals as in the example:

1. (play in the garden/get dirty)
   …If he hadn't played in
   …the garden, he wouldn't
   …have got dirty.
   …(3rd type, unreal past)

2. (not take his umbrella/get wet)

3. (win £1,000,000/buy a yacht)

4. (not fight/get a black eye)

5. (set the alarm/not oversleep)

6. (be taller/reach the cupboard)

7. (weather be nice/go fishing)

8. (run faster/catch the thief)

9. (keep bothering the dog/bite)

# 7. Conditionals – Wishes

## 139) Fill in the correct form of the verbs adding will, would or should if necessary.

1. If you ............*should see*............ (see) Ann, will you give her this message? **(slight possibility)**
2. We'll go skiing in the mountains if it ................................................ (snow). **(possibility)**
3. If he ................................................ (keep) talking, he'll never learn anything! **(insistence)**
4. Perhaps I could sit there too if you ................................................ (move) over a little. **(polite request)**
5. If you ................................................ (lend) me your car, I'll get to work on time. **(request)**
6. What will you do if you ................................................ (lose) your ticket? **(slight possibility)**
7. If you ................................................ (eat) so many sweets, you will get stomach-ache. **(insistence)**
8. If I ................................................ (arrive) earlier than planned, I'll phone you. **(slight possibility)**

## 140) Match the parts of the sentences.

| | | |
|---|---|---|
| 1. You can see the boss | A. unless it rains. | 1. ............*B*............ |
| 2. I would have bought it | B. provided that he is not too busy. | 2. ........................ |
| 3. We'll go to the beach tomorrow | C. if I'd had enough money with me. | 3. ........................ |
| 4. He would go by plane | D. she wouldn't have missed the train. | 4. ........................ |
| 5. If she hadn't slept late, | E. if it was cheaper. | 5. ........................ |

## 141) Put the verbs in brackets into the correct tense.

Neil isn't happy with his life. If he 1) *had listened* (listen) to his mother's advice, he 2) ........................ (stay) at school and gone on to university. He 3) ........................ (can/find) a good job if he had got a degree. Neil hates the job he is doing now. He thinks he 4) ........................ (go) crazy if he 5) ........................ (stay) there much longer. If he 6) ........................ (be) offered another job, he would take it immediately. In fact, he 7) ........................ (leave) if he 8) ........................ (can) afford to, but he can't. Life 9) ........................ (be) easier if he 10) ........................ (not/have) two children to support.

## 142) Put the verbs in brackets into the correct tense.

1. He'll be furious if he ever .............*finds out*............. (find out) about this.
2. The animals at the zoo ................................................ (die) unless they're fed.
3. I ................................................ (run) home if I'd known the football match was on TV.
4. The teacher ................................................ (not/shout) at her if she did her homework.
5. He ................................................ (buy) a car provided that he passes his driving test.
6. We ................................................ (miss) the lecture unless we hurry.
7. If she'd passed her exams, she ................................................ (go) to university.
8. If I ................................................ (understand) the question, I might be able to answer it!
9. I ................................................ (tell) you if I should hear from him.
10. If he ................................................ (forget) his ticket, they wouldn't have let him in.

## 143) Fill in : if, unless, provided or as long.

1. You will not be allowed into the building .............*unless*............. you have a security pass.
2. ................................................ that you book your flight early, you will get a seat.
3. ................................................ as you follow the instructions exactly, you won't have any difficulty.
4. ................................................ you meet Darren, give him my regards.
5. You can hire a car in France ................................................ as you have a driving licence and you're over 23.
6. You can't enter the country ................................................ you have a passport.
7. The kidnappers won't release the child ................................................ the ransom is paid.

# 7. Conditionals – Wishes

**144** Complete the following sentences with an appropriate conditional clause.

1. If I found a gun in the street, ........ *I would take it to the police.* ............
2. You wouldn't have been punished ............
3. If you drink all that juice, ............
4. If you drive so fast, ............
5. If you should see Mark this evening, ............
6. If you had taken my advice, ............
7. Unless the weather improves, ............
8. My father would have bought me a bicycle ............
9. He would have been very angry ............
10. If you aren't enjoying the film, ............

## Mixed Conditionals

All types of conditionals can be mixed. Any tense combination is possible if the context permits it.

|  | If - clause | Main clause |  |
|---|---|---|---|
| Type 2 | If nobody **phoned** him, | he **won't come** to the meeting. | Type 1 |
| Type 2 | If he **knew** her, | he **would have spoken** to her. | Type 3 |
| Type 3 | If he **had found** a job, | he **wouldn't be searching** for one now. | Type 2 |

**145** Fill in the blanks with the correct form of the verbs in brackets.

Yesterday the famous bank robber, Fingers Smith, robbed another bank in the centre of town. As usual, he only stole £10. If he 1) ........ *had left* ............ (leave) any clues, he 2) ............................ (be) in prison now, but he's much too clever. He disconnected the security cameras; if he 3) ............................ (not/do) that, the police 4) ............................ (have) him on film now. The strange thing is, Fingers doesn't seem to be interested in the money; if he 5) ...................... (be), he 6) ............ (can/steal) thousands of pounds by now. The police are determined to catch him, and the Chief is confident that they will. He says that if he 7) ............................ (think) they weren't going to arrest Fingers eventually, he 8) ............................ (leave) the police force long ago.

## Oral Activity 14

The students in two teams read the text and in turn make Conditionals. Each correct sentence gets 1 point.
**One night Paul was bored so he decided to go to the cinema. But the cinema was full because the film was very popular. Paul's friend lives near the cinema so he went to visit him. When he arrived, he heard his friend shouting for help. The door was open so Paul was able to get into the house. His friend had been painting and had fallen off the step-ladder. His leg was broken so he couldn't move. It was lucky that the cinema was full and Paul called round on him.**

Teacher: If Paul hadn't been bored, he wouldn't have decided to go to the cinema.
Team A S1: If the film hadn't been popular, the cinema wouldn't have been full. etc

## 7. Conditionals – Wishes

### Wishes

|  | Form | Use |
|---|---|---|
| **I wish** (if only) (regret about the present) | **+ Past Simple** | regret about a present situation which we want to be different |

*I wish I **were/was** more patient. (It's a pity I'm not patient enough.)*

|  | Form | Use |
|---|---|---|
| **I wish** (if only) (wish/ regret about the present) | **+ subject + could + bare inf.** | wish or regret in the present concerning lack of ability |

*I wish I **could ride** a bicycle. (But I can't.)*

|  | Form | Use |
|---|---|---|
| **I wish** (if only) (impossible wish for a future change) | **+ subject + would + bare inf.** (a. "wish" and "would" should have different subjects. We never say: ~~I wish I would, He wishes he would~~ etc. b. wish + inanimate subject + would is used to express the speaker's lack of hope or disappointment.) | wish for a future change unlikely to happen or wish to express dissatisfaction; polite request implying dissatisfaction or lack of hope |

*I wish he **would study** for his exams. (But I don't think he will. – wish for a future change unlikely to happen)*
*I wish Jane **would go** to university. (Jane has refused to do so and I'm unhappy about it. – dissatisfaction)*
*I wish you **would be** quiet. (Please be quiet; but I don't expect you will. – request implying lack of hope)*
*I wish **it would stop** snowing. (But I'm afraid it won't stop snowing. – wish implying disappointment)*

|  | Form | Use |
|---|---|---|
| **I wish** (if only) (regret about the past) | **+ Past Perfect** | regret that something happened or didn't happen in the past |

*I wish I **had gone** to Ann's party last night. (But I didn't. – It's a pity I didn't go.)*

**In wishes, we go one tense back. This means that we use Past Simple in the present and Past Perfect in the past.** *I'm poor. I wish I **were** rich.* **(present)**/*I lost my watch yesterday. I wish I **hadn't lost** it.* **(past)**
**After I wish we can use were instead of was in all persons.** *I wish I **was/were** taller.*
**If only means the same as I wish but it is more dramatic.** *If only I **was/were** taller.*

# 7. Conditionals – Wishes

**146** Fill in : wish about the present, regret about the past, wish or polite request implying dissatisfaction or lack of hope – then write what the people wish.

1. ...*regret about the past*....
   ..*I wish I hadn't opened*....
   ..*the gate.*....................
   He opened the gate.

2. ..................................
   ..................................
   She wants him to stop talking.

3. ..................................
   ..................................
   Ann cut Kate's hair very short.

4. ..................................
   ..................................
   She lost her earring.

5. ..................................
   ..................................
   He is very shy.

6. ..................................
   ..................................
   He spends a lot of money.

**147** Using the bold type in the sentences, write wishes as in the example:

1. You are leaving for the airport. **You can't find your passport.**
   You say : ....."*I wish I could find my passport.*"..........................................
2. You live in the suburbs. **You prefer the city centre.**
   You say : ..................................................................................
3. **You argued with your mother yesterday.** Today she is upset.
   You say : ..................................................................................
4. **You didn't clean your bedroom** and your mother is angry.
   You say : ..................................................................................
5. You want to go on holiday but **you can't afford it**.
   You say : ..................................................................................

**148** Write sentences as in the example:

1. You want to visit your friend but you've got too much work to do.
   *I wish I didn't have so much work to do. If I didn't have so much work to do, I could visit my friend.*
2. You went to bed late and didn't wake up in time for work.
   ..................................................................................
3. You want to go to the safari park with Michael, but you're afraid of lions.
   ..................................................................................

## 7. Conditionals – Wishes

4. You would like to write a letter to Fred but you don't have his address.
   ...........................................................................................................

5. You went skiing and broke your leg.
   ...........................................................................................................

6. You didn't go to the concert because you didn't know about it.
   ...........................................................................................................

7. You have to stay in bed because you've got the flu.
   ...........................................................................................................

8. You are lost in London because you don't have a map.
   ...........................................................................................................

**149** Read what Andy says and write what he wishes as in the example:

I had an argument with my wife. I was driving my car too fast. I had that accident. I can't control my temper. My wife won't come and visit me. My leg hurts. The man in the next bed won't stop talking. I can't get out of bed.

1. *...I wish I hadn't had an argument with my wife.*
2. ................................................
3. ................................................
4. ................................................
5. ................................................
6. ................................................
7. ................................................
8. ................................................

### Oral Activity 15

Students in teams take turns to give their reactions to the following picture situations. The teams should be able to invent at least 2 situations per picture using conditionals. Each correct answer gets 1 point.

Team A S1: If a wasp stung me, I would cry.          Team A S2: If a wasp stung me, I would see a
Team B S1: If a wasp stung me, it would hurt.                              doctor. etc

# 7. Conditionals – Wishes

## Oral Activity 16

Students in teams take turns inventing wishes and conditionals by using the following pictures as stimuli. The teams should be able to invent at least 2 situations per picture. Each correct sentence gets 1 point.

Team A S1: I wish the police would catch the thieves. If they catch them, I'll get my car back.
Team B S1: I wish I had locked my car. If I had locked it, they wouldn't have stolen it. etc

**150** Use Ann's thoughts to write wishes and conditionals as in the example:

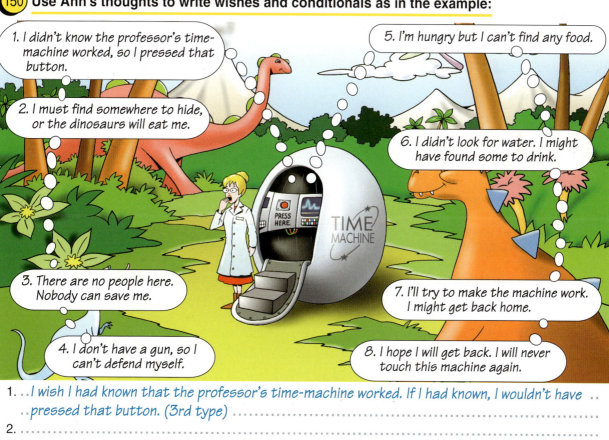

1. I didn't know the professor's time-machine worked, so I pressed that button.
2. I must find somewhere to hide, or the dinosaurs will eat me.
3. There are no people here. Nobody can save me.
4. I don't have a gun, so I can't defend myself.
5. I'm hungry but I can't find any food.
6. I didn't look for water. I might have found some to drink.
7. I'll try to make the machine work. I might get back home.
8. I hope I will get back. I will never touch this machine again.

1. I wish I had known that the professor's time-machine worked. If I had known, I wouldn't have pressed that button. (3rd type)
2. 
3. 
4. 
5. 
6. 
7. 
8.

# 7. Conditionals - Wishes

**Writing Activity 8**

Read the following letter, then rewrite it using wishes and conditionals.

*Dear Anyone,*
*I am on an island somewhere in the Pacific Ocean. I've been here for a week. I lost my watch in the sea so I don't know what time it is. Going on that cruise was the worst thing I've ever done. I'm not a good swimmer so I couldn't reach the lifeboat when the ship sank. I've thought about making a raft to sail away from the island, but I don't know which way to go. There is no one to talk to here. I feel so lonely! I haven't got a personal stereo so I can't listen to music. The only thing to eat is fish and I don't like fish! I didn't bring a knife with me so I can't build a shelter. I hope someone will find me soon!*

## Tense Review

**151) Fill in the correct tense.**

When Paul 1) ..*got*.. (get) to work yesterday his boss 2) ........................ (wait) for him. "I wish you 3) ........................ (try) to get here on time," his boss said. "If you 4) ........................ (be) late again, I 5) ........................ (dismiss) you." "But I 6) ........................ (be) on time!" Paul exclaimed. "If I 7) ........................ (leave) the house late, I 8) ........................ (phone), but in fact I 9) ........................ (leave) on time." His boss 10) ........................ (look) at his watch, and then at the clock on the wall. "Oh dear," he said, "I 11) ........................ (forget) to put my watch back to winter time. I do wish someone 12) ........................ (remind) me!"

## In Other Words

| | |
|---|---|
| If you don't study, you'll fail the test.<br>Unless you study, you'll fail the test. | Eat your soup, otherwise/or else/or you can't have any dessert.<br>If you don't eat your soup, you can't have any dessert. |
| You'd better go home.<br>If I were you, I'd go home. | |
| I stayed at home because I had a cold.<br>If I hadn't had a cold, I wouldn't have stayed at home. | If you come home early, we'll go to the cinema.<br>We'll go to the cinema as long as/provided that you come home early. |

**152) Rephrase the following sentences using the beginnings given.**

1. You'd better see a doctor.
   If ..*I were you, I'd see a doctor.*..................................
2. He won't help you if you don't ask him.
   Unless ............................................................
3. Take your medicine, otherwise you won't get better.
   If ............................................................
4. You won't make any spelling mistakes provided you use a dictionary.
   If ............................................................
5. If you park here, you'll be fined £20.
   Don't ............................................................
6. You'd better confess your crime.
   If ............................................................
7. She went home early because she was exhausted.
   If ............................................................

# 7. Conditionals - Wishes

8. You won't understand the story unless you finish the book.
   If ...........................................................................................
9. She can't go out if she doesn't promise to be back early.
   Unless .....................................................................................
10. The bee won't sting you as long as you stay still.
    Provided ..................................................................................

| Phrasal Verbs 7 | |
|---|---|
| look after : | take care of sb/sth |
| look for : | search for |
| look forward to : | anticipate with pleasure |
| look into : | investigate |
| look out (for) : | watch for |
| look through : | examine quickly |
| look up : | look for an address, name, word etc in a book |

**153** Fill in the correct preposition or adverb.

1. They had been looking ...*for*... a house for over a week before they found one.
2. My neighbour looks ..................... my cat when I'm away.
3. I'll look ..................... her telephone number in the directory.
4. The police are looking ..................... the case of the missing diamonds.
5. Look ..................... pickpockets when you're in the market; they're everywhere.
6. He's really looking ..................... the party. He can't stop talking about it.
7. Look ..................... this letter to see if there are any mistakes.

**154** Look at Appendix 1 and fill in the correct preposition.

1. You need to show your passport as proof ...*of*... your identity.
2. If you are unpleasant ..................... people, of course they won't like you.
3. We were prevented ..................... going sailing by the stormy weather.
4. If he doesn't understand at first, be patient ..................... him and explain it again.
5. It was very impolite ..................... Liz to leave without saying goodbye.
6. My grandmother is really proud ..................... me for going to university.
7. The technicians wore gloves to protect themselves ..................... the dangerous chemicals.
8. The hotel receptionist was polite ..................... everybody.
9. We were provided ..................... pencils and paper to write the exam.
10. Sharon was really pleased ..................... her birthday present since it was exactly what she wanted.

| Idioms 7 | |
|---|---|
| make allowances (for sb) : | consider sb's weaknesses etc |
| put the blame on sb : | say sb is responsible for sth bad |
| put an end/ a stop to sth : | end sth completely |
| put sth by for a rainy day : | save for future times of need |
| no kidding? : | used to express surprise or irony |
| (do sth) behind someone's back : | act without sb else's knowledge |

**155** Fill in the correct idiom.

1. Don't try to ...*put the blame on*... your sister. I know the accident was your fault.
2. "I'm top of my class this term."
   ".....................? I'm glad you're doing so well."
3. Don't talk about me ............................. If there's a problem, tell me to my face.
4. The government is trying to ..................... crime by putting more policemen on the streets.
5. You should ..................... the fact that she has just learnt to drive.
6. You should never spend all the money you earn, but always ......................................

## 8. Clauses

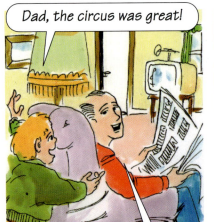

### Time Clauses

**Time clauses are introduced with:** after, as, as long as, as soon as, just as, since, before, by the time, when, while, until/till, the moment (that), whenever etc.

**As soon as** he (had) finished studying | he turned on the TV.
(Time clause) (Main clause)

**Time clauses follow the rule of the sequence of tenses.** This means that when the verb of the main sentence is in a present or future form, the verb of the time clause is in a present form. When the verb of the main sentence is in a past form, the verb of the time clause is in a past form too.
She'**ll come** when she **is** ready. (**not:** when she will be ready) You **can** wait here until she **comes**. (not: until she will come) She **did** the cleaning after she **had done** the washing-up. (not: after she does)

**We never use will/would** (future forms) in time clauses; we normally use a present form.
He'll go out **after** he **has finished** his job. (not: after he will finish or will have finished)
He'll be a lawyer **when** he **grows** up. (not: when he will grow up)

Note: when (time conjunction) + present — I'll take you out to dinner **when** I **get** paid.
when (question word) + future or present — Do you know **when** she **will arrive/is arriving**?

**156** Match the parts of the sentences and put the verbs into the correct tense.

1. She'll phone her mother
2. He bought a car
3. We'll leave
4. The doorbell rang
5. The phone had stopped ringing
6. She was watching the baby
7. We'll do our Christmas shopping
8. He'll watch TV

A. while she ........................... (have) a bath.
B. after he ........................... (do) his homework.
C. as it ........................... (sleep) peacefully.
D. as soon as we ........................... (be paid).
E. when she ....*gets*........... (get) to London.
F. by the time I ........................... (reach) it.
G. after he ........................... (pass) his driving test.
H. as soon as the baby-sitter ........................... (arrive).

1. ...*E*...  2. ......  3. ......  4. ......  5. ......  6. ......  7. ......  8. ......

# 8. Clauses

**157** Put the verbs in brackets into Present Simple or Future.

1. I ..'ll tell... (tell) you all about my holiday when I ..get.. (get) home.
2. Do you know when he ............................... (leave)?
3. When he ........................... (see) her, he ........................... (be) very surprised.
4. When ........................... (you/learn) that it's wrong to tell lies?

> **If** is used for things which may possibly happen. *I'll help you if I have time.*
> **When** is used for things which are sure to happen. *I'll phone you when I get to my hotel.*
> **By the time** means **before, not later than**. *She had finished cooking by the time her guests arrived.*
> **Until** means **up to the time when**. It is also used with a negative verb.
> *They waited until the building had been evacuated. They didn't take off until the weather improved.*

**158** Fill in: when or if.

1. I might have a party. ...If... I do, I'll invite you.
2. He promised to call us ........ he reached Rome.
3. She'll be very happy ........... she wins the race.
4. You will catch cold ......... you go out in the rain.
5. ........... he finishes school he'll go to university.
6. ................... anyone calls, tell them I'm busy.

**159** Fill in: by the time or until.

1. ...By the time.... he is thirty, he will have been playing in that team for twelve years.
2. He didn't travel abroad ..................... he was an old man.
3. He had left the gallery ............ we got there.
4. You mustn't leave the office ............... you've typed those letters.
5. ................... we get there it will be midnight.
6. No one can leave the room ........................ the examiner has collected the papers.

**160** Underline the correct item.

1. We'll leave **as/as soon as** we're ready.
2. Don't forget to lock up **until/before** you go to bed.
3. We can buy tickets **when/until** we get on the boat.
4. **While/After** I was watching TV, the programme was interrupted.
5. **As/After** I was cooking, the oven exploded.
6. **Until/By the time** we got to the party, nearly everyone had left.
7. You mustn't talk **while/until** you are sitting an exam.
8. We went into the lecture hall **just as/while** the professor began speaking.
9. He didn't get home **until/after** 12 o'clock.

**161** Fill in: until, while, before, as, when, as soon as, by the time or as long as.

1) ......By the time........ King Henry VIII of England was 18 years old, he was already the ruler of his country. He is probably remembered by so many people because he married six times 2) ........................... he was King. His first wife, Catherine of Aragon, gave him a daughter but no sons to take the throne after him. It seemed that 3) ........................ she was his wife, he would not have a son. Henry wanted to marry Anne Boleyn, but 4) ........................ he could marry her he had to divorce Catherine. Anne gave Henry another daughter but no sons, and for this reason he had her beheaded. 5) ........................ she was dead he found a new wife. She did have a son but she died just 6) ........................ the baby was born. Henry remained King 7) ........................ he died in 1547. 8) ........................ he died his only son, Edward, came to the throne, but 9) ........................ he was 16, he died too.

**162** Join the following sentences using the correct time conjunction.

1. He received the telegram. He left immediately. ....*He left as soon as he received the telegram.*....
2. She left the house. She locked the windows. ...........................................................

## 8. Clauses

3. They finished their meal. She made some coffee. ..................................
4. She was working in the garden. He was painting the garage. ..................................
5. She heard the bad news. She began to cry. ..................................

### Clauses of Purpose

**Purpose is expressed with :**

| | |
|---|---|
| **to-infinitive** (informal - we use the infinitive of purpose only when the subject of the verb and the subject of the infinitive are the same) **in order not /so as not + to-infinitive** are used in negative sentences | He phoned **to invite** her to dinner. (less formal) He phoned **in order to invite** her to dinner. (formal) They hurried **so as not to/in order not to miss** the train. (not: They hurried not to miss the train.) |
| **so that + will/can/may** (present or future reference) **so that + would/could/might** (past reference) | She**'ll save** money **so that** she **can buy** a flat. She **saved** money **so that** she **could buy** a flat. I **moved** that vase **so that** the dog **wouldn't break** it. |
| **in case + present** (present/future reference) **in case + past** (past reference) "in case" is never followed by "will/would" | I**'ll buy** some cake **in case** they **come**. I **bought** some cake **in case** they **came**. (not: I'll buy some cake in case they will come.) |
| **for + noun or -ing form** | A pen is used **for writing**. He went out **for a walk**. |

Clauses of purpose follow the rule of the sequence of tenses (see p. 76).
**I'll leave** early so that I **can catch** the train.     He **locked** the door in case someone **broke in**.

**Compare: in case - if**
She'll buy some cola **if** they come. (She'll buy some cola after they come.)
She'll buy some cola **in case** they come. (She'll buy some cola before they come, because they might come.)

### 163) Underline the correct item.

1. He arrived at the office before the others **so that** / **in case** he could start work early.
2. These tools are **for** / **to** mending my car.
3. She went shopping **not to** / **so as not to** be short of food.
4. He took a sandwich **so that** / **in case** he got hungry.
5. I'll give you my phone number **in order that** / **in case** you need any information.

6. He speaks French **so that** / **in case** they can understand him.
7. She worked hard **so that** / **for** she could go to university.
8. She is saving money **to** / **so that** she can go on holiday.
9. Shall we book a table **if** / **in case** the restaurant is busy?
10. My mother gives me piano lessons **so that** / **in case** I can become a musician.
11. I'll take my gloves **so that** / **in case** my hands get cold.
12. My father works hard **not to** / **in order not to** lose his job.
13. They caught a taxi **to** / **so that** go to the station.
14. I'll give you my address **in case** / **so that** you want to write to me.

## Oral Activity 17

Looking at the pictures below, students in teams choose an object to take with them on holiday, and produce a sentence giving the reason for their choice. Each correct sentence gets 1 point.

Team A S1: I'll take an umbrella in case it rains. OR I'll take an umbrella so as not to get wet if it rains.
Team B S1: I'll take a ball so that we can play football. OR I'll take a ball with me to play football.

**164** Martin is leaving home to go to university. His father wants to know why he is taking certain things with him. Write Martin's answers using the words in brackets.

1. Martin, why are you taking three blankets? (in case) *I'm taking them in case it gets very cold.*
2. What do you need these pans for? (so that) ..................
3. Why are you taking these cookery books? (so as not to) ..................
4. What's this hammer for? (for) ..................
5. And what's this radio for? (so that) ..................
6. And why do you need a camera? (to + infinitive) ..................

**165** Fill in the correct tense.

1. She opened the letter immediately in case it ........*was*........ (be) important.
2. Don't leave those matches there in case the children .................. (play) with them.
3. He turned the TV on so that he .................. (can) watch the news.
4. The police surrounded the area so that the robbers .................. (not/escape).
5. He took some extra money in case he .................. (need) it.
6. She learnt Spanish so that she .................. (can) get a job in Spain.

**166** Join the sentences using the words in brackets.

1. I'll leave you my address. You can send me a postcard. (so that)
   *....I'll leave you my address so that you can send me a postcard.*

## 8. Clauses

2. We bought some more coffee. We didn't want to run out. (so that)
   ......................................................................
3. Mrs Brown bought some sweets. Her grandchildren might visit her. (in case)
   ......................................................................
4. Put some pepper in the soup. That will make it taste better. (to -infinitive)
   ......................................................................
5. Take more money. You may run out. (so as not to)
   ......................................................................
6. The teacher explained the exercise again. Some of the students didn't understand. (in case)
   ......................................................................
7. Debbie hid her diary. She didn't want anyone to read it. (so that)
   ......................................................................

### Clauses of Concession

Clauses of Concession express contrast and they are introduced with : although, even though, though, despite, in spite of, despite the fact that, in spite of the fact that, while, but or whereas.

| | |
|---|---|
| **Although/Even though + clause**<br>**Even though/Although** he has lived in Spain for five years, he can't speak Spanish. | **despite/in spite of + noun/-ing form**<br>She came to work **despite** her cold.<br>She came to work **in spite of** having a cold.<br>**in spite of the fact/despite the fact that + clause**<br>**In spite of the fact/Despite the fact that** she had a cold, she came to work. |
| **Though + clause** is informal. We can use "though" at the beginning or the end of the sentence.<br>**Though** she has been warned, she wants to take the risk.<br>She's been warned. She wants to take the risk, **though**. | **while/whereas/but + clause**<br>She did well in the test **while/whereas/but** Tom didn't. |

**167** Fill in the blanks with : despite, in spite of, while, whereas, although or though.

Dear John,
I am having a great time in England, 1) ...*despite/in spite of*... the bad weather! We arrived safely in London, 2) ........................ the train was two hours late. 3) ........................ the fact that I miss America, I'm still enjoying myself. Tomorrow my friend is leaving for home, 4) ........................ I still have three more days here. I'm going to visit Buckingham Palace, 5) ........................ the fact that I've been there before. I'm looking forward to going home. I think I'll miss England a little, 6) ........................ .
Love,
Sarah

# 8. Clauses

**168** Underline the correct item.

1. **Despite** / **Although** it was snowing, the road was clear.
2. **Although** / **Despite** the traffic, we made it to school on time.
3. **In spite of** / **Although** the fact that I didn't study, I passed the exam.
4. I can't stand classical music, **whereas** / **in spite of** my mother loves it.
5. Tom loves playing football, **while** / **despite** Paul prefers basketball.
6. **Although** / **Despite** Johnny eats fish, his brother won't touch it.

**169** Rephrase the following sentences using the beginnings given.

1. Even though he's a millionaire, he hates spending money.
   **In spite of** *being a millionaire, he hates spending money.*
2. She attended the meeting in spite of her illness.
   **Although**
3. They managed to arrive on time, despite the heavy snowstorm.
   **Even though**
4. She's a managing director although she's only 25.
   **Despite the fact**
5. Although he has been told to stop, he still smokes.
   **In spite of**
6. In spite of losing thirty kilos, she's still overweight.
   **Although**

**170** Rephrase the following sentences in all possible ways as in the example:

1. Even though the music was quiet, the neighbours complained.

   *Although the music was quiet, the neighbours complained.*
   *Despite the fact that the music was quiet, the neighbours complained.*
   *In spite of the music being quiet, the neighbours complained.*
   *Despite the music being quiet, the neighbours complained.*
   *In spite of the fact that the music was quiet, the neighbours complained. etc*

2. Geoff has lots of friends but he doesn't go out very often.
3. Although the weather was bad, they enjoyed their day out.
4. This car is very old. However, it still runs well.
5. He looked everywhere for a job, but he didn't find anything.
6. It was raining hard. The aeroplane took off.
7. Richard is very rich, but he isn't happy.

## Oral Activity 18

Students in teams invent contrasting ideas. Each correct answer gets 1 point.

1. *Although she's fifty*, she looks younger.
2. ................................, she isn't wearing a coat.
3. ................................, he is mean with his money.
4. ................................, he failed the test.
5. ................................, she put on seven kilos.
6. ................................, he went to work.
7. ................................, my car got stolen.
8. ................................, I was still hungry.
9. ................................, we went swimming.
10. ................................, he plays with toy trains.
11. ................................, she can't speak French.
12. ................................, he doesn't have a car.
13. ................................, he felt homesick.
14. ................................, she didn't get any presents.
15. ................................, he saves a lot of money.
16. ................................, he was sent to prison.
17. ................................, he's very clever.
18. ................................, he refuses to give up smoking.
19. ................................, she still got sunburnt.
20. ................................, he's quite strong.

## 8. Clauses

### Clauses of Result - Clauses of Reason

### Clauses of Result

Clauses of Result are introduced with: such/so...that, (and) as a result or therefore.

**such a(n) + adjective + singular countable noun.** "Such" is also used before "a lot of".
She's **such a good teacher that** all her students like her.
She bought **such a lot of** presents **that** she couldn't carry them.

**so + adjective/adverb. So** is also used before **much, many, few** or **little**.
The suitcase was **so heavy that** she couldn't carry it.
He drove **so carelessly that** he crashed into a tree.
He ate **so much** last night **that** he had stomach-ache.
How can you sleep **so little** and not look tired?

**such + adjective + uncountable/plural noun**
It was **such nice weather that** we went to the beach. **So** and **such** can be used without "that".
She's **such** a clever lady everybody admires her.

**as a result/therefore + clause**
He didn't do well in the test **and as a result/therefore** he had to take it again.

### Clauses of Reason

Clauses of Reason are introduced with: as, since, because. (because usually answers a why-question.)
"Why do you have to move to another house?" "**Because** this one is too far from the tube station."

**As** and **since** are normally used at the beginning of the sentence.
**Since/As** it's your birthday, I'll let you borrow my best suit.

**171 Join the sentences using the word in brackets.**

1. Brian can't play football on Saturday. He has broken his leg. **(because)**
   ...Brian can't play football on Saturday because he has broken his leg.....
2. Darren hates flying. He can't go to Australia. **(since)**
   ..................................................................................
3. I couldn't go to the concert. I'd spent all my money. **(as)**
   ..................................................................................
4. Martin is away for Christmas. He'll miss the party. **(since)**
   ..................................................................................
5. Sarah missed the wedding reception. She fell ill. **(because)**
   ..................................................................................

# 8. Clauses

6. It's the end of term. We'll play some games. **(as)**

7. I've always dreamt of going to Russia. I studied Russian history at university. **(because)**

8. He really likes Guns 'n' Roses. I bought him their latest album for his birthday. **(since)**

9. He's lazy. He'll fail his exams. **(because)**

10. There was so much traffic. I was late for work. **(because)**

### 172) Fill in : so, such or such a(n).

1. I am .......... *so* .......... tired of the long journey to work every day that I wish I could just stay at home.
2. I had .......... awful headache that I spent the day in bed.
3. It's .......... lovely day! We should go for a picnic.
4. You are .......... rude to all my friends that none of them want to see you.
5. The book was .......... exciting that he couldn't put it down.
6. She has .......... pretty eyes that everyone admires them.
7. It was .......... big party that I couldn't speak to half the people there.
8. You talk .......... fast that I can't understand you.
9. He eats .......... lot of food, I'm not surprised he's fat.
10. You shouldn't spend .......... much. You'll end up without any money one day.

### 173) Fill in: so, such or such a.

Yesterday Peter put his dinner in the oven to cook. It was 1) ...*such a*.......... nice day that he decided to mow the lawn while he was waiting. It was 2) .......... hard work and took 3) .......... long time that his dinner began to burn, but he was 4) .......... busy in the garden that he didn't notice the smell. As he was working, he heard a fire engine arrive, and he went to the front of his house. His neighbour said, "Peter, there was 5) .......... bad smell and 6) .......... much smoke that we thought your house was on fire. We were 7) .......... worried that we called the fire brigade." Peter had 8) .......... shock! He ran into the kitchen, but the oven was 9) .......... hot that he couldn't touch it. The fireman had sprayed it with 10) .......... much water that the kitchen was wet all over. Finally, everybody went home. Peter was left with a kitchen that was 11) .......... mess and a dinner that was 12) .......... burnt that he decided never to cook and mow the lawn at the same time again.

### 174) Rewrite the following sentences adding so or such and a result clause.

1. I was happy. I cried.
   .... *I was so happy that I cried.* ..........
2. It was a nice day. We went swimming.

3. Their dog is frightening. I won't go near it.

4. This is disgusting food! I can't eat it.

5. He's a gentleman! He often sends her flowers.

6. The house was dirty. It smelled awful.

7. They had a terrible fight. They hate each other now.

8. She's a sweet child. Everyone loves her.

9. It was cold. The river froze.

10. It's an interesting film. I want to see it again.

## 8. Clauses

11. It was a difficult book. I couldn't understand it.
    ..................................................
12. It was a good play. I saw it twice.
    ..................................................
13. Her house is big. She only uses half of it.
    ..................................................
14. He is handsome. He could be an actor.
    ..................................................

### Exclamations

Ah! Watson! You're wearing your green boxer shorts today.

Elementary, my dear Watson. You forgot to put your trousers on!

How amazing! What a detective, you are, my dear Holmes! How did you guess?

Exclamations are words and phrases used to express surprise, shock etc. They take an exclamation mark (!). Some exclamations are : Good heavens! Goodness! Oh dear! Ah! Really! Good grief! etc.
**Good heavens!** You've cut yourself!
We also use **what (a/an), how, such, so** or a **negative question** to make a comment or exclamation.
**What** a fast runner! **How** fast he runs! He is **such** a fast runner! He runs **so** fast! **Doesn't he** run fast! **Wouldn't** it be fantastic!

Exclamations are introduced by **what** or **how** as follows :

| | |
|---|---|
| **what a(n) + (adjective) + singular countable noun** | **What a boring** film! |
| **what + (adjective) + uncountable/plural noun** | **What horrible** weather! **What beautiful** roses! |
| **how + adjective/adverb** | **How clever** he is! **How quickly** he speaks! |

**175** Fill in: "What ...", "What a(n) ..." or "How ...".

1. ...How... elegant you look this evening!
2. ............ noisy children they are!
3. ............ amazing sight the Pyramids are!
4. ............ great idea!
5. ............ strange his story was!
6. ............ interesting life he's led!
7. ............ beautiful garden!
8. ............ thoughtful of you!
9. ............ stupid questions he asks!
10. ............ nice of you to come!
11. ............ awful sweater!
12. ............ expensive meal!
13. ............ tired you look today!
14. ............ delicious food!
15. ............ kind he is to everyone!
16. ............ terrible news!
17. ............ boring book this is!
18. ............ exciting it all sounds!
19. ............ brave man!
20. ............ enormous house you live in!
21. ............ careless of you!
22. ............ interesting story!

# 8. Clauses

**176** Rephrase the following sentences in all possible ways as in the example:

What a cold day it is today! *How cold it is today! Isn't it cold today! It's so cold today! It's such a cold day today!*

1. What a happy girl!
2. How thin she is!
3. What a delicious cake!
4. What naughty children!
5. How rude he is!
6. How slowly he walks!
7. What a stupid woman!
8. Aren't they clever!
9. What a strong man!
10. How beautiful she is!
11. What an exciting story!
12. You're so silly!

## Oral Activity 19

Students in teams produce an exclamation and a result clause. Each correct item gets 1 point.
eg. Team A S1: What a big meal she's had! She's had such a big meal that she has stomach-ache.

**177** Read the story and fill in the gaps using "what (a/an)" or "how".

There was once a lion who thought he was the king of the jungle. 1) "..*What a*.. brave lion I am!" he said to himself. 2) "............................ frightened everyone is of me!" To prove his point he went up to a monkey and said, 3) "............................ foolish you look! Tell me, who's the king of the jungle?" 4) "............................................................ silly question!" replied the monkey. "Why, you are, of course."

The lion then went up to a giraffe and said, 5) "................ long neck you have! Tell me, who's the king of the jungle?" 6) "............................ kind of you to ask!" said the giraffe. "Why, you are, of course."

The lion then went up to a hippopotamus and said, 7) "............................ fat you are! Tell me, who's the king of the jungle?" 8) "............................ good manners you have!" said the hippopotamus. "Why, you are, of course."

The lion then went up to a parrot and said, 9) "............................ talkative you are! Tell me, who's the king of the jungle?" 10) "............................ easy question!" said the parrot. "Why, you are, of course."

Finally the lion went up to an elephant and said, 11) "............................ big ears you have! Tell me, who's the king of the jungle?" 12) "............................ rude animal you are!" replied the elephant, lifting the lion with its trunk, swinging him in the air and throwing him on the ground.

The lion, picking himself up, exclaimed, 13) "............................ bad-tempered elephant you are! There's no need to be so rude just because you don't know the answer!"

## 8. Clauses

### Relative Clauses

Relative clauses are introduced with a) relative pronouns i.e. **who**, **whom**, **whose**, **which** or **that** and b) relative adverbs i.e. **when**, **where** or **why** as follows:

**Relative Pronouns**

| | Subject of the verb of the relative clause (cannot be omitted) | Object of the verb of the relative clause (can be omitted) | Possession (cannot be omitted) |
|---|---|---|---|
| **used for people** | who/that | who/whom/that | whose |
| | There's **the boy** who/that started the fight. | Here's **the woman** (who/that) I told you about last week. | This is **Mrs Smith**, whose daughter works in my office. |
| **used for things/ animals** | which/that | which/that | whose/of which |
| | I saw **a film** which/that was very good. | This is **the book** (which/that) I read last week. | This is **the house** whose roof/the roof of which was destroyed. |

**Who**, **whom**, **which** or **that** can be omitted when there is a noun or personal pronoun between the relative pronoun and the verb, that is, when they are the objects of the relative clause. When **who**, **which** etc are subjects of the relative clause, they cannot be omitted.
*The dress (which/that) **you** bought yesterday is very nice.* ("Which/that" is the object and can be omitted.)
*The man **who** called just now is my dentist.* ("Who" is the subject and cannot be omitted.)

**What** can be used as subject or object or to emphasize a word or phrase. *He didn't do **what** I told him.*
**That** can be used instead of **who**, **whom** or **which** but is never used after commas or prepositions.
*He's the man **who/that** gave me your address. That hotel, **which** (not: that) is by the sea, is where we stayed.*
**That** usually follows superlatives and words such as: something, nothing, anything, all, none, many and few. *There's **nothing that** he can't do.*

**Relative Adverbs**

| Time | when (= in/on/at which) | August is the month **when** a lot of tourists visit the place. |
|---|---|---|
| Place | where (= in/at/on/to which) | That's the hotel **where** the President is staying. |
| Reason | why (= for which) | Lack of money is the reason (**why**) we are not going on holiday. |

# 8. Clauses

**Prepositions in Relative Clauses**

We normally avoid putting prepositions before relative pronouns.
That's the boy **with whom** I shared the room. (formal – not usual)
That's the boy **who/that** I shared the room with. (less formal)
That's the boy I shared the room with. (more usual)

**178) Fill in: which or whose.**

Broadstairs, 1) ..*which*.. is a town on the south coast of England, is famous for its Dickens Festival, 2) .................... is held every June. Dickens, 3) .................... first name was Charles, was a famous English writer 4) .................... most famous books are "A Christmas Carol" and "Oliver Twist". "A Christmas Carol", 5) .................... is about a mean man 6) .................... life is changed by the visits of three ghosts, has been made into several films 7) .................... are often shown at Christmas on television. Another one of his novels is called "Bleak House", 8) .................... is actually the name of the house in 9) .................... Dickens lived in Broadstairs. The people of Broadstairs all love the festival, 10) .................... brings a lot of money to the town and is fun for everyone. I'm sure Dickens, 11) .................... life and books are celebrated, would have loved it too.

**179) Read the letter and add the sentences in brackets using relative clauses.**

Dear Donna,
I must tell you about a man 1) ....*(who/that) I met on holiday*.... (I met him on holiday). I met him in Rome 2) .................... (I was staying there overnight). I was walking around the Forum, 3) .................... (it's one of Rome's ancient sites). The guide, 4) .................... (he'd been feeling unwell all day), suddenly fainted! Someone shouted, "Doctor!" and a man .................... (he was standing nearby), came rushing up to help. He took the guide into the shade, 6) .................... (it was cooler there), and rushed to a telephone, 7) .................... (it was nearby) to call an ambulance. Fortunately, it proved to be nothing serious, 8) .................... (we were all relieved to hear it). Anyway, we got chatting, and guess what! This man, 9) .................... (David is his name), comes from Birmingham, 10) .................... (I studied History there). We found out we had a lot in common, and I'm going to see him again next week. I'll keep you posted.
Love,
Kim

**180) Correct the mistakes.**

Mrs Jones, 1) whom lives in Wales, is a farmer. The farmhouse 2) which she lives has been in her family for generations. She has made many changes to the buildings 3) so as to life will be easier for everyone. 4) But in the old days everything was done by hand, now there are a lot of machines 5) who do the hardest jobs, and only Mrs Jones knows 6) how a difference this has made. The surrounding countryside, 7) that she has loved 8) from she was a girl, is 9) such green that it still amazes her. 10) Where she has free time she loves walking in the hills, but this happens 11) such rarely that sometimes she forgets 12) how it is like. 13) While her children have grown up she plans to move to a smaller house, but she will never leave the countryside because she knows 14) what unhappy she would be 15) when she did.

1. ..*who*..  4. ............  7. ............  10. ............  13. ............
2. ............  5. ............  8. ............  11. ............  14. ............
3. ............  6. ............  9. ............  12. ............  15. ............

87

## 8. Clauses

### Defining / Non-Defining Relative Clauses

A **defining** relative clause gives **necessary information** and is essential to the meaning of the main sentence. The clause is not put in commas. **Who**, **which** or **that** can be omitted when they are the object of the relative clause.
He's the actor **who** was killed in a car crash. ("Who" as subject is not omitted.)
That's the letter **(which/that)** Sally sent me. ("Which/that" as object can be omitted.)

A **non-defining** relative clause gives **extra information** and is not essential to the meaning of the main sentence. In non-defining relative clauses the relative pronouns cannot be omitted. **That** cannot replace **who** or **which**. The relative clause is put in commas.
John, **who** is very lazy, failed his test again. (not: John, ~~that~~ is very lazy, failed his test again.)

**181)** Fill in the appropriate relative, say whether the relative clauses are essential or not to the meaning of the main sentence, then add commas where necessary.

1. My wallet**,** .. *which* .................. was in my handbag**,** has disappeared. .....*not essential*.....
2. Brian ........................... is still at school is the captain of our local team. ...........................
3. London ................. is the capital of England attracts many foreign visitors. ...........................
4. The man ........................................ wife is seriously ill is very sad. ...........................
5. This parrot ........................... comes from Africa is a clever mimic. ...........................
6. The children ........................ play with my son are coming round for tea. ...........................
7. Brighton ........................... my boyfriend lives has a famous pier. ...........................
8. English weather ............. is often bad is the subject of many conversations. ...........................
9. The woman ................ car was stolen last night has called the police. ...........................
10. Kate's job ................. involves working long hours makes her very tired. ...........................
11. George ........................... is American is the best student in our class. ...........................
12. The soldier ........... fought the most bravely is being awarded a medal. ...........................
13. The house ............... my grandparents lived is being demolished. ...........................
14. Their argument ......... continued throughout the night was finally resolved. ...........................
15. The Sussex coast ............. is in the south of England is very beautiful. ...........................
16. Not everybody ............... is coming to my party is bringing me a present. ...........................
17. California ............. is on the west coast of America attracts actresses, surfers and musicians. ...........................
18. This cake ........................... I bought yesterday tastes delicious. ...........................

**182)** Fill in the correct relative pronoun. Then write (S) for subject and (O) for object. Finally, state if the relatives can be omitted or not in the box provided.

1. This is the window ....... *which/that* ............ I repaired last week. .*O*. ..*can be omitted*..
2. He is the man ........................... interviewed me for the job. .... ...........................
3. The fish ........................... I am cooking smells delicious. .... ...........................
4. She is the woman ........................... I'm going on holiday with. .... ...........................
5. The doctor ................. examined me on Friday was well-qualified. .... ...........................
6. The film ............. you have just seen was directed by Orson Welles. .... ...........................
7. This is the shop ........................... sells the best fruit. .... ...........................
8. Isn't he the man ........................... plays the violin in the orchestra? .... ...........................
9. Those are the shelves ........................... John made. .... ...........................
10. The house ........................... I was born in is that one. .... ...........................
11. Look out! That's the dog ........................... attacked John! .... ...........................
12. He is married to a woman ........... is much better looking than he is. .... ...........................
13. There were some parts of the book ............. I found really boring. .... ...........................
14. Anne Hathaway was the woman ....... William Shakespeare was married to. .... ...........................
15. "Tom Sawyer" is the story ........................... I enjoyed most as a child. .... ...........................
16. She is the woman ........................... helped me with my homework. .... ...........................

## 8. Clauses

**183** Fill in the relative pronoun and put commas where necessary. Write (D) for defining, (ND) for non-defining and if the relative clause can be omitted or not.

1. My sister, ..who.. works as a scientist, lives in America.   ND   ..omitted..
2. This icecream ............... comes from Italy is delicious.   ....   ..............
3. The town ............... I grew up was very small.   ....   ..............
4. James ............... hobby is rock climbing has broken his leg.   ....   ..............
5. The sweater ............... Jenny bought me is too big.   ....   ..............
6. The subjects ............... I am studying are very difficult.   ....   ..............
7. The school ............... I first went has closed down.   ....   ..............
8. The country ............... I want to visit most of all is China.   ....   ..............
9. Angela ............... best friend lives in Madrid has gone on holiday to Spain.   ....   ..............
10. The boutique ............... is by my house is having a sale.   ....   ..............
11. The book ............... I'm reading is very exciting.   ....   ..............
12. Miss Hunter ............... works at the bank has been promoted.   ....   ..............
13. Terry ............... father is also a mechanic has just repaired our car.   ....   ..............

### Oral Activity 20

Students in teams give definitions of the persons, things or places below using **who**, **which**, **where**, or **that**. Each correct definition gets 1 point.
Team A S1: A knife is an object which is used for cutting bread or meat.

    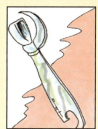 

**184** Join the sentences using who, when, where, which or whose.

1. Jim is the man. He met the Queen last year.   *Jim is the man who met the Queen last year.*
2. That's the beach. I used to go swimming there.
3. Steven lives in Bradford. It is a city in the north of England.
4. July was the month. My sister was born then.
5. This is my new coat. I bought it in yesterday's sale.
6. This is the factory. My father used to work here.
7. That's the man. His wife is a famous actress.
8. America is the country. The best hamburgers are made there.
9. Jo is an actress. She has just finished making her first film.
10. That's the dog. It always barks when you approach it.
11. 1666 was the year. A great fire destroyed much of London.
12. Christmas is the time. People buy each other presents.

## 8. Clauses

13. Sheena is a pop star. She had a hit record last year. ................................................
14. Smoking is a bad habit. It causes many deaths every year. ................................................
15. These are the children. Their mother is a policewoman. ................................................
16. That's the hospital. I had an operation there. ................................................

### Tense Review

**185) Put the verbs in brackets into the correct tense form.**

Jane 1) ..*had always wanted*... (always want) to be a nurse ever since she 2) ................ (be) a child but her father 3) ................ (tell) her that nursing 4) ................ (is) not a suitable profession for her to follow 5) ............ (leave) school, she 6) ................(offer) a job working as a doctor's receptionist. She didn't want to take the job, so she 7) ................(decide) to talk to her friend, Anne, about what she should do. Jane and Anne 8) ........................ (be) friends for a long time and 9) ......... (live) in the same street. When Jane 10) ........................(arrive) at Anne's house, Anne 11) ..............(sit) in the garden 12) ...............(read). She 13) ........................ (look up) and smiled as Jane 14) .............. (approach) "Hello, Jane. How are you? Why are you looking so miserable?" Jane 15) .............. (explain) the situation and her friend 16) ........................(listen) sympathetically. As Jane finished speaking, Anne's mother 17) ........................(come out) of the house and 18) ............(shout) to the two girls to come over. "I'm dreadfully sorry Jane, but I'm afraid your father had an accident this morning in work and is in hospital. They weren't able to give me many details, but they 19) ..............(tell) me he's going to be all right. I'll drive you over there now." When they 20) ........................(arrive) at the hospital Jane was amazed to see her father sitting up in bed and smiling broadly as they walked into his hospital room. "Father, I 21) ............(be) so worried, I thought something dreadful 22) ............(happen)." "Oh, there's no need to worry. I've broken my arm but the nurses here have taken such good care of me, they've been wonderful. And Jane, I've been thinking... ." Jane smiled at her friend, and knew that everything was going to be all right!

### In Other Words

| | |
|---|---|
| I didn't phone him because I didn't want to disturb him.<br>I didn't phone him so as not to disturb him.<br>I didn't phone him in case I disturbed him. | That's the village where I was born.<br>That's the village I was born in.<br>That's the village in which I was born. |
| It was such a nice vase that I bought it.<br>The vase was so nice that I bought it. | Although it was raining, we went out.<br>Despite the rain, we went out. |
| He was so busy that he couldn't phone us.<br>He was too busy to phone us. | What a nice day!<br>It's such a nice day! |
| It was such a warm day that we went fishing.<br>The day was very warm so we went fishing. | How quickly he walks!<br>He walks so quickly! |

**186) Rephrase the following sentences.**

1. We spoke quietly because we didn't want to wake the baby.
   ....*We spoke quietly so as not to wake the baby./We spoke quietly in case we woke the baby.*....
2. He was such a naughty boy that his father punished him. ................................................
3. It was so hot that I didn't leave the house. ................................................
4. That's the church where I got married. ................................................
5. Although he was ill he still went to work. ................................................
6. What a lovely house! ................................................
7. How happy you look! ................................................
8. He is too weak to lift that suitcase. ................................................
9. The room was so crowded that we couldn't go inside. ................................................
10. Despite being over 60, she was very beautiful. ................................................

## 8. Clauses

11. You talk so quietly! ................................................
12. She has such lovely eyes! ................................................
13. She was too tired to go on with her work. ................................................
14. This is the University I went to. ................................................
15. What a beautiful dress! ................................................
16. Although she was tired she still watched the late film. ................................................
17. She went to bed early. She didn't want to be tired the next morning. ................................................
18. I didn't tell you because I thought you'd be upset. ................................................

### Phrasal Verbs 8

| | |
|---|---|
| make out : | 1) distinguish/see |
| | 2) understand |
| make up : | 1) invent |
| | 2) put cosmetics on |
| | 3) end a quarrel |
| make up one's mind : | decide |

**187** Fill in the correct preposition or adverb.

1. He made ...*up*.. his face to look like a clown's for the party.
2. I can't make .............................. whether to buy the dress or not.
3. His handwriting is so bad I can't make ............ what he has written.
4. They finally made .............................. after their argument.
5. I've read this poem twice but I still can't make ..... .............................. what it is about.
6. Everything he has said is a lie. He made ............ .............. the whole story.

**188** Look at Appendix 1 and fill in the correct preposition.

1. I can't think of any reason ..*for*.. your not getting the job.
2. You shouldn't have to rely ........................ a calculator to do your Maths homework.
3. I'm sorry it's taken me so long to reply ............ your letter.
4. What was your boss's reaction ........................ your request for a week off work?
5. There has been a dramatic rise .................... unemployment in the past ten years.
6. She married him because he reminded her ....... Sylvester Stallone.
7. Why didn't you remind me ........................ the party last night? I really wanted to go.
8. I think there is a relationship ............ his poor performance at school and his unhappy home life.
9. It's important to develop a good relationship ....... ........................ your colleagues at work.
10. Do you know who was responsible .................... breaking this computer?

### Idioms 8

| | |
|---|---|
| feel/be/look worn out : | feel/be/look exhausted |
| learn sth by heart : | memorise |
| lose one's head : | panic; lose self-control |
| lose heart : | become discouraged |
| lose one's temper : | become angry |
| change one's mind : | decide to do sth different |
| tell the world : | tell everybody |
| spend money like water : | spend money quickly or in large amounts |

**189** Fill in the correct idiom.

1. He ..*was*... completely ...*worn out*........ after working for twelve hours without a break.
2. If there is a fire in the building, it is important to stay calm and not to ................................ .
3. I know some lines from the "Iliad", but I wouldn't like to have to .................... it all ................ .
4. When Kelly agreed to marry him, he was so happy he wanted to ................................ .
5. You'll never be rich because you ................ ................................................
6. I was going to go out last night, but then I ........ ................................ and stayed at home.
7. Don't ........................ just because you failed your driving test - I'm sure you'll pass eventually.
8. When Billy didn't stop talking, the teacher ........ ................ and threw him out of the classroom.

# Revision Exercises II

**190. Choose the correct item.**

1. This factory …C… more cars this year than ever before.
   A) produces   B) produced
   C) has produced   D) producing

2. …B… helpful man he is!
   A) How   B) What a
   C) What   D) Such

3. We …D… be going to France this summer, but we're not sure yet.
   A) can   B) must
   C) would   D) might

4. This car …B… to use less petrol than any other.
   A) designs   B) was designed
   C) has designed   D) was designing

5. That boy, …C… father is a footballer, is very good at sports.
   A) that   B) who's
   C) whose   D) which

6. I wish I …C… the answer.
   A) was knowing   B) know
   C) knew   D) would know

7. I'm glad you remembered …A… some tea because I haven't got any.
   A) to bring   B) bringing
   C) to have brought   D) bring

8. By the end of the month the estate agent …B/D… twenty houses.
   A) will sell   B) will have sold
   C) will be selling   D) is going to sell

9. Swansea, …B… my father was brought up, is a beautiful town.
   A) who   B) where
   C) that   D) which

10. "Why hasn't your company moved yet?"
    "They …C… to find new offices for months."
    A) have tried   B) had tried
    C) have been trying   D) were trying

11. She was …A… tired that she fell asleep.
    A) so   B) such
    C) enough   D) too

12. You mustn't leave the office …B… the manager returns.
    A) while   B) until
    C) by the time   D) during

13. "Have they found out who stole the money?"
    "Yes, a clerk pretended …A… it when in fact he was hiding it."
    A) to have lost   B) having lost
    C) losing   D) have lost

14. "Everything in this room is wet from the rain."
    "I …D… the windows!"
    A) mustn't have shut   B) must have shut
    C) would have shut   D) should have shut

15. "Why aren't you writing the test?"
    "I can't remember what the teacher said. I wish I …A… more attention."
    A) had paid   B) am paying
    C) would pay   D) pay

16. "Can you lend me some money?"
    "I'll give you some …B… I get paid."
    A) while   B) as soon as
    C) whenever   D) until

17. Take some money in case you …D… to do some shopping.
    A) will want   B) had wanted
    C) wanted   D) want

18. "Why didn't you ring me?"
    "I would have rung you if I …B… the time."
    A) have had   B) had had
    C) have   D) had

19. He …D… the best pianist alive.
    A) thinks to be   B) is thought being
    C) is thought be   D) is thought to be

20. Do you know …A… that man standing near Tom is?
    A) who   B) whom
    C) whose   D) who's

21. "Did you play football yesterday?"
    "Yes we did, …B… the snow."
    A) although   B) despite
    C) in spite   D) even though

22. …A… big ears he's got!
    A) What   B) What a
    C) How   D) Such

23. If I …D… her before, I would have recognised her.
    A) saw   B) would see
    C) see   D) had seen

24. Will you taste this milk? It …C… have gone off.
    A) will   B) can
    C) may   D) would

## Revision Exercises II

### 191) Choose the correct item.

Johnny Starrstruck is one of the 1) ...*most*........ (most/more/much) famous actors in Hollywood today. Recently, Johnny 2) ..................... (wins/has won/had won) 7 Oscars and he now earns over 6 million dollars 3) ..................... (per/the/for) film. However, Johnny hasn't always been 4) ..................... (so/such/such a) rich. He was born 5) ............. (in/on/at) Siberia where his father worked as a carpenter. Johnny's family 6) ..................... (moved/had moved/was moving) to America when Johnny was five 7) ........ (year/years/years') old. He went 8) ............. (in/at/to) school in America and 9) ..................... (until/when/ before) he left school he worked as an insurance salesman. A Hollywood director saw Johnny 10) ........ (in/at/on) a beach in California and asked 11) ..................... (him/he/his) to star in a film about 12) ..................... (surf/surfing/to surf). Since then Johnny 13) ..................... (has made/made/will have made) 15 films. He 14) ............ (has bought/bought/will buy) a house in Beverly Hills and he has a yacht in Hawaii. Next week he 15) ..................... (gets/shall/is getting) married 16) ..................... (with/to/for) Sylvia Sunshine, the Australian singer. They won't be able to have a honeymoon 17) ..................... (because/for/in order) Johnny 18) ..................... (is starting/ started/will start) work on a new film the day after the wedding. 19) ..................... (On/In/At) Christmas they will fly to Australia to visit 20) ..................... (Sylvia's/Sylvia/Sylvias') family.

### 192) Rewrite the following passage in the Passive.

People from the village of Puddle held a meeting last night after somebody discovered a large object in the local park. Nobody has identified it yet. The villagers have called in experts. They'll examine the object on Sunday. People believe that it could be a spaceship from another planet!

...................................................................................
...................................................................................
...................................................................................
...................................................................................
...................................................................................

### 193) Rephrase the following sentences using the words in bold type.

1. They stayed up all night because they wanted to see the comet.
   **order** ...*They stayed up all night in order to see the comet.*..................
2. Could you explain this to me?
   **mind** ...................................................................................
3. It's possible that she won't ring after all.
   **may** ...................................................................................
4. People say that he was treated unfairly.
   **said** ...................................................................................
5. It wasn't necessary for you to send us a cheque.
   **needn't** ...................................................................................
6. If you don't remember his number, how can you phone him?
   **unless** ...................................................................................
7. The day was so wet that I stayed at home.
   **such** ...................................................................................
8. This is the school I studied at.
   **where** ...................................................................................
9. It is not possible that he has spent so much money.
   **can't** ...................................................................................
10. You should get some house insurance because you may be burgled.
    **case** ...................................................................................
11. His remark was irritating.
    **I** ...................................................................................

## Revision Exercises II

12. How gracefully that horse jumps!
    **so** ............................................................
13. When did you get back from France?
    **since** ............................................................
14. It's too hot to work in the garden.
    **cool** ............................................................
15. Someone should have told her about it.
    **been told** ............................................................
16. John's father made him pay for the damage.
    **was made** ............................................................

**194** Put the verbs in brackets into the correct tense.

"Good evening ladies and gentlemen. I 1) ..*am*.. (be) Charles Trump. I 2) ................ (report) from BBC news headquarters. Earlier this evening, at 6.24 pm, an earthquake 3) ................ (hit) Cairo, Egypt. Many people 4) ................ (kill); many more 5) ................ (injure) and much of the city 6) ................ (destroy). Emergency teams 7) ................ (already/set up) all over the city. They 8) ................ (help) the injured. Firemen and local people 9) ................ (dig) in the wreckage as many people 10) ................ (still/trap). A BBC special news team 11) ................ (leave) for Cairo immediately after we 12) ................ (receive) news of the earthquake. We 13) ................ (expect) a special, in-depth report from them at any moment. As soon as we 14) ................ (hear) from them we will release another news bulletin. Anyone who 15) ................ (wish) to enquire about family or friends should ring the following emergency numbers - 010 367 - 38291/2/3/4 for information. We'll be back with the special bulletin."

**195** Fill in: can, would, could, or will.

Library asst: 1) ..*Can*.. I help you?
    Student: Yes, I'd like some books on World War I. 2) ................ you show me where to look?
Library asst: Yes of course. What exactly 3) ................ you like?
    Student: Well, I'm doing a project at school.
Library asst: Come with me. I 4) ................ show you where the books are.
    Student: 5) ................ you help me choose some too?
Library asst: Well, I 6) ................ for a few minutes, but I'll have to get back to the desk soon.
    Student: I 7) ................ need to take some home with me, too. 8) ................ that be alright?
Library asst: Yes, of course, but you'll need to bring them back by next week.

**196** First identify the meaning of the modal verb, then rephrase the sentences as in the example:

1. The scissors **must** be in this drawer. — *probability - I think the scissors are in this drawer.*
2. This **can't** be the right way!
3. **Shall** I help you with your homework?
4. He **should** try to give up smoking.
5. You **can't** come in without a membership card.
6. You**'d better** cut the grass soon.
7. You **may** leave now.
8. **Could** I see the manager?
9. You **ought to** drive more carefully.
10. There **might** be some shops open on Sunday.
11. We**'ve got to** escape or else we'll die.
12. **Would you like** me to fetch it for you?
13. It **can't** be 2 o'clock!

# Revision Exercises II

**197** Fill in the correct preposition or adverb.

1. There wasn't enough cake to go ..round.. at the wedding.
2. My father has given .............. smoking.
3. I prefer tea .............. coffee.
4. Most people hope .............. a white Christmas.
5. No one laughed .............. the comedian's jokes.
6. He made .............. an excuse to avoid her.
7. The ice on the roads called .............. careful driving.
8. There has recently been an increase .............. the price of petrol.
9. The police are looking .............. the matter of the missing painting.
10. Don't be mean .............. your sister. Give her the book back, please!

**198** Read the numbered lines and correct the mistakes in the spaces provided. Some lines are correct. Indicate these lines with a tick ( ✓ ).

1. In the last twenty years, the Rancine Corporation brought you  ......has brought......
2. over a hundred wonderful new products. Today, I'm feeling
3. proud to announce another. We haven't known what we are
4. going to call it yet, but at the moment we are referring to it
5. like "Minus 10". This is because this product will make any
6. woman to look ten years younger. These photographs show
7. a sixty-years-old woman before and after she had tried the
8. cream. The active ingredient is a rare plant who one of our
9. scientists discovered while he has done research in the
10. Amazon. In our initial experiments, we observed women
11. who use "Minus 10" over periods of one month, two
12. months and six months. Since then we improved it even
13. more and by next summer we will perfect it.

**199** Use Gavin's thoughts to write conditionals, then identify the type.

1. I was curious. I came to investigate this strange spaceship.
2. These aliens speak strangely. I can't understand them.
3. I may get home one day. No one will believe this story.
4. I didn't bring my camera. I can't take any pictures.
5. I hope they have some food, or I'll starve to death.
6. There's no telephone here. I can't phone home.

1. *If I hadn't been curious, I wouldn't have come to investigate this strange spaceship. (3rd type)*
2. ...........................................................................................
3. ...........................................................................................
4. ...........................................................................................
5. ...........................................................................................
6. ...........................................................................................

## 9. Reported speech

| | |
|---|---|
| **Direct speech** is the exact words someone said. We use quotation marks in Direct speech. | "I'll go to London," she said. |
| **Reported speech** is the exact meaning of what someone said but not the exact words. We do not use quotation marks in Reported speech. | She said **she would go to London**. |

### Say - Tell

We can use **say** and **tell** both in Direct and Reported speech. **Tell** is always followed by a personal object (told me). **Say** is used with or without a personal object. When it is used with a personal object **say** is always followed by **to** (said to me).

| Direct speech | Reported speech |
|---|---|
| She **said**, "I can't drive." | She **said** (that) she couldn't drive. |
| She **said to me**, "I can't drive." | She **said to me** (that) she couldn't drive. |
| She **told me**, "I can't drive." | She **told me** (that) she couldn't drive. |

| | |
|---|---|
| **Expressions with say** | say good morning/evening etc, say something, say one's prayers, say a few words, say so etc |
| **Expressions with tell** | tell the truth, tell a lie, tell sb the time, tell sb one's name, tell a story, tell a secret, tell sb the way, tell one from another etc |

**200** Fill in "say" or "tell" in the correct form.

1. Can you ...*tell*... me what time the film starts?
2. She ..................... she would never speak to him again.
3. I promise to ..................... the truth, the whole truth and nothing but the truth.
4. She always ..................... "good morning" to her neighbours.
5. Ruth ..................... her prayers and went to bed.
6. Sometimes it's hard to ..................... one twin from another.
7. Who ..................... you I was married?
8. I couldn't believe what he ..................... to me.
9. Would you mind ..................... me what you're doing?
10. "Go and tidy your room," he ..................... to his son.

# 9. Reported speech

| We can report: | A. **statements** | B. **questions** | C. **commands**, **requests**, **suggestions** |
|---|---|---|---|

## Reported Statements

1. To report statements we use a reporting verb (**say**, **tell**, **explain** etc) followed by a that-clause. In spoken English **that** can be omitted. He said, "I feel sick." He **said (that)** he felt sick.

2. Pronouns and possessive adjectives change according to the context.
   **Direct speech:** He said, "**I'll** lend **you my** car."   **Reported speech:** He said **he** would lend **me his** car.

3. Time words and tenses can change as follows depending on the time reference:

| Direct speech | Reported speech |
|---|---|
| tonight, today, this week/month/year | that night, that day, that week/month/year |
| now | then, at that time, at once, immediately |
| now that | since |
| yesterday, last night/week/month/year | the day before, the previous night/week/month/year |
| tomorrow, next week/month/year | the following day/ the day after, the following/ next week / month/year |
| two days/months/years etc ago | two days/months/years etc before |

"Tom is leaving **tomorrow**," she said. She said Tom was leaving **the next day**. (Speech reported after Tom had left.)
"Bob is leaving **tomorrow**," she said. She said Bob is leaving **tomorrow**. (Speech reported before Bob has left.)

4. When the reporting verb is in the past, the verb tenses change as follows:

| Direct speech | Reported speech |
|---|---|
| **Present Simple**<br>"He **likes** walking," she said. | **Past Simple/Present Simple**<br>She said he **liked/likes** walking. |
| **Present Continuous**<br>"He **is watching** TV," she said. | **Past Continuous**<br>She said he **was watching** TV. |
| **Present Perfect**<br>"He **has just left**," she said. | **Past Perfect**<br>She said he **had just left**. |
| **Past Simple**<br>"He **left** an hour ago," she said. | **Past Perfect**<br>She said he **had left** an hour before. |
| **Future**<br>"He**'ll be** back in an hour," she said. | **Conditional**<br>She said he **would be** back in an hour. |
| **Present Perfect Continuous**<br>"I**'ve been typing** since morning," she said. | **Past Perfect Continuous**<br>She said she **had been typing** since morning. |

5. If the direct verb is already in the Past S., in Reported speech it can change into the Past Perfect or remain the same. "I **was** late for work," she said.   She said she **was/had been** late for work.

6. If the direct verb is in the Past Perfect, it remains the same in Reported speech. "I **had** already **written** to him," he said. He said he **had** already **written** to him.
   Past Continuous usually remains the same in Reported speech.
   **Direct speech:**       "I **was reading** while my parents **were watching** TV," she said.
   **Reported speech:**   She said she **was reading** while her parents **were watching** TV.

## 9. Reported speech

**7.** Certain words change as follows depending on the context.

| Direct speech: | this/these   here   come | (in his office) He said, "I'll be **here** again on Monday." |
| Reported speech: | that/those   there   go | (outside the office) He said he'd be **there** again on Monday. |

**8.** There are no changes in the verb tenses in Reported speech when the direct sentence expresses a general truth, is Conditional Type 2 or Type 3 or a wish.

"The earth **is** a planet," he said.   He said the earth **is** a planet. (general truth)
"If you **studied** more, you**'d pass** your test," he said.   He said that if I **studied** more, I**'d pass** my test.
"I wish I **were/was** rich," he said.   He said he wished he **were/was** rich.

**9.** When the introductory verb is in the Present, Future or Present Perfect, there are no changes in the verb tenses.

"Nina **can** read," she **says**.   She **says** that Nina **can** read.

**10.** The verb tenses can change or remain the same in Reported speech when a sentence expresses something which is up to date or still true. However, the verb tenses usually change when something is not true or out of date.

"I **like** ice-cream," he said.   He said he **likes/liked** ice-cream. (still true)
"I **am** rich," he said.   He said he **was** rich. (but we know he isn't; not true)

**201** Report what the Jones family said when they came home from their holiday.

1. Mr Jones ...*said that he had had a brilliant time.*.................................
2. Jimmy ..................................................................
3. Grandmother ..........................................................
4. Judy ..................................................................
5. Mrs Jones ............................................................
6. Paul ..................................................................
7. Patrick ................................................................
8. Tracy ................................................................
9. Danny ................................................................
10. Tina ................................................................

## 9. Reported speech

### Reported Questions

In **Reported questions** we use affirmative word order and the question mark is omitted. To report a question we use: a) **ask + wh-word** (who, what etc) when the direct question begins with such a word, b) **ask + if / whether** when the direct question begins with an auxiliary verb (do, has, can etc). Pronouns, possessive adjectives, tenses, time expressions etc change as in statements.

| Direct speech: | He said, "Where did he stay?" | He said, "Did you have a nice time?" |
|---|---|---|
| Reported speech: | He **asked where** he had stayed. | He **asked if/whether** I had had a nice time. |

**Indirect questions** are different from **Reported questions**. We use Indirect questions when we ask for information, whereas we use Reported questions to report someone else's questions. Indirect questions are introduced with **Could you tell me ...?, Do you know ...?, I wonder ..., I want to know ...** etc and their verb is in the affirmative. There are no changes in the verb tenses as in Reported questions. If the Indirect question starts with **I wonder ...** or **I want to know ...**, then the question mark is omitted.

| Direct questions | Reported questions | Indirect questions |
|---|---|---|
| He asked me, "How old is he?" | He asked me **how old he was**. | Do you know **how old he is**? |
| He asked me, "Where has he gone?" | He asked me **where he had gone**. | I wonder **where he has gone**. |

**202** Report the tourists' questions to the tour guide.

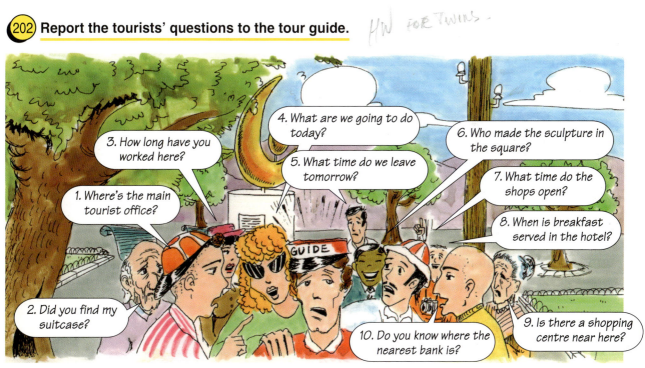

1. The boy with the cap ...*asked the tour guide where the main tourist office was.*
2. The old man
3. The woman with the hat
4. The woman with the glasses
5. The tall man
6. The Chinese boy
7. The man with the moustache
8. The boy with the camera
9. The old woman
10. The bald man

## 9. Reported speech

### Reported Commands / Requests / Suggestions

To report commands, requests, suggestions etc we use a reporting verb (advise, ask, suggest, beg, offer, order, tell etc) followed by a **to-infinitive**, a **not to-infinitive** or an **-ing form** according to the construction of the introductory verb. (see page 102)

| Direct speech | Reported speech |
| --- | --- |
| He said to me, "Come with me." | He told me **to go** with him. |
| He said to me, "Don't lie to me." | He told me **not to lie** to him. |
| He said, "Let's go out." | He suggested **going** out. |

**203** Mrs Baxton is giving her cleaner instructions about what to do for the day.

1. Clean the bathroom.
2. Make the beds.
3. Don't forget to tidy the bedroom.
4. Feed the dogs.
5. Sweep the kitchen floor.
6. Don't leave the rubbish in the kitchen.
7. Remember to water the plants.
8. Do the washing-up.
9. Hoover the sitting room.
10. Don't let anyone into the house.

1. ...She told her to clean the bathroom.
2. ............
3. ............
4. ............
5. ............
6. ............
7. ............
8. ............
9. ............
10. ............

**204** First state whether the following statements are true (T) or false (F), then turn them from Direct speech into Reported speech.

1. "Ostriches can fly," he said. ...He said (that) ostriches could fly. ...F...
2. "The Amazon is the widest river in the world," she said.

3. "The Earth is the largest planet in the universe," he said.

4. "Penguins live in the desert," she said.

5. "It's hot at the South Pole," he said.

6. "Luxembourg has the best football team in the world," he said.

7. "Dolphins are mammals," he said.

8. "The Sahara desert is the largest desert in the world," he said.

# 9. Reported speech

9. "British weather is always wonderful," she said.
.................................................................................................
10. "The Mediterranean is the deepest sea," he said.
.................................................................................................

**205** Turn from Direct speech into Reported speech.

1. "I've finished all my work," she said. ........ *She said (that) she had finished all her work.*
2. "Why are you looking at me like that?" she asked him.
3. "Don't play with matches," his mother said.
4. "I've forgotten to bring my lunch with me," he said.
5. "Will you be home soon?" she asked her husband.
6. "Go to bed!" Father said to the children.
7. "I'll clean the car tomorrow," Tim said to his father.
8. "Where have you been?" Gary asked his wife.
9. "I've been working for the same company since 1960," he said to me.
10. "Do you know Garfield?" she asked me.

## Modals in Reported speech

There are changes in the verb tenses of some modal verbs in Reported speech:

will/shall ➡ would, can ➡ could (present)/ would be able to (future), may ➡ might, shall ➡ should (asking for advice) or would (asking for information), must ➡ must/had to (obligation) (* must remains the same when it expresses possibility or deduction)

**Would, could, used to, mustn't, should, might, ought to** and **had better** remain the same.

| Direct speech | Reported speech |
| --- | --- |
| She said, "I'll do it later." | She said (that) she **would** do it later. |
| She said, "I **can** speak German." | She said (that) she **could** speak German. |
| She said, "I **can** come next Monday." | She said (that) she **would be able to** go next Monday. |
| She said, "I **may** speak to Ann." | She said (that) she **might** speak to Ann. |
| She said, "How **shall** I do this?" | She asked how she **should** do that. (advice) |
| She said, "When **shall** we reach York?" | She asked when they **would** reach York. (information) |
| She said, "You **must** be back at 10.00." | She said (that) I **must/had to** be back at 10.00. (obligation) |
| She said, "He **must** be a liar." | She said (that) he **must** be a liar. (deduction) |
| She said, "You **should** try harder." | She said (that) I **should** try harder. |
| She said, "You **had better** phone him." | She said that I **had better** phone him. |

**206** Turn the following sentences into Reported speech.

1. "How shall I tell Tom the bad news?" she said.... *She asked how she should tell Tom the bad news.*
2. "You must try my home-made pie," he said.
3. "Can I go home now?" he asked.
4. "May I call you by your first name?" he asked her.
5. "You can come in, but you mustn't make any noise," she said to him.
6. "What time shall we arrive in London?" he asked.
7. "She must try harder if she wants to succeed," he said.
8. "My father will be angry with me if he finds out," she said.
9. "You ought not to drive so fast," he said to her.
10. "They don't have to come if they don't feel like it," he said.
11. "You had better speak to the manager," she said to him.
12. "I may not be able to meet you at the airport," he said to her.

## 9. Reported speech

### Introductory Verbs

| Introductory verbs | Direct speech | Reported speech |
|---|---|---|
| **agree + to-inf** <br> offer <br> promise <br> refuse <br> threaten | "Yes, I'll help you." <br> "Shall I open the door?" <br> "Of course I'll pay you." <br> "No, I won't go with you." <br> "Stop crying or I'll punish you." | He **agreed to help** me. <br> He **offered to open** the door. <br> He **promised to pay** me. <br> He **refused to go** with us. <br> He **threatened to punish** me if I didn't stop crying. |
| **advise + sb + to -inf** <br> ask <br> beg <br> command <br> invite <br> order <br> remind <br> warn | "You should see a lawyer." <br> "Could you help me?" <br> "Please, please don't hurt her!" <br> "Stand to attention!" <br> "Will you have dinner with me?" <br> "Leave the cat alone!" <br> "Don't forget to ring Ann." <br> "Don't go near the rocks." | He **advised** me **to see** a lawyer. <br> He **asked** me **to help** him. <br> He **begged** me **not to hurt** her. <br> He **commanded** the soldiers **to stand** to attention. <br> He **invited** me **to (have)** dinner with him. <br> She **ordered** me **to leave** the cat alone. <br> She **reminded** me **to ring** Ann. <br> He **warned** me **not to go** near the rocks. |
| **admit + gerund** <br> accuse sb of <br> apologise for <br> boast of/about <br> complain to sb of <br> deny <br> insist on <br> (say one) prefers <br> suggest | "Yes, I told her the secret." <br> "You took the money." <br> "I'm sorry I arrived so late." <br> "I'm the fastest of all." <br> "I have a toothache." <br> "I didn't take the book." <br> "You must come with us." <br> "I'd rather do it myself." <br> "Let's have a party." | He **admitted (to) telling/having told** her the secret. <br> He **accused me of taking/having taken** the money. <br> He **apologised for arriving/having arrived** so late. <br> He **boasted of/about being** the fastest of all. <br> He **complained to me of having** a toothache. <br> He **denied taking/having taken** the book. <br> He **insisted on** me/my **going** with them. <br> He **said he preferred doing/to do** it himself. <br> He **suggested having** a party. |
| **agree + that-clause** <br> complain <br> deny <br> explain <br> exclaim/remark <br> promise <br> suggest | "Yes, it's a big house." <br> "You're always lying to me." <br> "I didn't take that book." <br> "That's why I didn't take it." <br> "What a sunny day it is!" <br> "Of course I'll help you." <br> "You'd better see a doctor." | He **agreed that** it was a big house. <br> He **complained that** I was always lying to him. <br> He **denied that** he had taken the book. <br> He **explained** to me **why/that** he hadn't taken it. <br> He **exclaimed/remarked** that it was a sunny day. <br> He **promised that** he would help me. <br> He **suggested that** I (should) see a doctor. |

Note: admit, advise, boast, insist, threaten, warn, remind can also be followed by a that-clause in Reported speech.

**207** First write the appropriate introductory verb then report the following situations.

1. "You should go to bed."  ...advise...  ...He advised me to go to bed...
2. "Please, please don't leave me."
3. "Do it now!"
4. "No, I did not kill him."
5. "Oh, alright. I'll do the washing-up."
6. "Don't forget to take the dog out."
7. "Everybody, stand up now!"
8. "No, I will not give you my money."
9. "Could I use your phone?"
10. "I'm sorry I shouted at you."
11. "I'll punish you if you don't behave."
12. "It was me who stole the book."
13. "It only works if you press the green button."
14. "You're right. It was a brilliant film."

# 9. Reported speech

15. "I've been feeling dizzy all day."
16. "Of course I'll write to you."
17. "I'll give you a lift home, if you like."
18. "Let's go for a swim."
19. "It was you who broke the TV."
20. "If I were you, I would tell them the truth."

**208) Use an appropriate introductory verb to report the following.**

1. "It wasn't me who stole the car," said Henry. *Henry denied stealing / having stolen the car.*
2. "May I have a piece of cake please?" she said.
3. "Yes, okay. I'll tell him about the accident," he said.
4. "I must have the report by tomorrow," the boss said.
5. "Please, please let me go to the party," Sue asked her mother.
6. "I'll never be naughty again," Ted said to his father.
7. "Stand up straight!" said the sergeant to the soldier.
8. "Yes, it was me who robbed the bank," he said.
9. "I didn't come to work because I was ill," she said to her boss.
10. "Let's play chess," he said.
11. "I'm sorry I forgot to phone you," he said to her.
12. "Don't forget to go to the bank," she said to him.
13. "You should relax more," the doctor said to him.
14. "Mark is always shouting at me," she said.
15. "Yes, it is a nice dress," he said.
16. "Shall I carry your bag, Tracy?" he said.
17. "No, I certainly won't do your homework Graham," said Bill.
18. "You scratched my record," he said to her.
19. "Leave now or I'll phone the police," she said to the salesman.
20. "Oh alright, I'll lend you my car, Tom," she said.
21. "It's true, I broke the window," he said.
22. "I'll phone you as soon as I arrive," she said to me.
23. "You're right, she is beautiful," she said.
24. "No, I won't marry you, John," she said.
25. "If you try to escape, I'll shoot you," he said to the prisoner.
26. "Why don't we have chicken for dinner?" he said.
27. "You must sign the contract, Mr Harrison," she said.
28. "I'll punish you if you do that again!" he said to the boy.
29. "Would you like me to show you how to use this computer?" she said to me.
30. "Yes, it is a good idea," he said.

## Reporting a dialogue or conversation

In conversations we use a mixture of statements, commands and questions. When we turn them into Reported speech we use **and, as, adding that, and he/she added that, explaining that, because, but, since, and then he/she went on to say, while, then,** etc. or the introductory verb in present participle form. Words or expressions such as **Oh, Oh dear, Well** etc are omitted in Reported speech.

| Direct speech | Reported speech |
|---|---|
| "Oh, this is a very nice dress," she said. "How much does it cost?" | She remarked/exclaimed that that was a very nice dress **and** she asked how much it cost. ("Oh" is omitted) |
| "I can't buy it," she said. "I can't afford it." | She said she couldn't buy it, **explaining** that she couldn't afford it. |
| "Shall I help you?" he said. "We can work on it together." | He offered to help me, **suggesting** that we could work on it together. |

## 9. Reported speech

**209** Report the following using an appropriate introductory verb from the list below:

| complain | advise | refuse | warn | beg | suggest | agree | exclaim |
|---|---|---|---|---|---|---|---|
| deny | offer | insist | apologise | threaten | accuse | prefer | |

1. "You should take more exercise," the doctor said. *The doctor advised me to take more exercise.*
2. "This film is so boring," he said to his mother.
3. "Please, please let me go out to play, Mum," she said.
4. "Shall I carry your shopping for you?" he said to her.
5. "Don't get dirty in the garden," she said to Jane.
6. "I'm not going to tidy Helen's bedroom," Tim said.
7. "I didn't eat the cake," he said to her.
8. "What a silly thing to say!" she said.
9. "You really must get your hair cut," she said to him.
10. "You broke my record player," she said to him.
11. "I'm sorry I didn't write to you," she said to him.
12. "Let's go to Jamaica for our holiday," he said to her.
13. "Yes, that is a nice colour," the sales assistant said to her.
14. "I'd rather watch a film than the news," she said to her.
15. "How rude he is!" she said to me.
16. "I think you should go on a diet," she said to him.
17. "I didn't take your dress," she said to her sister.
18. "What a nice gift!" he said.
19. "I'll hit you if you don't stop talking," the boy said to his brother.
20. "I'm sorry I spoke to you like that," he said to his mother.

**210** Rewrite the following sentences in Reported speech.

1. "What time does the next bus leave?" he said. "I need to get to the station."
   *He asked what time the next bus left because he needed to get to the station.*
2. "Don't go swimming in the lake," she said. "The water is filthy."
3. "Let's go shopping tomorrow," she said. "The sales have started."
4. "Stand up," the teacher said to the pupils. "The headmaster is coming."
5. "Please don't take my ring," she said to him. "It was a present."
6. "It's very late, Martin," his mother said. "Where have you been?"
7. "Shall I cook the dinner?" he said to her. "You look very tired."
8. "Please stop making that noise!" she said to him. "I can't concentrate."
9. "Yes, I dropped your vase," she said. "I was cleaning the shelf."
10. "Can I use the car, please?" she said. "I need to run some errands."
11. "I'm sorry I'm late," he said. "The car wouldn't start."
12. "Why are you teasing your sister?" she asked him. "You know it makes her unhappy."
13. "Why won't you come to the party?" he said to her. "Everyone would love to see you."
14. "It was Rob who broke the window," he said to her. "He was kicking the football."

# 9. Reported speech

**211** Turn the following passage into Indirect speech.

"How do you like your course, Sarah?" Jane asked.
"I didn't like it at first," Sarah replied. "I'm really enjoying it now."
"Why did you have doubts about it?" Jane asked.
"Well, there was too much reading, and none of the other students seemed very friendly," Sarah said. "But now I've got used to it and I like it a lot. Do you like your course?"
"Well, the course is all right, though I'm not as interested in History as I thought I was," Jane said.
"Why don't you study something else, then? What about studying English?" Sarah said.
"That is a really good idea, Sarah. Then we could help each other with our work," Jane said.

...Jane asked Sarah how she liked her course.

**212** Turn the following dialogue into Reported speech.

A: Mum, please, will you let me stay at Sally's house tonight?
M: No, I won't.
A: Why?
M: The last time you stayed there, you stayed up late and you were too tired to go to school the next day.
A: That's true. But we won't do that again.
M: And you were both smoking cigarettes.
A: That's not true! I've never smoked in my life.
M: Well, all right then, you can go, but only if you promise to behave.

...Ann begged her mother to let her stay at Sally's house that night but her mother refused.

**213** Turn the following into Reported speech.

1. The policeman ...asked the driver if he had been speeding.
2. The driver
3. Then the driver
4. Mr Thompson
5. Mr Brown
6. Mr Jones
7. Tim
8. Mr Smith
9. Dr Baker

## 9. Reported speech

**214** Write the exact words Judge Pickles said to Fletcher.

He asked him why he did it. Then he told him he was obviously guilty. He told him to look at him when he was speaking to him. He asked him if he was sorry for what he had done. He told him that the bank manager was still in hospital. He said he would go to prison for a long time for that crime. He asked him if he had anything to say in his defence. Then he told the policeman to take him away.

1. Why did you do it?
2. ...........
3. ...........
4. ...........
5. ...........
6. ...........
7. ...........
8. ...........

### Oral Activity 21

The teacher finds a recorded dialogue with short exchanges and plays it in class. Students in turn report what the speakers said or asked.

### Oral Activity 22

Students in teams take turns to ask a question for each picture, then report the exchanges. Each correct item gets 1 point. eg. Why haven't you tidied your room? She asked him why he hadn't tidied the room and he answered he had been too busy. etc

Why haven't you tidied your room?
I've been too busy.

No, thanks.

Yes, I am. I'm very hungry.

It's 6 o'clock.

I'm trying to fix the tap.

No, I made it myself.

Yes, get in.

Bob gave it to me.

## 9. Reported speech

### Tense Review

**215** Fill in the correct tense forms.

Yesterday I 1) ..received.. (receive) a phone call from an old friend who I 2) ..................... (not/hear) from for months. I asked him what he 3) ............. (do), and he told me that he 4) ................ (spend) the past three months sailing around the world on an old-fashioned sailing ship. I 5) ................ (always/ love) everything to do with the sea, so I was very excited to hear that he 6) ........................ (manage) to do something so thrilling. I asked him if we 7) ................ (can) get together soon, and made him promise that he 8) ........................... (bring) all the photos he 9) .......................... (take). When he 10) ............. (come) next week, I'll expect him to tell me exactly what the trip 11) .............. (be) like.

| Phrasal Verbs 9 | |
|---|---|
| put down : | write down |
| put forward : | propose |
| put off : | postpone |
| put on : | 1) dress oneself in<br>2) increase in weight |
| put out : | extinguish (fire, cigarette etc) |
| put through : | connect by phone |
| put sb up : | provide a place to stay |

**216** Fill in the correct preposition or adverb.

1. They've put ...off..... the meeting until tomorrow.
2. Put .......... gloves and a scarf before going out.
3. The receptionist put me ......... to the manager's secretary.
4. Put ............... everyone's name on a piece of paper and I'll see them later.
5. When he gave up smoking, he put ......... nearly ten kilos.
6. Some friends put me .............. when I visited York so I didn't have to pay for a hotel.
7. At the staff meeting Ann put ........ the idea of using recycled paper and everybody agreed it was a good idea.
8. The firemen put ............ the fire in less than 10 minutes.

**217** Look at Appendix 1 and fill in the correct preposition.

1. She felt very sorry ..for.. the injured boy.
2. The student was satisfied .............. his exam results.
3. The young hooligans were sentenced ............ four months in prison.
4. Fiona takes after her mother; they look very similar ............... each other.
5. My friends shouted ............ me from across the road.
6. I always cry when someone shouts .......... me.
7. My brother telephoned to say he was sorry ......... my accident.
8. He said he was sorry .................... breaking the windows.
9. The doctor informed her that, fortunately, she wasn't suffering ................ a serious illness.
10. She became suspicious .............. the strange man who was following her.

| Idioms 9 | |
|---|---|
| fit like a glove : | (of clothes) fit very well |
| sleep like a log : | sleep very deeply |
| have sth on the tip of one's tongue : | (be) on the point of remembering and saying sth |
| pour with rain : | rain heavily |
| be hard of hearing : | be rather deaf |

**218** Fill in the correct idiom.

1. She went to the best dressmaker to ensure that her wedding dress ..fitted her like a glove... .
2. She couldn't quite remember the man's name but she ................................................. .
3. You'll have to speak clearly because he's rather ................................................. .
4. I ................... last night in spite of the storm.
5. We couldn't play tennis as it was ................................................. .

**107**

## 10. Nouns - Articles

**There are four kinds of nouns :** **abstract** (love, beauty etc), **common** (chair, table etc), **collective** (class, audience, family, government, staff, team etc), **proper** (Ann, Ted, Spain etc).

### Gender

**Masculine** = men, boys, animals when we know their sex (he)
**Feminine** = women, girls, ships, animals when we know their sex (she)
**Neuter** = things, babies/animals when we don't know their sex (it)

Most personal nouns have the same form whether male or female (doctor, teacher etc). Some nouns have different forms, though. Some of these are:

| | | | |
|---|---|---|---|
| actor - actress | emperor - empress | king - queen | prince - princess |
| barman - barmaid | father - mother | landlord - landlady | son - daughter |
| boy - girl | gentleman - lady | lord - lady | steward - stewardess |
| (bride)groom - bride | grandfather - grandmother | monk - nun | uncle - aunt |
| brother - sister | hero - heroine | nephew - niece | waiter - waitress |
| duke - duchess | husband - wife | policeman - policewoman | widower - widow |

**219** Put (M) for male, (F) for female or (M/F) for both in the spaces.

1. doctor .....M/F.....
2. nurse .........
3. teacher .........
4. typist .........
5. student .........
6. bride .........

7. pilot .........
8. waiter .........
9. wife .........
10. driver .........
11. barman .........
12. king .........

13. child .........
14. lord .........
15. queen .........
16. lady .........
17. scientist .........
18. prince .........

19. landlord .........
20. stewardess .........
21. grandfather .........
22. policeman .........
23. engineer .........
24. musician .........

**220** Write the masculine or feminine of the following if there is a difference.

1. husband .....wife.....
2. politician .........
3. brother .........
4. uncle .........
5. student .........

6. nephew .........
7. policeman .........
8. lawyer .........
9. waiter .........
10. actor .........

11. doctor .........
12. monk .........
13. duke .........
14. clerk .........
15. shop assistant .........

## 10. Nouns - Articles

### The Plural of Nouns

**Nouns are made plural by adding:**

| | |
|---|---|
| **-s** to the noun. (pen - pen**s** etc) | **-es** to nouns ending in **-o** (tomato - tomato**es**) |
| **-es** to nouns ending in **-s, -ss, -x, -ch, -sh**. (bus - bus**es**, glass - glass**es**, box - box**es**, torch - torch**es**, bush - bush**es** etc) | **-s** to nouns ending in: **vowel + o** (radio - radio**s**), **double o** (zoo - zoo**s**), **abbreviations** (photograph/photo - photo**s**), **musical instruments** (piano - piano**s**) and **proper nouns** (Eskimo - Eskimo**s**). Some nouns ending in **-o** can take either **-es** or **-s**. These are : buffalo, mosquito, volcano etc. |
| **-ies** to nouns ending in **consonant + y**. (baby - bab**ies**, lady - lad**ies** etc) | |
| **-s** to nouns ending in **vowel + y**. (boy - boy**s**, day - day**s** etc) | **-ves** to some nouns ending in **-f/-fe**. (leaf - lea**ves**) (but: chiefs, roofs, cliffs, handkerchiefs, safes etc) |

**Compound nouns** form their plural by adding **-s/-es**:

| | |
|---|---|
| to the second noun if the compound consists of two nouns. girlfriend - girlfriend**s** | to the first noun if the compound consists of two nouns connected with a preposition. sister-in-law – sister**s**-in-law |
| to the noun if the compound consists of an adjective and a noun. frying pan - frying pan**s** | at the end of the compound if this is not made up of any nouns. breakdown - breakdown**s** |

**Irregular Plurals**

man - **men**, woman - **women**, foot - **feet**, tooth - **teeth**, louse - **lice**, mouse - **mice**, child - **children**, goose - **geese**, sheep - **sheep**, deer - **deer**, fish - **fish**, trout - **trout**

**221** Write the plural of the following nouns:

1. city ....cities..
2. brother-in-law ............
3. headline ............
4. photo ............
5. bank robbery ............
6. stepfather ............
7. couch ............
8. dish ............
9. tray ............
10. roof ............
11. sit-in ............
12. hold-up ............
13. mouse ............
14. tooth ............
15. knife ............
16. potato ............
17. sleeping pill ............
18. calf ............
19. water-bottle ............
20. sunshade ............
21. trout ............

**Some nouns take only a plural verb.** These are objects which consist of two parts: **garments** (trousers, pyjamas etc), **tools** (scissors, compasses etc), **instruments** (binoculars, spectacles etc) or nouns which have a plural meaning such as : belongings, cattle, clothes, congratulations, earnings, goods, greens, (good) looks, outskirts, people, police, riches, stairs etc.

**Some nouns take only a singular verb.** These are: **mass nouns** (bread, tea, sugar etc), **abstract nouns** (advice, love, death etc), **words ending in -ics** (athletics, mathematics etc), **games/diseases ending in -s** (billiards, mumps etc), **nouns such as:** weather, luggage, furniture, money, news etc.

**Group nouns** refer to a group of people. These nouns can take **either a singular or a plural verb** depending on whether we see the group as a whole or as individuals.
Such group nouns are : army, audience, class, club, committee, company, council, crew, family, government, press, public, staff, team etc.

The **team was** the best in the country. (the team as a group)
The **team were** all given medals. (each member separately as individuals.)

## 10. Nouns - Articles

**Some nouns have a different meaning in plural**

| Singular | Plural |
|---|---|
| The needle of a **compass** always points north. | You can draw a perfect circle with **compasses**. |
| It is an English **custom** to celebrate the Queen's birthday. | When he got off the plane his bag was searched at **Customs**. |
| She has a lot of **experience** working with children. | We had lots of exciting **experiences** on our journey through Africa. |
| Would you like a **glass** of milk? | He can't see very well without his **glasses**. |
| She has got long, blonde **hair**. | There are two **hairs** in this soup! |
| They were shocked at the **scale** of the disaster. | She weighed herself on the **scales**. |
| This door is made of **wood**. | The boy got lost in the **woods**. |
| He goes to **work** every day except Sunday. | Picasso's **works** are really fascinating. |

### 222 Fill in: is or are.

1. Where ...*are*.... your trousers?
2. Could you tell me where the scissors ............ ?
3. Tonight, there ............ athletics on TV.
4. Money ......... easy to spend and difficult to save.
5. Gloves ................ worn in cold weather.
6. This student's knowledge ............ amazing.
7. Love ........... the reason for much happiness in the world.
8. This bread ............ stale.
9. Your pyjamas ............ on the bed.
10. My luggage ............ too heavy to carry.
11. My advice to you ............ to stay in bed.
12. Physics ............ my favourite subject.
13. Measles ............ a common illness.
14. The glasses ............ in the cupboard.
15. My mum's hair ............ really long.
16. Our bathroom scales ............ quite accurate.
17. Darts ............ a popular game in England.
18. This work ............ too hard for me.
19. People ..... unhappy with the new tax system.

### Countable - Uncountable Nouns

Nouns can be **countable** (those that can be counted, eg. *1 bag, 2 bags etc*) or **uncountable** (those that can't be counted eg. *sugar*). Uncountable nouns take a singular verb. They are not used with a/ an. **Some**, **any**, **no**, **much** etc can be used with them. eg. I need **some** help. (not: ~~a help~~) There isn't **much** sugar left.

The most common uncountable nouns are: accommodation, advice, anger, baggage, behaviour, blood, bread, business, chess, coal, countryside, courage, damage, dirt, education, evidence, food, fruit, furniture, gold, hair, happiness, help, homework, housework, information, jewellery, knowledge, laughter, luck, luggage, meat, money, music, news, rubbish, seaside, shopping, soap, spaghetti, traffic, trouble, water, weather, work, writing etc.
Note that the nouns for types of meat are also uncountable: beef, mutton, venison etc

Many uncountable nouns can be made countable by means of partitives.
a **piece** of cake/information/advice/furniture; a **glass/bottle** of water; a **jar** of jam; a **tin** of beans; a **pint** of milk; a **box** of chocolates; a **packet** of biscuits/tea; a **slice/loaf** of bread; a **pot** of yoghurt; a **pot/cup** of tea; a **kilo/pound** of meat; a **bottle** of vinegar; a **tube** of toothpaste; a **bar** of chocolate/soap; a **bit/piece** of chalk; an ice **cube**; a **lump** of sugar; a **sheet** of paper; a **bag** of flour; a **pair** of trousers; a **game** of soccer; a(n) **item/piece** of news; a **drop/can** of oil; a **can** of cola; a **carton** of milk; a **block** of wood etc.

### 223 Write (C) countable or (U) uncountable.

1. sugar ...U...
2. bird ........
3. pen ........
4. transport ........
5. housework ........
6. ball ........
7. soap ........
8. bridge ........
9. water ........
10. news ........
11. house ........
12. luggage ........
13. boy ........
14. fruit ........
15. chess ........
16. food ........
17. dog ........
18. furniture ........
19. weather ........
20. sausage ........

## 10. Nouns - Articles

**224** Make the following uncountable nouns plural as in the example:

| 1. ice | two | *ice cubes* | 8. advice | two | ............ | 15. paper | two | ............ |
|---|---|---|---|---|---|---|---|---|
| 2. toast | three | ............ | 9. sugar | two | ............ | 16. hockey | two | ............ |
| 3. soap | two | ............ | 10. yoghurt | two | ............ | 17. chocolate | three | ............ |
| 4. tea | two | ............ | 11. wood | three | ............ | 18. spectacles | two | ............ |
| 5. lamb | three | ............ | 12. news | two | ............ | 19. toothpaste | three | ............ |
| 6. ink | two | ............ | 13. jam | three | ............ | 20. information | two | ............ |
| 7. cola | two | ............ | 14. beef | three | ............ | 21. spaghetti | three | ............ |

### A/An - The

**A/An** is used only with singular countable nouns to talk about things in general. We don't use **a/an** with uncountable or plural nouns. We can use **some** instead. **A/An** is often used after the verbs **be** and **have**.
**A** cat is **a** domestic animal. (Which cat? Cats in general.) Bring me **some** milk, please!

We can use **a/an** or **the** before a singular countable noun to refer to a class of people, animals or things. However, we omit **a/an** or **the** before a noun in the plural when it represents a class.
**A/The** dolphin is a mammal. Also: **Dolphins** are mammals. Exception: **Man** is a mammal too. (not: ~~The man~~)

**The** is used with singular and plural nouns, countable and uncountable ones, to talk about something specific, or when the noun is mentioned for a second time.
Whose is **the** van parked in front of our house? (Which van? The one parked in front of our house.)
He found a cat in the park. He took **the** cat home. (The word "cat" is mentioned for a second time.)

**The** is also used with the words **beach, cinema, country(side), ground, jungle, radio, sea, seaside, theatre, world** etc. eg. He likes going to **the** theatre. We usually say "television" without "the". We often watch television. but: Turn on **the** television (set). We also say : He lives near **the sea**. but: They are **at sea** (= they are sailing.) We normally omit "the" before the words **last** and **next** when we talk about a period of time immediately before or after the moment of speaking. He graduated **last** year. I'll meet you **next** week. I went to work on Monday but **the next** day I stayed at home.

**225** Fill in: a, an or the.

1) ..*The*.... tiger is 2) ............ large carnivorous animal which belongs to 3) ............ cat family. 4) ............ males are about three feet high and can be as long as twelve feet, including 5) ............ tail. There are about eight varieties of tiger found around 6) ............ world. 7) ............ tiger is 8) ............ wild animal, which lives in 9) ............ jungle where water and prey are plentiful. 10) ............ tiger will only attack 11) ............ person if it is starving or if it is threatened. 12) ............ tiger is 13) ............ easily recognized animal as it has 14) ............ thick yellow or white coat with distinctive black stripes.

**226** Fill in: a, an or the where necessary.

Last summer we went to 1) ..*the*.... seaside for two weeks. Unfortunately, we hadn't booked 2) ............ accommodation before we went, and we had 3) ............ awful time finding 4) ............ room to stay in. 5) ............ only room we could find was very small, but it had 6) ............ lovely view of 7) ............ sea and was only two minutes from 8) ............ beach. 9) ............ weather was very hot, and on 10) ............ first day I stayed out so long, I got 11) ............ terrible sunburn and had to stay in bed 12) ............ next day. After that, however, everything went well and we had 13) ............ wonderful holiday.

## 10. Nouns – Articles

| The is used before: | The is omitted before: |
|---|---|
| **nouns which are unique.** *the Earth, the Eiffel Tower* | **proper nouns.** *Jim comes from New York.* |
| **names of cinemas** *(the Rex)*, **hotels** *(the Sheraton)*, **theatres** *(the Apollo)*, **museums** *(the Prado)*, **newspapers/magazines** *(The Guardian,* **but:** *Newsweek)*, **ships** *(the Marie Celeste)*, **institutions** *(the RSPCA)*, **galleries** *(the Tate Gallery)*. | **names of sports, games, activities, days, months, holidays, colours, drinks, meals and languages** (not followed by the word "language"). *She plays squash well. She likes red. We speak English.* **but:** *The English language is spoken all over the world.* |
| **names of rivers** *(the Seine)*, **seas** *(the Black Sea)*, **groups of islands/states** *(the Bahamas, the USA)*, **mountain ranges** *(the Alps)*, **deserts** *(the Sahara desert)*, **oceans** *(the Atlantic)*, **canals** *(the Suez Canal)* **and names or nouns with "of"** *(the Tower of London, the Statue of Liberty)*. **Note:** *the equator, the North/South Pole, the north of England, the South/West/North/East* | **names of countries** *(Italy)*, **cities** *(Rome)*, **streets** *(Oxford Street,* **but:** *the High Street)*, **squares** *(Trafalgar Square)*, **bridges** *(Tower Bridge* **but:** *the Golden Gate Bridge, the Severn Bridge)*, **parks** *(Hyde Park)*, **stations** *(Victoria Station)*, **individual mountains** *(Everest)*, **islands** *(Cyprus)*, **lakes** *(Lake Michigan)*, **continents** *(Europe)* **but:** *the Argentine, the Netherlands, (the) Sudan, the Hague, the Vatican.* |
| **musical instruments, dances.** *the piano, the tango* | **possessive adjectives.** *This isn't your bag.* |
| **names of families** *(the Browns)*, **nationalities ending in -sh, -ch or -ese** *(the English, the Dutch, the Japanese)*. **Other plural nationalities are used with or without the** *(the Greeks, the Italians etc)*. | **two-word names whose first word is the name of a person or place.** *Kennedy Airport, Westminster Abbey* **but:** *the White House, (because the first word "White" is not the name of a person or place.)* |
| **titles** *(the Queen, the Prince)*. **"The" is omitted before titles with proper names** *(Queen Victoria)*. | **pubs, restaurants, shops, banks and hotels which have the name of their founder and end in -s or -'s.** *Harrods, Lloyds Bank, Emma's pub* **but:** *the White Horse (pub) (because "White" is not a name)* |
| **adjectives used as plural nouns** *(the poor, the rich, the young, the blind etc)* **and the superlative degree of adjectives/adverbs** *(the worst)*. *She's the **most** beautiful girl in her class.* **Note:** "most" used as a determiner followed by a noun, does not take "the". *Most people believe he's a liar.* | **bed, church, college, court, hospital, prison, school, university**, when we refer to the purpose for which they exist. *Tom was sent to prison. (He is a prisoner.)* **but:** *His mother went to the prison to see him last week. (She went to the prison as a visitor.)* **Work** (place of work) never takes "the". *She's at work.* |
| **the words station, shop, cinema, pub, library, city, village etc.** *She went to **the station** to see Jim off.* | **the words home, father/mother** when we talk about our own home/parents. *Mother is at home.* |
| **morning, afternoon, evening, night.** *I'll be at home in **the** evening.* **but:** *at night, at noon, at midnight, by day/night, at 4 o'clock etc.* | **means of transport:** *by bus/by car/by train/by plane etc* **but:** *in the car, on the bus/train etc. She travelled **by plane**.* **but:** *She left **on the 6 o'clock plane** yesterday.* |
| **historical references/events.** *the Renaissance, the Middle Ages, the First World War* (**but:** *World War I*) | |
| **only, last, first** (used as adjectives). *He was **the last** person to come.* | **illnesses.** *He's got malaria.* But we say: **flu/the flu, measles/the measles, mumps/the mumps** |

## 10. Nouns – Articles

**227** Fill in "the" where necessary.

Dear Sue,
Well I've been here in 1) ..X.. New York for two months now. I'm having 2) ...... time of my life. I'm staying with my father's friends, 3) ...... Bronsons. So far I'm not missing 4) ...... home at all. 5) ...... Americans are very different from 6) ...... English. I noticed this 7) ...... moment I arrived at 8) ...... Kennedy Airport, where 9) ...... most people were very friendly. I've done a lot of sightseeing since I arrived. I think I've seen all 10) ...... famous sights. 11) ...... ones I liked best were 12) ...... Statue of Liberty and 13) ...... Times Square. We're going to 14) ...... Washington 15) ...... next week. I'm looking forward to visiting 16) ...... President's home, 17) ...... White House. Mr Bronson won't be able to come with us as planned though, because he has 18) ...... flu. He was going to drive us there but now we're going by 19) ...... bus instead. Well, I'll have to sign off now as we're going to 20) ...... cinema tonight and then we're going for 21) ...... dinner at 22) ...... Delaney's restaurant. Give my love to 23) ...... Mother and 24) ...... Father and 25) ...... family. I'll be 26) ...... home for 27) ...... Christmas.
Write soon.
Love,
Jessica

**228** Underline the correct item.

1. All of his belongings **was / were** in one small suitcase.
2. Soccer **is / are** a popular game in England.
3. Aerobics **do / does** you a lot of good.
4. Chocolate **makes / make** you put on weight.
5. Most people **enjoy / enjoys** Christmas.
6. The money he makes **is / are** enough to live on.
7. The police **is looking / are looking** for the murderer.
8. Her good looks always **gets / get** her what she wants.
9. The young couple **is getting / are getting** married next year.
10. My advice **is / are** to stop smoking immediately.
11. Measles, which **is / are** a children's disease, **is / are** dangerous for adults.
12. The audience **was / were** given free tickets to the next show.
13. The economics I learnt at school **is / are** out of date now.
14. Her grandparents' death in a car accident **was / were** a great shock.
15. Fish **is / are** easy to look after as pets.
16. Television news **gives / give** you more information than radio news.
17. The stairs to the first floor **is / are** over there.
18. The information I got **was / were** very helpful.

**229** Fill in "the" where necessary.

1) ..The..... Larkins are a very interesting family. 2) ......... Mr Larkin is a travel-writer who has been all over 3) ......... world and written books about 4) ......... China and 5) ......... Chinese. He has also published articles in newspapers such as 6) ......... Times and 7) ......... Observer. 8) ......... His wife, Sylvia, is a journalist who has interviewed people like 9) ......... Prince of Wales and 10) ......... President Reagan. At the moment, she is writing an article about 11) ......... homeless. Their son, 12) ......... Jack, is a professional footballer who plays in 13) ......... USA. He has been playing 14) ......... football since he was a child. Jack met his wife, Sally, at 15) ......... Chicago Airport 16) ......... morning after he had left 17) ......... home to live in 18) ......... States. She is a musician who plays 19) ......... drums in a rock band. In 20) ......... summer the whole family meet at 21) ......... Maxim's in 22) ......... Paris, then travel by 23) ......... car around 24) ......... Europe for a month. 25) ......... Last year they spent 26) ......... whole month of 27) ......... July in Portugal before going back to 28) ......... work.

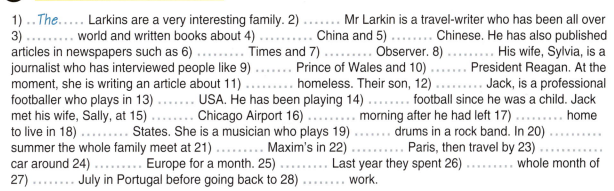

## 10. Nouns – Articles

**230** Fill in "the" where necessary.

1) ..X.. Last summer we went to stay in 2) ........ village where my grandmother was born. I had never been there before, so when we arrived at 3) ........ station I was surprised to see how small it was. As in 4) ........ many villages in 5) ......... north of 6) ......... England, all 7) ......... houses are built of 8) ......... same stone. Running through the village is 9) ...... River Tyne. The village has a church which was built in 10) ...... Middle Ages. Although 11) ......... population is only about 500 people, this village has 12) ............ best cricket team in 13) ......... county, and many people play 14) ........ rugby as well. Apart from 15) ......... sport, though, so little happens there that many of 16) ........ people still remember 17) ........ time 18) ...... Queen visited their village in 19) ......... 1955.

**231** Fill in: a, an or the where necessary.

Last week I had 1) ..an... accident in 2) ....... Italy. I was skiing in 3) ..... Alps. One day I was going too fast down a mountain, when I crashed into 4) ....... tree. I broke both my legs and cut my arm. There was so much 5) ...... blood, I had to be rushed to 6) ....... hospital in 7) ...... ambulance. When I got there, 8) ...... doctor told me that I would have to stay there for at least two weeks. I was very depressed. All I wanted to do was go 9) ....... home.

### Oral Activity 23

The teacher divides the class into two teams and says countable or uncountable nouns. The teams in turn add "a/an" or "some". Each correct answer gets 1 point. The team with the most points is the winner.

Teacher : bread　　　　　　　　　　　Teacher: book
Team A S1: some bread　　　　　　　Team B S1: a book etc.

### Oral Activity 24

The teacher divides the class into two teams and says nouns. The teams in turn add "the" where necessary. Each correct answer gets 1 point. The team with the most points is the winner.

Teacher: Taj Mahal　　　　　　　　　Teacher: Buckingham Palace
Team A S1: the Taj Mahal　　　　　　Team B S1: Buckingham Palace etc.

### Tense Review

 **232** Put the verbs in brackets into the correct tense forms.

Yesterday evening a fire badly 1) ..damaged....... (damage) the Grand Hotel in Bournemouth. The police 2) ............... (believe) that the fire was started deliberately. They 3) ............... (find) an empty petrol can and a box of matches in one of the hotel lifts. Broken glass 4) ..................... (injure) a number of the guests who 5) ..................... (enjoy) a New Year's Eve party at the hotel. Ten people 6) ..................... (take) to hospital where they 7) ..................... (treat) for shock. Police 8) ...... ................ (interview) guests and hotel staff since this morning to discover what 9) ......................... (happen). One guest 10) ..................... (tell) our reporter that he 11) ................. (see) two men enter the lift carrying a petrol can just before the time the fire 12) ....................... (think) to have started. He 13) ............................ (give) their descriptions to the police. So far the hotel management 14) ......................... (refuse) to comment on the situation.

## 10. Nouns – Articles

**233** Fill in : a, an or the where necessary.

1. ...The... Grand Canyon is in ........ — ........ Arizona.
2. He visited .................... Pyramids while he was in ................. — ........ Egypt.
3. .................... Morpeth is .................... town in .................... north of ............. England.
4. She lives in .................... castle near .................... River Rhine.
5. I went shopping at .................... Macy's and bought .................... expensive overcoat.
6. They are going for .................... walk near .................... London Zoo in ............. Regent's Park.
7. There is .................... cinema in .................... Bridge Street called ................. Odeon.
8. Anna comes from .................... Netherlands but she lives in ................. USA now.
9. .................... Malta is in .................... Mediterranean.
10. .................... Victoria Coach Station is near .................... Apollo theatre.
11. When we went to .......... Paris we saw .......... Eiffel Tower and .......... Louvre.
12. .......... Smith's book shop is in .............. High Street opposite .......... Barclays Bank.

### Expressions with "Do"

one's best/worst, business with sb, a crossword, damage to, one's duty, an exercise, an experiment, good, one's hair, harm, homework, housework, a job, lessons, sth for a living, miracles (for), research, right/wrong, a service, the shopping, a translation, the washing-up, work etc

### Expressions with "Make"

an appointment, an arrangement, the beds, a cake, certain, changes, coffee, a deal with sb, a decision, a discovery, an effort, an excuse, a fortune, an impression, improvements, a joke, a mess, a mistake, money, a noise, an offer, peace, preparations, progress, a success of sth, sure, a translation, trouble, war etc

**234** Fill in "make" or "do" in the correct form.

1. After he ...had done.. the washing-up he went out ..to do... the shopping.
2. Although I .................... my best, I'm afraid I .................... several mistakes.
3. When you .................... your homework, could you please .................... the beds?
4. You have to .................... a decision soon.
5. A few days in the country would ........ me good.
6. You will .................... more progress if you .................... the exercises carefully.
7. John .......... a fortune on the Stock Exchange.
8. Those children .................... so much noise!
9. Soldiers must always .................... their duty.
10. She .................... such good work that she always .................... a good impression.
11. To see the dentist, you'll have to .............. an appointment.
12. They've decided to .......................... some improvements before moving into the office.
13. After I .................... my Maths homework, I had my mother .................... sure it was all right.
14. She is used to .................... business with foreigners.
15. She .................... some research when she .................... the discovery.
16. To .................... a success of this business we will have to .................... some changes.
17. Would you .......... an effort to .......... this translation by next week?
18. She .................... her excuses for not attending the meeting.
19. Someone .................... an offer for the house.
20. Eating too many sweets can .................... harm to your health.

**235** Look at Appendix 1 and fill in the correct preposition.

1. Somebody threw a snowball ..at.... me as I was walking along the road.
2. I'm bored! Can't you think .............. something we can do?
3. Can you translate this .................... French?
4. I wonder why Pam is so terrified .......... dogs.
5. Throw the ball ........ me so I can shoot a basket.
6. The manager would like to talk ................ you ................ your work.
7. I will think ................ the matter and give you my decision tomorrow.
8. The children teased Sally ................ being fat.

# 11. Causative Form (Having something done)

**We use have + object + past participle** to say that we arrange for someone else to do something for us.
Jim **arranged for the plumber** to fix the tap. Jim **had the tap fixed**. (He didn't do it himself - the plumber did it.)

| | | |
|---|---|---|
| **Present Simple** | She **cleans** her house. | She **has** her house cleaned. |
| **Present Continuous** | She **is cleaning** her house. | She **is having** her house cleaned. |
| **Past Simple** | She **cleaned** her house. | She **had** her house cleaned. |
| **Past Continuous** | She **was cleaning** her house. | She **was having** her house cleaned. |
| **Future Simple** | She **will clean** her house. | She **will have** her house cleaned. |
| **Future Continuous** | She **will be cleaning** her house. | She **will be having** her house cleaned. |
| **Present Perfect** | She **has cleaned** her house. | She **has had** her house cleaned. |
| **Present Perfect Cont.** | She **has been cleaning** her house. | She **has been having** her house cleaned. |
| **Past Perfect** | She **had cleaned** her house. | She **had had** her house cleaned. |
| **Past Perfect Cont.** | She **had been cleaning** her house. | She **had been having** her house cleaned. |
| **Infinitive** | She must **clean** her house. | She must **have** her house cleaned. |
| **Gerund** | She likes **cleaning** her house. | She likes **having** her house cleaned. |

The verb **to have** used in the Causative forms its negations and questions with **do/does** (Present Simple) and **did** (Past Simple). **Don't have** this letter posted yet! **Did** you **have** your hair cut?

**Get** can be used instead of **have** in spoken English. **Have + object + past participle** can be used instead of passive forms to express an accident or misfortune.

You should **get** your skirt washed. (= You should **have** your skirt washed.)
She **had** her bag stolen. (Her bag was stolen.)

**(236)** Read the situations, then write sentences using the Causative form.

1. Mary took her blouse to the cleaner's. What did she do? *She had her blouse cleaned.*
2. My watch is broken. What should I do?
3. Michael is at the hairdresser's because he needs a haircut. What is he doing?
4. A man is cleaning our swimming pool. What are we doing?
5. A dressmaker has made a dress for Sue. What has Sue done?
6. His milk is delivered every morning. What does he do?
7. Tom's tooth needs filling. He's going to the dentist's tomorrow. What's he going to do?

## 11. Causative Form (Having something done)

8. Sarah's car needed petrol so she took it to the garage. What did she do? ......................................
...........................................................................................................................................................
9. We don't have a garage. A builder is going to build one for us next week. What are we going to do? ........
...........................................................................................................................................................
10. An architect designed a house for him. What did he do? ......................................................................

**237** Bill Smith does everything himself. Lord Hornby pays other people to do it. Write what Lord Hornby says.

**Bill Smith**

1. I painted my house last week.
2. I'm mending my car.
3. I've put in new windows.
4. I'll build a swimming pool next year.
5. I clean my shoes every day.
6. I wash my car once a week.
7. I'm installing a new shower next month.
8. I made a rocking chair for my wife.
9. I check my son's homework every night.

**Lord Hornby**

1. *I had my house painted last week.* ...............
2. ...........................................................................
3. ...........................................................................
4. ...........................................................................
5. ...........................................................................
6. ...........................................................................
7. ...........................................................................
8. ...........................................................................
9. ...........................................................................

**238** Jane and Naomi are models. Jane does everything herself but Naomi is lazy and has everything done for her. Put the verbs in brackets into the Causative form.

Jane: I like doing my own hair. I usually wash it every two days.
Naomi: I don't. I 1) ...*have mine washed*... (wash) every day by my hairdresser.
Jane: I dyed my hair yesterday.
Naomi: Oh! I 2) ............................................................... (dye) last week.
Jane: I enjoy doing my own make-up too, don't you?
Naomi: Oh no. I 3) ............................................................... (do) by a beautician.
Jane: I make my own clothes. I like things you can't buy in shops.
Naomi: I 4) ............................................................... (make) by my dressmaker. She's very good.
Jane: Sometimes I even repair my own car. I'm quite a good mechanic.
Naomi: How horrible! I 5) ............................................................... (repair) at the garage. It's cheap and I don't get my clothes dirty.
Jane: But it's easy to wash your clothes, isn't it?
Naomi: I prefer 6) ............................................................... (wash) at the cleaner's.
Jane: I like to relax by tidying the garden.
Naomi: Well I relax while I 7) ............................................................... (tidy) by the gardener.
Jane: I've got to go now. I'm going to polish my nails.
Naomi: You should do what I do. I 8) ............................................................... (polish) by a manicurist.

## 11. Causative Form (Having something done)

**239** Write about these people's misfortunes using the Causative form.

1. Ted's car was damaged.
   ..Ted had his car damaged.

2. Martha's car was stolen.
   ....................................

3. Terry's leg was broken.
   ....................................

4. Rick's house was broken into by a burglar.
   ....................................

5. Gary's windows were smashed by hooligans.
   ....................................

6. The police have taken away Todd's driving licence.
   ....................................

**240** Write sentences in the Causative form as in the example:

1. Mike is going to ask a carpenter to put the doors up. ..Mike is going to have the doors put up.
2. Tony asked a mechanic to fix the car.
3. You should ask a plumber to unblock the toilet.
4. Ask the maid to tidy your room.
5. Simon is going to ask a tailor to make a suit for him.
6. Did he ask the optician to test his eyes?
7. Tommy asks his brother to do his homework.
8. The girl asked her mother to read the story to her.
9. They will ask a chef to cook the meal.
10. The report is being typed by his secretary.
11. She will ask a decorator to decorate the lounge.
12. You should ask someone to fix your car brakes.
13. When will your new shower be installed?
14. Bruce may ask a builder to repair his roof.
15. Are you going to ask someone to service your motorbike?
16. I've asked the secretary to rewrite the whole report.
17. Her children are being taught computer science.
18. James asked the messenger to send the flowers round to his girlfriend's house.
19. Can't you ask someone to repair the washing machine?
20. You should ask them to install a telephone.
21. Mary's lawn was mowed yesterday.
22. Jane wants someone to make her a dress.
23. Bob's hair has just been cut.
24. Sharon might ask someone to dye her hair red tomorrow.
25. Debbie has asked someone to fit new carpets in her house.
26. Someone is massaging Sue's feet at the moment.
27. I used to ask the dentist to polish my teeth every six months.
28. Our house needs to be painted.

## 11. Causative Form (Having something done)

### In Other Words

**241** Rephrase the following using the words in brackets.

1. My sister is in hospital where they are taking her appendix out. **(having)**
   ..*My sister is in hospital having her appendix taken out.*..
2. A tailor made his new suit. **(had)**
3. A naughty boy broke Jim's shop window. **(had)**
4. My friend will ask someone to organise his party. **(organised)**
5. She asked a caterer to prepare the food for the reception. **(had)**
6. Is your friend feeding the dog while you're away? **(fed)**
7. He's going to ask an accountant to check his receipts. **(checked)**
8. A plumber repaired Mrs Smith's sink. **(got)**
9. Her dad will shorten her jeans. **(shortened)**
10. His finger was shot off in the war. **(had)**
11. His car is in the garage where they are changing its wheels. **(having)**
12. Tommy's bicycle was stolen. **(had)**
13. She will ask someone to build a shed for her. **(built)**
14. Did you get your brother to fix your motorbike? **(have)**

### Tense Review

**242** Put the verbs in brackets into the correct tense forms.

Last month Gertrude 1) ..*received*... (receive) an invitation to her best friend's wedding. Her friend's name is Susan and they 2) .......................... (know) each other for years. Susan 3) .................. (be) very rich and 4) ................................. (invitations/print) in gold letters on expensive card. Gertrude was worried because she 5) ........................ (not/have) anything nice to wear to the wedding. "I can't afford to 6) ............................ (dress/make), so I 7) ........................ (have to) make one myself," she 8) ...................... (say) to herself. Then she 9) ........................ (look) in the mirror. "Oh dear," she said, "I 10) ............................. (hair/not do) for months. I 11) ........................ (go) to the hairdresser's tomorrow." She also 12) ............................ (think) that it would be a good idea to 13) ..................................... (nails/manicure) by a professional. "I must look my best because I'm sure everyone 14) ................ (be) so well dressed," she thought anxiously. But she needn't have worried because on the day of the wedding she 15) ......................... (look) very nice indeed.

### Oral Activity 25

Lord Mountebank has just bought an old castle in Scotland. It's a birthday present for his new wife. Students look at the picture and the word cues, and say sentences in the Causative.

    **new windows/put in/at the moment**
S1:  He's having new windows put in at the moment.
    **hole in wall/repair/last week**
S2:  He had the hole in the wall repaired last week.
    **swimming pool/build/next month**
    **trees/plant/yesterday**
    **living room/decorate/at the moment**
    **statue of himself/erect/next week**
    **solar panels/install/already**
    **walls/clean/last week**
    **stables/build/at the moment**
    **horses/not deliver/yet**
    **the whole castle/wrap in ribbon/for his wife's birthday**

## 11. Causative Form (Having something done)

### Writing Activity 9

Look at Oral Activity 25 and write the letter that Lord Mountebank wrote to his wife telling her all about the castle. Use the causative form.

**Dear Patricia,**
    I have just bought a wonderful old Scottish castle for your birthday. At the moment I'm having new windows put in ...

### Phrasal Verbs 10

| | |
|---|---|
| run across : | find by chance |
| run after : | chase |
| run away : | escape; get away by running |
| run down : | 1) knock down<br>2) say bad things about sb |
| run into sb/sth : | 1) meet unexpectedly<br>2) collide with |
| run out of : | reach the end (of a supply) |

**243** Fill in the correct preposition or adverb.

1. I ran ....*across*...... an interesting article about fashion while I was reading the newspaper.
2. We've run ................. flour and sugar – how can I make a cake?
3. The bank guard ran ................. the thief.
4. You mustn't run ................. your teachers.
5. David lost control of the car and ran ............. a tree.
6. When the dog barked, the children ran ............ .
7. I ran ............. an old friend of mine yesterday.
8. Our neighbour was run ............. by a taxi and was very badly injured.

**244** Look at Appendix 1 and fill in the correct preposition.

1. This offer is only valid ...*for*....... children under twelve.
2. She's good at Maths, but she's a bit weak ......... Physics.
3. We've been waiting ......... you for an hour!
4. Buying badly made clothes is a waste ............. money.
5. I don't know what Laura is so upset ............. .
6. His parents warned him ............. misbehaving in school.
7. Dorothy is worried ............. her daughter as she hasn't heard from her for weeks.
8. What's the use ............. complaining when nobody listens?

### Idioms 10

| | |
|---|---|
| be hard on sb : | treat sb in a strict or unfair way |
| be short of sth : | not have enough |
| be sound asleep : | be sleeping deeply |
| be flat out : | be exhausted |
| be out of work : | be unemployed |
| be out of practice : | lack practice |
| be thick : | be stupid |
| be in sb's shoes : | be in sb's position |

**245** Fill in the correct idiom.

1. I*'m flat out*..... - I think I'd better go to bed.
2. He's a nice boy, but he ................. a bit ......... when it comes to schoolwork.
3. You mustn't ....................... your daughter – she's doing the best she can.
4. George ....................... for nearly a year before he found a job.
5. If I ..........................................., I'd try to find a better place to live.
6. I ............................... money this week – can I pay you next week?
7. By the end of the film my friend ................. ................................. on the sofa.
8. I'd like to play tennis, but I am completely ......... ................. so I'm sure I'll lose.

120

# 12. Adjectives - Adverbs - Comparisons

## Adjectives

**Adjectives** describe nouns. They have the same form in both the singular and the plural. They normally go before nouns. They also go alone (without nouns) after the verbs: appear, be, become, feel, seem, smell, taste etc. *She had a **bad** dream. (What kind of dream? A bad one.) The egg smells **awful**.*

## Adverbs

**Adverbs** normally describe verbs, adjectives or other adverbs. *She drives **carefully**. (How does she drive? Carefully.)* They say **how** (adverbs of manner), **where** (adverbs of place), **when** (adverbs of time), **how much/to what extent** (adverbs of degree) or **how often** (adverbs of frequency) something happens. There are also **sentence adverbs** (certainly, surely, probably, possibly etc) and **relative adverbs** (where, why, when).

## Formation of Adverbs from Adjectives

Most adverbs are formed by adding **-ly** to an adjective eg. *quick* ➡ *quickly*. Adjectives ending in **-ic** add **-ally** to form their adverbs eg. *dramatic* ➡ *dramatically*. Adjectives ending in **-le** drop **-le** and add **-ly** to form their adverbs eg. *terrible* ➡ *terribly*. Adjectives ending in **consonant + y** drop **-y** and add **-ily** to form their adverbs eg. *happy* ➡ *happily*. Adjectives ending in **-ly** (friendly, lonely, lovely, fatherly, motherly, silly, lively, ugly etc) form their adverbs with **in a ... way** eg. *in a friendly way*. Adjectives ending in **-e** form their adverbs adding **-ly** without dropping **-e** eg. *rare* ➡ *rarely*. Exceptions: *whole* ➡ *wholly*, *true* ➡ *truly*.

The adverb of **good** is **well**. Some adverbs are the same as their adjectives (daily, early, fast, hard, late, monthly, best, easy, low etc) eg. *He works **hard**. This is a **hard** job.* In spoken English the adverbs **loud**, **quick**, **slow**, **cheap** are the same as their adjectives. In formal English we use: **loudly**, **quickly**, **slowly**, **cheaply**. eg. *He speaks **loud**. (spoken English) He speaks **loudly**. (formal English)*

**246** Write the correct adverbs.

| + -ly | -ic + -ally | -le ➡ -ly | consonant + y ➡ -ily |
|---|---|---|---|
| quick ... *quickly* | tragic ............. | horrible ............. | cosy ............. |
| safe ............. | comic ............. | sensible ............. | sleepy ............. |
| stupid ............. | dramatic ............. | impossible ............. | witty ............. |

**247** Fill in the correct adjective or adverb using the words in brackets.

1. Gillian behaved very ............. *badly* ............. at the party last night. **(bad)**
2. You are quite ............. at playing the piano, aren't you? **(good)**

## 12. Adjectives - Adverbs - Comparisons

3. Think about it ............................................................. before you make a decision. **(careful)**
4. I like my bedroom because it's so ............................................................................. **(cosy)**
5. It makes me feel ............................................................. to think of you living alone. **(sad)**
6. If you can't talk ............................................................., don't talk at all. **(sensible)**
7. Her whole family died in a ............................................................. accident. **(tragic)**
8. I was not ............................................................. convinced by her reasoning. **(whole)**
9. ............................................................., I can't help you. **(unfortunate)**
10. You look ............................................................. in your new dress. **(lovely)**
11. The ability to think ............................................................. is an important skill. **(logical)**
12. I ............................................................. believe this to be the finest novel ever written. **(true)**
13. You'd better work ............................................................. if you want to keep your job. **(hard)**
14. Please don't drive so ............................................................. . **(fast)**
15. Linda washes her hair ............................................................. . **(daily)**
16. That chicken tastes ............................................................. . **(delicious)**
17. You're bound to make mistakes if you write so ............................................................. . **(careless)**
18. Your perfume smells ............................................................. . **(beautiful)**
19. Charles and Camilla have been living together ............................................................. for years. **(happy)**
20. Although I had only met him once, he greeted me ............................................................. . **(friendly)**

**248** Put the adverbs from the list below into the correct column.

| why | where | away | today | far | usually | possibly | drastically |
| here | well | hard | only | fast | perhaps | always | in the park |
| badly | off | up | never | there | probably | suspiciously | tomorrow |
| hardly | near | now | then | slowly | foolishly | immediately | |
| once | at once | wholly | twice | upstairs | definitely | absolutely | |
| clearly | quite | still | when | lately | carefully | frequently | |
| soon | almost | often | certainly | honestly | obviously | occasionally | |

| How | Where | When | How much | How often | Sentence Adverbs | Relative Adverbs |
|---|---|---|---|---|---|---|
| manner | place | time | degree | frequency | | |
| fast | here | soon | almost | often | certainly | when |

### Some pairs of adverbs have different meanings

- **deep** = a long way down (He dug **deep** into the ground.) **deeply** = greatly (The scientist was **deeply** respected.)
- **free** = without payment (Children travel **free** on buses.) **freely** = willingly (He spoke **freely** about his past.)
- **hard** = with a lot of effort (He works **hard**.) **hardly** = scarcely (I **hardly** see him.)
- **high** = to/at a high level (The pilot flew **high** above the clouds.) **highly** = very much (She is **highly** regarded by her employers.)
- **last** = after all others (He got here **last**.) **lastly** = finally (**Lastly**, read the instructions then do the test.)
- **late** = after the arranged or proper time (They arrived **late**.) **lately** = recently (I haven't seen him **lately**.)
- **near** = close (I live **near** the school.) **nearly** = almost (I have **nearly** finished.)
- **pretty** = fairly (I thought the film was **pretty** awful.) **prettily** = in an attractive way (She smiled **prettily**.)
- **short** = suddenly (The driver stopped **short**.) **shortly** = soon, not long (He will be arriving **shortly**.)
- **wide** = far away from the right point (He threw the ball **wide**.) **widely** = to a large extent (It's **widely** believed that the Prime Minister will resign soon.)

## 12. Adjectives – Adverbs – Comparisons

**249** Underline the correct item.

1. The arrow flew **wide**/widely of the target.
2. Computers are wide/**widely** used in schools nowadays.
3. Students can enter the museum **free**/freely on Saturdays.
4. He free/**freely** admitted to being a liar.
5. I like sitting **near**/nearly the fire.
6. Be careful! You near/**nearly** crashed into that cyclist.
7. She left too **late**/lately to catch the train.
8. Have you seen any good films late/**lately**?
9. The death of his friend affected him deep/**deeply**.
10. To find water, they had to dig **deep**/deeply into the ground.
11. I think he's a **pretty**/prettily good singer, actually.
12. The little girl laughed pretty/**prettily** at the sight of the puppy.
13. He tries very **hard**/hardly to make her happy.
14. She used to be a great musician, but she hard/**hardly** plays at all now.
15. Tommy came **last**/lastly in the 100m sprint.
16. **Last**/Lastly, I would like to thank the caterers for providing such delicious food.
17. Mr Tibbs isn't in at the moment, but he'll be here short/**shortly**.
18. The policeman stopped **short**/shortly when he saw the robber had a gun.
19. The eagle was flying **high**/highly above the mountains.
20. My father is a high/**highly** respected surgeon.

### Order of Adjectives

- **Adjectives normally go before nouns.** *She bought an **expensive** house.* **Adjectives can also be used without a noun after certain verbs (appear, be, feel etc).** *He felt **nervous**.*
- **The adjectives** afraid, alone, alive, awake, asleep, glad **etc are never followed by a noun.** *The baby was **asleep**. (not : an asleep baby)*
- **Nouns can be used as adjectives if they go before another noun. They have no plural form in this case.** *Could you repair the **garden** gate? a **morning** class, a **two-week** holiday (not : a two-weeks holiday)*
- **Certain adjectives can be used as plural nouns referring to a group of people in general. These are:** the poor, the rich, the blind, the young, the old, the disabled, the hungry, the strong, the deaf, the living, the dead, the sick, the elderly **etc.**
  *We should have more respect for **the elderly**. (elderly people in general)*
  *The **rich** should help the **poor**. But in the singular : The **rich man** helped the **poor woman**.*
- **Opinion** adjectives (wonderful, awful etc) go before **fact** adjectives (large, old etc).
  *She lives in a **lovely big** flat. She bought a **beautiful leather** bag.*
- **When there are two or more fact adjectives, they normally go in the following order :**

|  | | | | Fact Adjectives | | | | |
|---|---|---|---|---|---|---|---|---|
|  | opinion | size | age | shape | colour | origin | material | used for/ be about | noun |
| That's a | wonderful | large | old | rectangular | black | Chinese | wooden | linen | chest. |

**250** Put the adjectives in the correct order.

1. a Chinese/little/pretty girl ...*a pretty little Chinese girl*.....
2. a(n) wedding/expensive/satin/white/dress
3. a detective/new/brilliant/French/film
4. a(n) Greek/ancient/fascinating/monument
5. a(n) pair of/leather/black/walking/old/shoes
6. a(n) German/brown/enormous/beef/sausage
7. a red and white/lovely/marble/Turkish/chess set

# 12. Adjectives – Adverbs – Comparisons

8. a round/gold/big/medallion .................................................
9. a grey/smart/cotton/new/suit .................................................
10. a(n) motorcycling/old/black/dirty/jacket .................................................

## Order of adverbs

Adverbs can go in **front**, **mid** or **end** position in a sentence. **Front** position is at the beginning of the sentence. **Mid** position is before the main verb or after the auxiliary. **End** position is at the end of the sentence.

            **Front**           **Mid**           **End**
        **Finally**, he will **probably** start working **here next week**.

**Adverbs of frequency** (often, usually, never, ever, regularly, barely, seldom, scarcely, rarely, sometimes etc) normally go before main verbs but after auxiliary verbs (mid position). However, in short answers they go before the auxiliary verb. He **often** brings me flowers. He is **always** coming late. "He is **always** telling lies, isn't he?" "Yes, he **always** is."
**Used to** and **have to** take the adverb of frequency before them. You **always have to** remind him to take his pills. Frequency adverbs can also go at the beginning or the end of the sentence for reasons of emphasis. **Sometimes** I get up late. I go to that park **occasionally**.

**Adverbs of time** usually go at the end of the sentence (She left Madrid **yesterday**.) or at the beginning of the sentence if we want to put emphasis on the time (**Yesterday** she left Madrid.).
Short time adverbs such as: **soon**, **now**, **still**, **then** etc. can go in mid position.
She is **now** having a lesson.

The adverbs: **already**, **no longer**, **normally**, **hardly**, **nearly**, **almost** usually go in mid position.
He **nearly** missed the train. They are **no longer** working here. There's **hardly** any cake left.

**Sentence adverbs** (probably, certainly, possibly, clearly, fortunately, luckily, maybe, perhaps, of course etc) go in any position, front, mid or end; the front position is the most usual though. **Probably** he believed you. He **probably** believed you. He believed you **probably**. In negations certainly, possibly and probably go before the auxiliary. He **probably didn't** believe you.

**Adverbs do not normally go between the object and the verb.** She likes sweets **very much**. (not: ~~She likes very much sweets.~~)

**Adverbs of degree** (absolutely, just, totally, completely, extremely, very, a lot, really, terribly, much, awfully, rather, quite, fairly, pretty, a little, a bit, slightly, enough, too etc) can go before the adjective or the adverb they modify. She's **quite** good at Maths. Most of these adverbs can also go before a main verb or after an auxiliary verb. I **rather** like this film. I can't **quite** understand it. The adverbs : a lot, much, a little, a bit, awfully, terribly, absolutely, completely and totally go in mid or end position. The train was delayed **a little**. or The train was **a little** delayed. The earthquake **completely** destroyed the area. or The earthquake destroyed the area **completely**.

**Adverbs of manner** (beautifully, badly, eagerly etc) and **place** (here, there etc) go after the verb or the object of the verb if there is one (end position). She looked at me **angrily**. Adverbs of manner can also go in mid position. She looked **angrily** at me. When there is more than one adverb in a sentence, their order is **manner - place - time**. However when there is a verb of movement (go, run, leave etc), the place adverb goes next to the verb of movement.

| | manner | place | time | | place | manner | time |
|---|---|---|---|---|---|---|---|
| He spoke | well | at the meeting | yesterday. | She goes | to work | on foot | every day. |

## 12. Adjectives - Adverbs - Comparisons

**251** Rewrite the sentences using the adverbs in brackets.

1. The dentist checks my teeth. *The dentist checks my teeth twice a year.* (twice a year)
2. I like spicy food. .................................................................................. (very much)
3. The weather is warm in Portugal. ............................................................ (quite)
4. He won't be late. ................................................................................... (probably)
5. Andrew drives. ...................................................................................... (carelessly)
6. He's so rude! ......................................................................................... (always)
7. There isn't any food left. ....................................................................... (hardly)
8. We caught our flight to Paris. ................................................................ (barely)
9. She carried the vase. ............................................................................. (carefully)
10. He helps in the house. ......................................................................... (rarely)

**252** Rewrite the letter putting the adverbs from the list in the best position.

**last week/there/soon/always/well/unfortunately/usually/possibly/really/next week**

Dear Sam,
Thank you for looking after my daughter while she was in London *last week*. She says she had a great time. I must come and visit you myself. We have got along. I work at weekends, but I'll be able to visit you in the summer holidays. I'm looking forward to seeing you again. I'll phone you.
Love,
Sue

**253** Rewrite the text putting the following adverbs from the list in the best position.

**always/late/quickly/nearly/luckily/strangely/that morning/suddenly/still**

Alf Roberts is ...*always*... doing stupid things. One morning he woke up for work. He got up and ran out of the house without having breakfast. He missed the 9 o' clock bus, but the bus driver waited for him. The other passengers were all looking at him and he didn't know why. Then he realised that he was wearing his pyjamas.

**254** Rewrite the text making corrections where necessary.

Cyril Morton had appeared always to most of the people in the town very mean. He lived an alone person in a Victorian old huge house on the side of the hill. Nobody saw ever him, and children were afraid persons to play near the house. Some people wondered if he was still an alive man. One day the local home for disabled received an anonymous note and a cheque for £5,000. The note read : "This is to pay for a two-weeks holiday in Brighton for all of you." Nobody knew where the cheque had come from but, obviously, they were to accept it glad. A year later, Cyril died at the age of 92. The whole town was surprised to find out that the old man had left all his money to disabled, including his house. This shows that we should judge never elderly just because they want often to be left alone people.

*Cyril Morton had always appeared* ..................................................................

**255** Rewrite the sentences putting the words in the correct order.

1. on Fridays/in the café/eats breakfast/always/he ...*He always eats breakfast in the café on Fridays.*...
2. safely/they/arrived/this morning/home ..................................................................
3. drinks coffee/in the evening/never/Sam ..................................................................

## 12. Adjectives – Adverbs – Comparisons

4. on a yacht/she sails/every summer/round the islands ........................................
5. quietly/in his bed/slept/the baby/all night ........................................
6. often/home/she goes/on Fridays/early ........................................
7. rarely/you/see/cricket/these days/on TV ........................................
8. in the garden/the nightingales/last night/loudly/were singing ........................................

### Regular Comparative and Superlative Forms

| Adjectives | Positive | Comparative | Superlative |
|---|---|---|---|
| of one syllable add -(e)r/-(e)st to form their comparative and superlative forms | short<br>big<br>large | shorter (than)<br>bigger (than)<br>larger (than) | the shortest (of/in)<br>the biggest (of/in)<br>the largest (of/in) |
| of two syllables ending in -er, -ly, -y, -w also add -er/-est | heavy<br>shallow | heavier (than)<br>shallower (than) | the heaviest (of/in)<br>the shallowest (of/in) |
| of two or more syllables take more/most | special<br>attractive | more special (than)<br>more attractive (than) | the most special (of/in)<br>the most attractive (of/in) |

Certain adjectives form their comparative and superlative in both ways, either by adding -er/-est to the positive form or taking more/most. Some of these are: clever, common, cruel, friendly, gentle, narrow, pleasant, polite, quiet, simple, stupid etc.
clever - cleverer - cleverest   ALSO   clever - more clever - the most clever

| Adverbs | Positive | Comparative | Superlative |
|---|---|---|---|
| adverbs having the same forms as adjectives add -er/-est | fast | faster | the fastest |
| "early" drops -y and adds -ier/-iest | early | earlier | the earliest |
| two syllable or compound adverbs take more/most (compound adverbs are adjectives + -ly. eg. careful - carefully) | often<br>safely<br>easily | more often<br>more safely<br>more easily | the most often<br>the most safely<br>the most easily |

We normally use than after a comparative. *I'm taller than you.* We normally use the before a superlative. We often use of or in after a superlative. We normally use in with places. *I'm the tallest of all. I'm the tallest in my school.*

126

## 12. Adjectives – Adverbs – Comparisons

**256** Fill in the blanks with the correct comparative and superlative forms.

| | | | | | | |
|---|---|---|---|---|---|---|
| 1. slow | ..slower.... | (the) slowest... | 5. lonely | ............ | ............ |
| 2. happy | ............ | ............ | 6. hard | ............ | ............ |
| 3. carefully | ............ | ............ | 7. fantastic | ............ | ............ |
| 4. often | ............ | ............ | 8. early | ............ | ............ |

### Irregular Forms

| Positive | Comparative | Superlative |
|---|---|---|
| good/well | better | best |
| bad/badly | worse | worst |
| much | more | most |
| many/a lot of | more | most |
| little | less | least |
| far | farther | farthest |
| far | further | furthest |

a) **further/farther (adv)** = longer (in distance)
He lives **further/farther** away than me.
**further (adj)** = more
For **further** details, consult your lawyer.

b) **very + positive degree.** It's a **very nice** day.
**even/much/far/a bit + comparative degree.**
This house is **even bigger** than the other. She's **much older** than my mother.

### Types of Comparisons

| | |
|---|---|
| as ...(positive degree)... as<br>not so/as ...(positive degree)... as<br>not such a(n)/so ... as | Ted is **as tall as** Jim.<br>Kate isn't **as/so clever as** her sister (is).<br>Dave **isn't such a** good footballer **as** he used to be. |
| less ...(positive degree)... than<br>the least ...(positive degree)... of/in | The red car is **less expensive than** the blue one, but the black one is **the least expensive of** all. |
| the + comparative..., the + comparative | **The earlier** you leave, **the earlier** you'll be back.<br>**The more reliable, the more expensive** a car is. |
| comparative + and + comparative | The story is becoming **more and more interesting**.<br>He walked **faster and faster**. |
| prefer + -ing form or noun + to + -ing form or noun (general preference) | I prefer **drinking tea to drinking coffee**.<br>I prefer **spaghetti to pizza**. |
| would prefer + to -inf + rather than + Inf without to (specific preference) | I would prefer **to go** on foot **rather than take** a taxi.<br>I would prefer **to stay** at home **rather than go** to the party. |

**257** Using fat, interesting, big, boring or small, fill in the blanks as in the example:

Tom is ..fatter than.. Sam. Sam isn't ............... Tom. Joe is ............... all and Sam is ............... fat ............... all.

Karen's book is ............ interesting ............ Kim's. Kim's book is ............ Karen's. Jane's book is ............ all.

A horse is ............ a dog and ............ an elephant. A dog isn't ............ a horse. An elephant is ............ all and a dog is ............ all.

127

# 12. Adjectives – Adverbs – Comparisons

**Like - As**

| **Like** is used: | **As** is used: |
|---|---|
| to say what sb or sth looks like. She looks **like** Madonna. (She isn't Madonna.) | to say what sb or sth is really or to talk about one's job or role. He works **as** a clerk. (He's a clerk.) |
| after feel, look, smell, sound + noun. It **smells like** fish. | in certain expressions: as usual, as...as, as much, such as, the same as. He plays the piano **as** well **as** I do. |
| with nouns/pronouns/-ing. She works **like** a robot. (She isn't a robot.) It was **like flying** in the air. | after the verbs : accept, be known, class, describe, refer to, regard, use. He is **regarded as** the best student in his class. |

**258** Fill in: like or as.

1. Charles Nichols is known ..*as*.. "Chuck" to his friends.
2. Her perfume smelt ............ roses.
3. People say she looks ............ Kim Basinger.
4. His father worked ............ an accountant in the city.
5. ............ usual, Terry was late for work.
6. Diving into the sea was ............ diving into an icy pool.
7. This is nice material - it feels ............ silk.
8. She doesn't sing ............ well ............ her mother.
9. I don't think you could describe Andy ............ an intelligent person.
10. Some politicians, such ............ John Major, are always in the news.
11. Ann looks ............ an angel.

**259** Fill in: like or as.

Sam Sanderson works 1) ..*as*.. a pianist in a restaurant in Chicago. No one in town plays the piano 2) ............ well 3) ............ he does. He looks a bit 4) ............ Stevie Wonder, which is why he is known to his friends 5) ............ "Stevie". One night he was playing in the restaurant 6) ............ usual, when he was approached by the leader of the biggest jazz band in America. He offered Sam a job 7) ............ lead pianist in his band. This made him so happy he felt 8) ............ dancing on his piano. So he did!

## 12. Adjectives - Adverbs - Comparisons

**260) Complete the sentences as in the example:**

1. She gets ...*more and more beautiful* ................................................... every day.            1. beautiful
2. My toothache is getting .................................................................................            2. painful
3. Your ability to remember things gets ............................... as the years go by.            3. bad
4. The meteor was coming .................................................................. the Earth.            4. near

**261) Complete each sentence as in the example:**

1. (It is dangerous.) The faster you drive, ...*the more dangerous it is.*......................
2. (Your marks will be good.) The harder you work, .................................................
3. (I feel fit.) The more I exercise, ...............................................................................
4. (We'll get there late.) The later we leave, ...............................................................
5. (It is quiet.) The further we are from the city, .........................................................
6. (The roads became busy.) The nearer we got to the city centre, .............................

**262) Choose the correct item.**

Dear Clare,
I'm 1) ..*really*.. (completely/really/slightly) sorry I haven't written earlier. I've been 2) ............ (a lot/enough/extremely) busy recently. The children are on holiday at the moment and so I'm 3) ............ (absolutely/much/enough) exhausted! I'll be 4) ............ (too/just/awfully) glad when they go back to school! Then I'll be 5) ............ (completely/a lot/rather) free during the day! The school holidays are 6) ............ (enough/just/too) long. The children get 7) ............ (terribly/much/enough) bored and I get 8) ............ (slightly/totally/a lot) exhausted! Well, write soon with your news.
Take care,
Joe

**263) Put the adjectives in the correct order.**

Dear Sir,
I am writing to you because I left a 1) ..*large brown leather*... (leather/large/brown) suitcase on the 7.45 train to London yesterday. In the suitcase there is a 2) ............ (plastic/digital/little) alarm clock and a pair of 3) ............ (silk/black/expensive) pyjamas. There is also a 4) ............ (lovely/satin/long) dress, which was a present for my wife, and a 5) ............ (Chinese/beautiful/gold) chain which I would hate to lose. Finally, there is a 6) ............ (black/large/plastic) folder containing confidential government papers, so it is very important that my suitcase is found and returned to me at the above address as soon as possible.
Yours faithfully,
Paul Daniels

**264) Fill in the blanks as in the example:**

Dear Wendy,
You asked me for advice on what to study at university, so I thought I'd write straight back because 1) ..*the sooner*.. (soon) you make a decision, 2) ............ (soon) you'll be able to apply for a place. You say you are not 3) ............ (interested) in the Sciences as you are in the Arts. That's all very well, but the Fine Arts are much 4) ............ (little/useful) than the Sciences when it comes to getting a job at the end of the course. As you know it's getting 5) ............ (difficult) for graduates to find work these days. You may prefer 6) ............ (paint/study) Physics but, let me tell you, Art is 7) ............ (little/useful) all the subjects you could do. Of course, the final decision is up to you, but I would prefer 8) ............ (see) you get a degree that would lead to a good job rather than 9) ............ (leave) university unable to find a job at all.
With love,
Aunty Audrey

## 12. Adjectives - Adverbs - Comparisons

**265** Fill in: very or much.

William has just bought a 1) ..*very*... nice new car. It is 2) .......... faster than his old one and 3) .......... more comfortable. He is 4) ............ proud of it as it is 5) ............. more stylish than any of his friends' cars. And so it should be, because it was 6) ............. expensive indeed. He spent 7) ............. more money on it than he could afford and his friends think he was 8) ............. foolish to buy it.

**266** Fill in the blanks with the correct forms. Add "the", "than" or "of" where necessary.

Last night I saw 1) ...*the worst*..... (bad) film I've ever seen. It was even 2) ............ (bad) ......... Rocky IV. It lasted 3) ................ (long) ......... three hours and, believe me, it was 4) .................. ............ (boring) three hours ............ my life. The acting was dull, and the story even 5) .................. (dull). I was very disappointed, as I'd left work 6) ................ (early) ............ usual especially to see it. My friend had recommended it, saying it was 7) ............... (good) film he had seen for months. I won't listen to him again. He has 8) .......................... (strange) taste ......... anyone I know.

**267** Fill in the blanks as in the example :

Dear Carmen,

Thanks for letting me stay in your villa in Spain last month. It was 1) ..*the best*... (good) holiday I've ever had; it was 2) ............... (much) fun than last year's in France. I think the Spanish people are 3) ............... (friendly) than the French, and I could communicate 4) ............... (easily) in Spanish, although I still found it 5) ................ (difficult) than German. The weather was much 6) ................ (warm) than in England, where we've had 7) ...................... (bad) summer in over ten years. I loved Spain so much that I think I could live there 8) ...................... (happy) than anywhere else in the world.

Love,
Larry

## Oral Activity 26

In teams, find the differences between picture A and picture B using comparisons. Each correct sentence gets 1 point. The team with the most points is the winner.

Team A S1: There are more pictures on the walls. | Team B S1: There are fewer pictures on the walls.

## 12. Adjectives - Adverbs - Comparisons

**268** Fill in: more, most, less, least or much.

A: Max, our new dog, is 1) ...much.... smaller than Sam, so he eats
2) ......................... food.
B: He sounds lovely. What does he look like?
A: He's the 3) ......................... beautiful dog I've ever seen. He's
also the 4) ......................... aggressive dog I've ever owned.
He's even 5) ......................... gentle than Sam.

**269** Complete the sentences as in the example:

1. Walk a bit ...more quickly...... (quickly). We're going to be late.
2. I went to bed much ................................. (late) than normal last night.
3. She is ................................. (well-qualified) than anyone else in the office.
4. Is your new car any ................................. (good) than your old one?
5. She's a far ................................. (experienced) player than her opponent.

### Oral Activity 27

Students in teams make comparisons looking at the pictures and the list of adjectives. Each correct answer gets 1 point. The team with the most points is the winner.

| pretty, happy, big, long, small, slim | faithful, friendly, big, useful, long, dangerous | safe, enjoyable, comfortable, fast, expensive | expensive, fast, old, modern, big, small, economical | healthy, juicy, sweet, big |

Team A S1: Betty is prettier than Sue.     Team B S2: Ann is the prettiest of all.

### Writing Activity 10

Your friend has asked you to help him find a place to buy in Brighton. You have found a flat, a small house and a big house. Write him a letter comparing the three, using the information in the boxes.

| £140,000, near town centre, quite small, noisy area, very modern, 2 years old | £255,000, on the edge of town, small, not too noisy area, 50 years old | £380,000, 3 miles from town, quite big, very quiet, beautiful area, 20 years old |

Dear Simon,
I have found three places which you may be interested in : a flat, a small house and a big house. The flat is the cheapest ...

## 12. Adjectives – Adverbs – Comparisons

**270** Complete Betty's letter using the adjectives from the list in the correct degree.

long, warm, nice, old, small, good, happy, easy, slow, old, fast, enjoyable.

Dear Paul,
I'm now in London, after the 1) ...longest... train ride I've ever had. It's 2) ................ than I expected. The city is 3) ................ than Birmingham and the buildings are 4) ................ . We're staying in the 5) ................ hotel I've ever seen but it has the 6) ................ service. John is 7) ................ than he's been for a long time. It's 8) ................ to get around than I had imagined but it's a good idea to avoid the Northern Line on the tube because it's the 9) ................ one. Tomorrow, we're going to visit Eton College, the 10) ................ school in England. We're going to travel by train because it's the 11) ................ and the 12) ................ way to get there. Bye for now.
Love,
Betty

### Tense Review

**271** Fill in the correct verb forms.

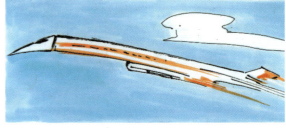

I ...remember... (remember) the first flight of Concorde, the aeroplane which 2) ................ (build) with the co-operation of the British and French Governments. I 3) ................ (stay) at my grandparents' house in Bristol. My grandad 4) ................ (be) retired by that time, but he 5) ................ (work) at the factory that built Concorde. That morning we 6) ................ (have) breakfast early, as grandad 7) ................ (promise) that he 8) ................ (take) us to the factory 9) ................ (watch) Concorde take off. As we 10) ................ (walk) towards the factory, we 11) ................ (join) by many other people. Finally, we 12) ................ (arrive) at a bridge near the factory where hundreds of people 13) ................ (stand). Some 14) ................ (wait) there for over two hours. Minutes later we 15) ................ (get) our first sight of Concorde. It 16) ................ (be) beautiful. It was the longest and thinnest plane I 17) ................ (ever/see). I'll never forget 18) ................ (watch) it take off and disappear into the clouds.

### In Other Words

| | |
|---|---|
| I've never seen such a nice dress. <br> It's the nicest dress I've ever seen. | A Porsche is much more expensive than a Fiat. <br> A Fiat is much/far less expensive than a Porsche. |
| She gave me a sad look. <br> She looked at me sadly. | If you leave early, you'll reach the office early. <br> The earlier you leave, the earlier you'll reach the office. |
| He is taller than John. <br> John isn't as tall as him/he is. | Ann is the best typist of all. <br> No other typist is as good as Ann (is). |
| That car is like this one. <br> That car is similar to this one. | Jenny has the same number of pencils as George. <br> George has as many pencils as Jenny (has). |

**272** Rephrase the following sentences using the words in bold type.

1. Their flat is similar to ours. **(LIKE)** ...Their flat is like ours. ................................
2. Paul is the best singer of all. **(OTHER)** ................................
3. That's the silliest thing I've ever heard! **(NEVER)** ................................

## 12. Adjectives - Adverbs - Comparisons

4. He gave me an angry look. **(LOOKED)** ...........................
5. Sam makes the same amount of money as Joe. **(MUCH)** ...........................
6. I run faster than Laura. **(DOESN'T)** ...........................
7. This book is much more interesting than that one. **(LESS)** ...........................
8. If you get up late, you'll have less time to get ready. **(LATER)** ...........................

### Phrasal Verbs 11

| | |
|---|---|
| **set off** : | start a journey; set out |
| **set out** : | 1) begin a journey  2) (+ full inf.) begin a job, task etc. |
| **set up** : | 1) start a business,  2) erect |
| **stand by sb** : | support sb, esp in a difficult situation |
| **stand for** : | represent |
| **stand in for** : | replace sb temporarily |
| **stand up** : | rise to one's feet |
| **stand up to** : | defend oneself against sb |

**273** Fill in the correct preposition or adverb.

1. If you want the day off, you'll have to find someone to stand ..*in for*.. you.
2. Everyone stood .................... when the judge entered the court.
3. We had to set .................... at 6 am to get to the village by 2 pm.
4. She loves travelling, so she's decided to set ........ a travel agency.
5. When she was accused of the crime, all her friends stood .................... her.
6. He was too shy to stand .................... his boss when she accused him of being lazy.
7. They set .......... their tent in the middle of a field.
8. He set .......................... to become a successful lawyer but never made it.
9. The letters CD stand .............. "compact disc".

**274** Look at Appendix 1 and fill in the correct preposition.

1. When she was ill she stayed ......*at*.... home for two weeks.
2. I met an old friend ............. chance while I was out shopping.
3. I like to spend a month ............... the seaside every summer.
4. We went into the centre of London ........... bus.
5. On his voyage round the world, he was ............ sea for six months.
6. She didn't mean to do that – she did it ............ accident.
7. I called her Mary instead of Martha ............... mistake.
8. They met while they were ............... university.

### Idioms 11

| | |
|---|---|
| **behind bars** : | in prison |
| **full of beans** : | lively |
| **out of the blue** : | suddenly and unexpectedly |
| **by and large** : | mainly |
| **take it easy** : | don't be worried or excited |
| **in a flash** : | very quickly |
| **keep an eye on sth** : | guard sth |
| **keep one's fingers crossed** : | wish for good luck |

**275** Fill in the correct idiom.

1. You should ..... *keep an eye on* ..... your bag or somebody might steal it.
2. After robbing the bank, he spent five years ........ .................... .
3. I'm going next door, but I'll be back ............... .
4. That child is so .......................... that it's tiring to be with him.
5. Everything will be alright. Just ...................... !
6. There are a few problems, but ...................... it's a good plan.
7. We were discussing politics when, ............... , she started talking about her daughter's boyfriend.
8. I don't know if they'll win the Cup, but I'm .......... .................... that they will.

# Revision Exercises III

**276** **Choose the correct item.**

1. Jane ...D... Spanish for five years now.
   A) teaches  B) is teaching
   C) taught  D) has been teaching

2. "Did you speak to John?" "Yes, he ............... his homework when I phoned him."
   A) did  B) has done
   C) was doing  D) does

3. "Are you coming out with us?" "I can't, I ............ ............... late tonight."
   A) will work  B) am working
   C) have worked  D) had worked

4. She is the smartest model ............ the world.
   A) in  B) of
   C) than  D) from

5. I ought ............... her this morning – now it's too late.
   A) to have phoned  B) phone
   C) phoning  D) to be phoning

6. Would you mind ............... the TV down?
   A) to turn  B) turn
   C) have turned  D) turning

7. "Did you grow up in the city?" "No. When we were children we ............... in the country."
   A) would live  B) have lived
   C) had lived  D) used to live

8. I think that Dave ............ a new car this year.
   A) had bought  B) will buy
   C) buys  D) have bought

9. She's looking everywhere – she seems ............ something.
   A) to have lost  B) to lose
   C) to be losing  D) to have been lost

10. She said that she ............ the actor several times before.
    A) met  B) was meeting
    C) meets  D) had met

11. My boss dislikes people ............... late.
    A) be  B) to have been
    C) being  D) having been

12. After we ............... , we can go to the cinema.
    A) eat  B) will eat
    C) ate  D) had eaten

13. He'll have sent in his application ............... the end of May.
    A) by  B) when
    C) until  D) yet

14. This is the village ............ I was born.
    A) that  B) which
    C) where  D) who

15. This room really ought ............... soon.
    A) to paint  B) be painted
    C) to be painted  D) to have been painted

16. If only I ............... them my secret!
    A) wouldn't tell  B) shouldn't tell
    C) don't tell  D) hadn't told

17. Despite ......... a lot of money, she's always broke.
    A) she earns  B) of earning
    C) earn  D) earning

18. That boy, ...... father is a violinist, is very musical.
    A) who  B) whose
    C) which  D) who's

19. "What did you think of her new novel?" "I think it is the ............... book she's ever written."
    A) most interested  B) most interesting
    C) more interesting  D) interested

20. The money ............ not enough to pay the bill.
    A) are  B) were
    C) has  D) was

21. That is the ......... incredible news I've ever heard.
    A) most  B) more
    C) very  D) far

22. He works ....... than anyone else in the company.
    A) slower  B) slowest
    C) slowly  D) more slow

23. "Can I help you?" "I'd like a ....... of milk, please."
    A) box  B) carton
    C) pot  D) rasher

24. Paul asked Sally when ............ go out with him.
    A) would she  B) will she
    C) she would  D) she will

25. David ......... to be the best player on the team.
    A) says  B) is said
    C) said  D) is saying

134

## Revision Exercises III

### 277) Rewrite the text correcting it where necessary.

The first night I spent alone in the castle was most terrifying night of my life. My grandmother recently died and had left me the place in her will. It was an old rather Scottish castle with a long and mysterious history. I didn't feel afraid strangely when I arrived in the evening there, but as night fell I began to feel coldly and lonely. I decided to go upstairs to bed at 11 o'clock, and fell soon into a deep sleep. I was awakened few hours later with a strange noise in the room. I turned on quickly the lamp and, to my horror, saw that there was an old ugly woman standing at the foot of my bed. She was wearing a black dress and her face totally was white. Her eyes were red and she was staring straight at me with a terrified evil smile on her face. I wanted to scream and to run out  from the room, but I was very afraid to move. Suddenly, she floated up on the air and flew at me, screaming horrible. I leapt out from bed, ran downstairs, out the castle door, jumped into my car and drove off at top speed. I never have been back to the castle from that day. At the moment, I try to sell it.

### 278) Choose the correct item.

After Laura had been living in Rome 1) ...*for*..... (since, before, for) several months, she realised that there were many things she hadn't seen. 2) ..................... (Even though, Despite, In spite of) she had plenty of free time, she hadn't even been to 3) ..................... (a, the, —) Vatican or the Coliseum, and she wished she 4) ..................... (sees, would see, had seen) more. People had told her that the Villa Borghese was worth 5) ..................... (see, to see, seeing), so she got up early one Saturday so that she 6) ..................... ..................... (could spend, spent, will spend) the day there. She considered taking her umbrella in case it 7) ..................... (would rain, rained, could rain). The morning was 8) ..................... (such, such a, so) lovely though, she decided it probably wouldn't, so she left it behind. When she got there she had her picture taken 9) ..................... (with, by, from) a man who told her he 10) ..................... (will send, sent, would send) her copies of it 11) ..................... (if, when, by) she gave him her address. In fact he kept 12) ..................... (ask, to ask, asking) her questions about herself 13) ..................... (by the time, If, until) she became suspicious. She knew she 14) ..................... (shouldn't, couldn't, mustn't) have given him her address at all, but it was 15) ..................... (much, such, too) late. An hour or so later it started to rain so she decided to go home at once. When she got there, she 16) ..................... (found, had found, finds) the door open; her house 17) ..................... (was burgled, had been burgled, had been stolen). The "photographer" had told her he would send her the pictures, but he hadn't 18) ..................... (said, asked, told) her that he would ring his friends and have them rob her house 19) ..................... (while, as soon as, until) she was out. If only she 20) ..................... (were, had been, would be) more careful, none of this would have happened.

### 279) Fill in "the" where necessary.

1) ...*The*.. Brown family invited 2) ......... Smiths round to 3) ......... their house last week to show them the video they had made while they were on 4) ............. holiday in 5) ............. Bahamas. They had travelled by 6) ......... plane to the islands and begun recording as soon as they landed. The video showed 7) ......... Mr Brown buying a newspaper, 8) ......... Independent, at the airport. They stayed at 9) ......... Holiday Inn and the video showed the family settling into 10) ............. their rooms. They were shown playing 11) ............. volleyball on 12) ......... beach, dancing in 13) ......... disco, having 14) ............. dinner in 15) ......... hotel and riding around 16) ............. islands on 17) ......... bicycles. The video lasted for three hours, and by the time it had finished, 18) ......... entire Smith family were asleep in front of 19) ......... TV.

## Revision Exercises III

**280** Complete the sentences keeping the meaning the same.

1. This is the best holiday I've ever had. I've never had ..... *such a good holiday* ..................... before.
2. She's never been skiing before. It's the .................................................................... skiing.
3. When did you move to this house? How long is it ............................................. this house?
4. The last time I saw Sally was a year ago. It's ............................................... saw Sally.
5. Despite his youth he can speak three languages. Although ................................ languages.
6. It's months since I saw a good film. I haven't ........................................................ months.
7. They arrived too late to meet the princess. They didn't ................................... the princess.
8. Do you mind checking this for me? Could .......................................................... for me?
9. It wasn't necessary for you to buy a ticket. You needn't ...................................... a ticket.
10. It's not possible that he's Italian! He ................................................................ Italian!
11. It was wrong of her to tell lies. She ................................................................... lies.
12. She is expected to win the competition. It ................................................. the competition.
13. People say that he is very talented. He ............................................................ talented.
14. If you don't book a table, we won't be able to eat there. We won't ........................ a table.
15. Ring him now, otherwise it will be too late. If you ............................................. too late.
16. Vandals destroyed Jack's car. Jack had ............................................................ vandals.
17. A famous artist has painted her portrait. She has ................................................. artist.
18. I've never seen such a tall man. He's ................................................................ seen.
19. Everyone thinks he's a dishonest businessman. He is regarded ....................... businessman.
20. "Don't tease the dog!" he said to me. He warned ................................................. dog.

**281** Fill in the correct preposition or adverb.

1. Two teams were organised to search ..*for*..... the missing boys.
2. He made ........................ an excuse to explain why he was late to work.
3. I'm worried ........................ Julie - she seems very unhappy lately.
4. This bus pass is valid ........................ one month.
5. Do you know what UFO stands ........................ ?
6. They couldn't make ................ which the right house was in the fog.
7. We've run ................ sugar again! Go and buy some!
8. He made ......... his face to look like a vampire's.
9. He was saved ................ the burning house by the fire brigade.
10. Be sure to put ............... your camp-fire before you leave the campsite.

**282** Put the verbs in brackets into the correct tense.

Before Lucy 1) ...*started*.. (start) her new job last month, she 2) ..................... (tell) by the manager that she 3) ............................. (have to) dress very smartly. Although she 4) ....................... (not/have) much money, she decided 5) ............................. (suit/make) by a tailor. She 6) ............................... (choose) the finest silk, which the tailor 7) ............................... (just/deliver) from China. Lucy knew it 8) ............................... (probably/cost) a lot but she 9) ............................... (think) she would be able to afford it. When the suit 10) ............................. (finish), she 11) ................ (shock) to find out that it cost £1000. She wished she 12) ............................... (ask) the price beforehand! If she had, she 13) ............................. (not/have to) sell her car to pay for it. Now she 14) ............................... (feel) silly in her silk suit when she 15) ........................... (ride) to work on a bicycle.

**283** Turn the following into Reported speech, using an appropriate introductory verb.

1. "Yes, OK. I'll buy some more cakes," he said. ...*He agreed to buy some more cakes.* ...................
2. "Don't forget to feed the cat," she said to him. .................................................................
3. "I'm sorry I forgot your birthday," I said to her. ................................................................
4. "It was you who broke my tape recorder," he said to me. ....................................................
5. "I feel tired and sick," she said to him. ...........................................................................

6. "Don't drive so fast or you'll be killed," he said to me. ..............................................
7. "You're right. It's very expensive," she said. ..............................................
8. "No, I didn't shoot the President," he said. ..............................................
9. "Would you like to come to Paris with me?" he said to her. ..............................................
10. "No, I certainly will not lend you my leather jacket," he said to me. ..............................................

### 284) Change from Active to Passive.

They sent John to boarding school at the age of ten. Before he left they gave him some spending money and his father told him to obey his teachers. They had never sent him away on his own before, so he felt a bit nervous on the train, although he knew that somebody would pick him up at the station. When he arrived at the school they showed him to his room and he realised that he would have to share it with twenty other boys! But after some older boys had taken him round the school and invited him to play football, he knew he would be happy there.

### 285) Turn into Reported speech using the appropriate introductory verbs.

James: I don't feel at all well.
Sue: What a shame! You should see a doctor.
James: Yes, I suppose I should. But don't forget that we are going to the theatre tonight.
Sue: Why don't we stay at home?
James: But we simply must go! We promised we'd be there.
Sue: I certainly didn't promise.
James: Oh Sue, you're always forgetting what you've said!

### 286) Fill in : whose, who, why, where, which or whom.

Last year my best friend, 1) ..whose.. name is Annie, invited me to stay with her during the summer holiday. Annie lives in Nancy, 2) .............. is a beautiful town in the east of France. She has a big apartment 3) .............. overlooks the river. The school 4) .............. she works is very close to her apartment. Annie studied French at university, 5) .............. is the reason 6) .............. she decided to live in France. Annie teaches English to students, most of 7) .............. are hoping to study in England or America and need to be able to speak English. I met some of Annie's students when I got to Nancy. I also met Annie's boss, 8) .............. struck me as being a very nice man. He offered me a job in his school as soon as he found out that I was a teacher too. I decided to accept his offer, 9) .............. is 10) .............. I'm still here in Nancy.

## Revision Exercises III

**287** Put the verbs in brackets into the infinitive or -ing form.

Dear Paul,
I'm sorry, but I forgot 1) ...to write.. (write) yesterday. I'm sorry 2) .......................... (tell) you this, but the trip is off. David Richter, who was supposed 3) .......................... (arrive) yesterday, rang this morning only 4) .......................... (say) that a back injury had prevented him from 5) .......................... (come), and that he would have to spend at least a month 6) .......................... (recover). I regret 7) .......................... (get) so excited about it now. I wonder if there's any chance of 8) .......................... (you/come) for a visit anyway? I haven't got enough enthusiasm left 9) .......................... (do) anything very adventurous, but it would be great 10) .......................... (see) you.
Love,
Greg

**288** Fill in the correct modal verb.

Mr Lewis, there are a few things you 1) ..will have to... do for me while I'm away. First of all, you 2) .......................... forget to ring Mr Jones about the contract. If you 3) .......................... get him on the phone, you 4) .......................... send him a fax about it. You 5) .......................... worry about the Baker account as I 6) .......................... take care of that when I get back. Also, you 7) .......................... remind Mrs Anderson about the meeting on Friday. She 8) .......................... forget if you don't remind her.

**289** Match the sentences with the correct tense description.

1. There was nobody in the school because lessons had finished.
2. Someone's been playing my tapes!
3. What were you doing at midnight on the 29th?
4. He opened the cabinet, took out a box and put the money in it.
5. Be careful! You're going to hit that car!
6. She's been working since 7 o'clock this morning.
7. They'll probably be a bit late.
8. Will you be going to the shops today?
9. Music was playing, people were dancing and talking...
10. He was killed in an accident.
11. Bobby's grown a lot since last year.
12. She was running when she twisted her ankle.

a. past actions which happened one after the other
b. prediction
c. action expressing irritation
d. background description to events in a story
e. past action which occurred before another action
f. action started in the past and continuing up to the present
g. past action in progress interrupted by another past action
h. personal experience/change
i. past action which is not connected with the present and happened at a definite past time not mentioned
j. action in the middle of happening at a stated past time
k. evidence that sth will happen
l. polite enquiry about people's arrangements

1...e.. 2...... 3...... 4...... 5...... 6...... 7...... 8...... 9...... 10...... 11...... 12......

**290** Rephrase the following using the appropriate modal verb.

1. It's possible that the plane will be late. ...The plane might be late.................................
2. It would have been better if you had told them the truth. ..........................
3. It's not possible that he said that. ..........................
4. You aren't allowed to smoke in the house. ..........................
5. Do you think you could type this for me? ..........................
6. Why don't we go swimming? ..........................
7. Do you mind if I shut the window? ..........................
8. There was no reason for her to come that early. ..........................
9. You nearly caused an accident. Be careful! ..........................
10. Is it possible for her to win? ..........................

# 13. Demonstratives – Pronouns – Possessives – Quantifiers

"You can't carry *those* cups, Bob. Why don't you take *this* tray?"

"But Pete, I've got enough to carry with *these* cups. I don't want to carry *that* tray, too."

## Demonstratives

| This/These are used: | That/Those are used: |
|---|---|
| for people or things near us.<br>**These** shoes over here are mine. | for people or things not near us.<br>**That** chair over there is broken. |
| for present or future situations.<br>I'm going to Disneyland **this** month. | for past situations.<br>We had a wonderful Christmas **that** year. |
| when the speaker is in the place he/she is referring to. **This** room is very untidy.<br>(The speaker is now in the untidy room.) | to refer back to something mentioned before.<br>"She failed her exams". "**That**'s too bad". |
| to introduce people or when we introduce ourselves on the phone.<br>"John, **this** is Ann and **this** is Tom."<br>"Hello? **This** is Pam Jones speaking." | when speaking on the phone to ask who the other person is.<br>"Hello? This is Jo Ryan. Who's **that** speaking?/Who's **that**, please?" |

This/these - that/those are not always followed by nouns.
**This** is the best I can do for you.  "I've won the lottery." "**That**'s too good to be true."

**291** Fill in: this, that, these or those.

1. ….*This*………… is David.  2. Whose are ………… books?  3. …. is Pam. Who's …, please?

4. ……………… isn't my coat.  5. ……………… is my car.  6. ……………… are my slippers.

## 13. Demonstratives – Pronouns – Possessives – Quantifiers

**292** Fill in with : this, that, these or those.

1. "Can you pass me ………… *that* ………………… book, please?" "Yes, of course. Here you are."
2. "Have you seen ………………………………… film before?" "No. I hope it'll be good."
3. "Look at ………………………………… people swimming in the canal! They must be crazy!"
4. "Could you come here and hold ………………………………… wires for me, please?"
5. "Did you see Ken and Liz when they came?" "No, we were away ………………………………… weekend."

### Pronouns

| | Personal pronouns | | Possessive adjectives | Possessive pronouns | Reflexive-Emphatic pronouns |
|---|---|---|---|---|---|
| | before verbs as subjects | after verbs as objects | followed by nouns | not followed by nouns | |
| | I | me | my | mine | myself |
| | you | you | your | yours | yourself |
| | he | him | his | his | himself |
| | she | her | her | hers | herself |
| | it | it | its | — | itself |
| | we | us | our | ours | ourselves |
| | you | you | your | yours | yourselves |
| | they | them | their | theirs | themselves |

### Personal Pronouns

- We use **personal pronouns** to refer to **people**, **things** or **animals**. *I've bought some **milk**. **It**'s on the table.* We don't use a noun and a personal pronoun together. *My umbrella is in the car.* (not: *My umbrella, it's in the car.*) *My aunt took me out to dinner.* (not: *My aunt she took me out to dinner.*)
- We use **I, you, he, she** etc before verbs as **subjects** and **me, you, him, her** etc after verbs as **objects**. *He gave **her** an expensive diamond ring but **she** didn't like **it**.*
- **There + be** is used for something mentioned for the first time or to say that something or someone exists. *There are some people in the waiting room. They want to see you.*
- **It + be** is used to give more details about something or someone already talked about. *There's someone at the door. It's the postman.*
- **It + be with to-infinitive or that-clause** is used to begin a sentence. *It's hard to believe her. It's bad luck that she failed.* It is also used for weather, distance, temperature, time expressions and in the following : *It seems that, It appears that, It looks like, It is said that* etc. *It's cold today, isn't it? It seems that it's going to snow.* But we say : *There seems to be a problem.*

## 13. Demonstratives – Pronouns – Possessives – Quantifiers

**293** Fill in the correct personal pronouns.

Ben: Have you seen Martin today?
Sue: Yes. 1) ...I... saw him this morning. 2) ........................ was coming out of the travel agent's.
Ben: Did 3) ........................ ask 4) ........................ where 5) ........................ was going?
Sue: Yes. He said 6) ........................ was going to Italy with Mary for two weeks. 7) ........................ was at the travel agent's as well. 8) ........................ both looked very excited and happy.
Ben: Shall 9) ........................ go on holiday together somewhere this year?
Sue: Mary told 10) ........................ that 11) ........................ had a great time in Italy last year. Shall 12) ........................ ask 13) ........................ how much 14) ........................ cost?

**294** Fill in : there or it.

Sam: Look, Tom! 1) ...There...'s a woman leaning against the wall. 2) ........................ 's Mrs Bentley, isn't it?
Tom: I think so. 3) ........................ 's something wrong with her. 4) ........................ looks like she's going to faint! Quick!
Sam: 5) ........................ 's somebody else with her now. I don't know who 6) ........................ is. Let's see if she is okay. 7) ........................ may be something we can do for her. 8) ........................ 's all right just to go and check, isn't it?
Tom: Yes, you're right. Although 9) ........................ does look as if she's a little better now. Let's go and see anyway.

### Possessive adjectives/pronouns – Possessive case

- **Possessive adjectives/pronouns** express possession. Possessive adjectives go before nouns, whereas possessive pronouns do not go before nouns. *This is **her** jacket. It's **hers**.* Sometimes possessive pronouns go at the beginning of a sentence. ***Yours** is in the bedroom.*

- We use **the** rather than a **possessive adjective** with this pattern:

  | verb | + person | + preposition | |
  |------|----------|---------------|---|
  | She | hit | Peter | in the face. |

  (not: in his face)

- **Own** is used with possessive adjectives to emphasise the fact that something belongs to someone and no one else. *We've got **our own** car.* or *We've got a car of **our own**.*

| Possessive case with 's or s' for people or animals | Possessive case with "of" for inanimate things |
|---|---|
| **singular nouns (person or animal) + 's**<br>the child**'s** trumpet, the cat**'s** tail, the waitress**'s** apron | **for inanimate things or abstract nouns**<br>the leaves **of** a tree, the cost **of** living |
| **regular plural nouns + '** *the girls' bedroom* | **of + possessive case/possessive pronoun when there is a determiner, (this, some etc) before the noun** *That's **a** poem **of** Ken's. (one of Ken's poems)* **some** books **of** mine (some of my books) |
| **irregular plural nouns not ending in s + 's**<br>the men**'s** suits, the women**'s** bags | |
| **compound nouns + 's** *my brother-in-law**'s** car* | **Note** : phrases of place + 's *at the butcher**'s**, the company**'s** headquarters*<br>**time or distance expressions + 's / '**<br>*Sunday**'s** paper, two days**'** leave, one mile**'s** walk*<br>We can use either "'s" or "of" when we talk about places or organisations<br>*Rome**'s** churches **or** the churches **of** Rome*<br>**and "of" with people in longer phrases**<br>*That's the car **of** one of my friends at work.* |
| **'s after the last of two or more names to show common possession**<br>Ted and Mary**'s** house (They live in the same house.) | |
| **'s after each name to show individual possession**<br>Tom**'s** and Kim**'s** houses (They live in different houses.) | |

## 13. Demonstratives - Pronouns - Possessives - Quantifiers

**295) Fill in the correct possessive adjectives, pronouns or personal pronouns.**

Ralph: Have you seen 1) ...*my*... keys, Amy? I can't find them.
Amy: Well, 2) ........................ are on the kitchen table. I haven't seen 3) ........................ anywhere. Perhaps they are in 4) ........................ coat pocket.
Ralph: No. I've looked. 5) ................ may have left 6) ................ at 7) ................ mother's house.
Amy: I remember seeing some keys on the table but I thought they were 8) ........................ mother's. I'll go over there and have a look for 9) ................ . Can you get dinner for yourself and Bill? And make sure he does 10) ........................ homework before he eats.
Ralph: I'm supposed to be meeting Mark and Barry at 8 o'clock.
Amy: Well, if you're a bit late, 11) ........ will wait for 12) ........ . Don't worry, 13) ........ won't be long. Bye!

**296) Rewrite the following sentences using the possessive.**

1. I'll see you at the hotel – the entrance later. ....*I'll see you at the entrance of the hotel later.*..........
2. We saw Mrs Jones – dog in the park. ...............................................
3. They spoke to Tim and Mary – daughter yesterday. ...............................................
4. I would like you to meet a friend – my. ...............................................
5. Here are two compositions – Tina. ...............................................
6. We will leave on tonight – the flight. ...............................................
7. This is the children – the classroom. ...............................................
8. Have you seen John – Sally – houses? ...............................................
9. I stayed at my mother-in-law – house last night. ...............................................
10. The cost – living is rising rapidly nowadays. ...............................................

**297) Write a phrase with "own" as in the example:**

1. They would like a house that is theirs and no one else's. ....*They would like a house of their own.*......
2. I will give you some of my books. ...............................................
3. They've got a private car to drive to work. ...............................................
4. Jane would like a dog just for her. ...............................................
5. We would like an island all to ourselves. ...............................................

**298) Here are the titles of some films. Write them using a possessive form or of.**

1. The Sword .........*of*............... Death
2. The Russian ............................. Plane
3. The Middle ............................. the Day
4. The Price ............................. Fame
5. The Smiths ............................. House
6. The Dog ............................. Life
7. The Spies ............................. Plan
8. The Day ............................. the Funeral
9. The People ............................. the Island
10. The Lights ............................. the City

**299) Fill in the correct pronoun.**

Dear Mum,
Well, I've arrived in Taipei without any problems. 1) ..*My*.. flatmates both seem very nice. 2) ........ spent all day yesterday cleaning the flat and tidying up. Later some of the other teachers came to visit 3) ........ and 4) ................ brought cakes and sweets with 5) ................ . One of the teachers, Sue, went to Newcastle University, like 6) ................ . 7) ................ looks familiar. 8) ................ think Bob might know 9) ................ because 10) ................ was in the same department as 11) ................ . 12) ................ timetables are quite good. Well 13) ................ is anyway! Some people are not very happy with 14) ................ timetables because 15) ................ finish late. Anyway 16) ................ doesn't matter here because everything is open until late. I hope that 17) ................ are all okay.
Write soon,
Jo

## 13. Demonstratives – Pronouns – Possessives – Quantifiers

### Reflexive / Emphatic Pronouns - myself, yourself etc

**Reflexive pronouns** are used after certain verbs (behave, burn, cut, enjoy, hurt, kill, look, laugh at, introduce, dry, teach etc) when the subject and the object of the verb are the same. *Did you hurt yourself? They look after themselves.*

**Reflexive pronouns** can be used after be, feel, look, seem to describe emotions or states. *She doesn't look herself these days.* They are also used after prepositions but not after prepositions of place. *You should take care of yourself.* but: *He is sitting in front of me.* (not : in front of myself)

Certain verbs do not normally take a reflexive pronoun. These are: wash, shave, (un)dress, afford, complain, meet, rest, relax, stand up, get up, sit down, wake up etc. *She washed and (got) dressed.* We don't say: She washed herself and dressed herself. However we can use a reflexive pronoun with wash or dress when we talk about young children or animals. *Although Eliza is only 3 years old, she can dress herself. That elephant is washing itself!*

**Emphatic pronouns** have the same form as reflexive pronouns but a different meaning. They emphasise the noun or the fact that one person, and not another, performs an action. *I myself found the murderer.* or *I found the murderer myself.* They also mean without help. *He painted the house himself.* (without help) They go after nouns, pronouns, at the end of a sentence, or after "but" and "than". *You should count on no one but yourself.*

**Note these idioms :** Enjoy yourself! (= Have a good time!) Behave yourself! (= Be good!) I like being by myself. (= I like being alone.) She lives by herself. (= She lives on her own.) Help yourself to coffee. (= You're welcome to take some coffee if you want some.) Do it yourself. (= Do it without being helped.) Make yourself at home! (= Feel comfortable.) Make yourself heard. (= Speak loudly enough to be heard by others.)

**Each other** means **one another**. Compare the examples below:

They have hurt **each other**.

They have hurt **themselves**.

### 300 Fill in the correct reflexive pronouns.

1. Take care of ........*yourself*........ when you go canoeing, Bob.
2. I've cut ............................................................ on this tin.
3. Did you enjoy ............................................................ last night, you two?
4. Ben's ashamed of ............................................................ for stealing your bike.
5. The boys behaved ............................................................ when they were at Auntie Mabel's.
6. I don't like Sheila. She thinks far too much of ............................................................ .
7. We can do it if we truly believe in ............................................................ .

### 301 Fill in "each other" or an appropriate reflexive or emphatic pronoun.

1. Billy and his penfriend wrote to ........*each other*........ for five years before they actually met.
2. The children were playing by ............................................................ in the garden when it started snowing.
3. Paul and Ted haven't spoken to ............................................................ for days. What's wrong with them?
4. We blame ............................................................ for leaving the house unlocked.

143

## 13. Demonstratives – Pronouns – Possessives – Quantifiers

5. They bumped into .................................................................................. last weekend.
6. We can manage by .................................................................., thank you very much.
7. They looked at ............................................................. in the mirror and laughed.
8. We saw ......................................................................... on television last week.
9. Tom made these chairs .............................................................................. .
10. We gave ............................................................................ presents for Christmas.
11. Don't worry about us. We're old enough to look after ........................................... .
12. The kettle will switch ........................................................... off when it has boiled.

**302** Fill in the correct pronouns then identify them : reflexive or emphatic?

1. *emphatic pronoun*
2. ........................
3. ........................
4. ........................

They're painting the house *themselves*.
This man has cut .............. .
Oh no! I've burnt .............. .
She's repaired the car .............. .

5. ........................
6. ........................
7. ........................
8. ........................

She's drying ............. .
They've cut their hair .............. .
We make our clothes .............. .
The cat is washing .............. .

**303** Complete the sentences using one of the words in the list below and a -self pronoun.

enjoy, built, wrap, blames, seem, upset, behave, lives by

1. Is Bill okay? He doesn't ...... *seem himself* ........................................ at the moment.
2. Mary .................................................................................. for the car crash.
3. " .................................................................. in this blanket to keep warm, Tim."
4. The Jones' have ............................................................... a swimming pool.
5. She shouldn't ................................................................. like that. He's not worth it.
6. " ........................................................ children," the mother said to her naughty boys.
7. She feels lonely. She ............................................................................. .
8. Did you ................................................................................. at the party?

**304** Fill in: my, your, their or the.

1. I wish you wouldn't keep biting ........ *your* ................. nails; you're making me nervous.
2. I was so nervous ................................................................. hands were shaking.
3. Peter was seriously injured when he was hit on ................................... head with a baseball bat.
4. In many European countries people kiss each other on ........................ cheek when they meet.
5. All the football supporters had red and white scarves around ............................... necks.

144

## 13. Demonstratives – Pronouns – Possessives – Quantifiers

### Some – Any – No – Not Any – Every

|  | Adjectives | Pronouns | Adverbs | |
|---|---|---|---|---|
|  |  | people | things | places |
| **Positive** | some<br>any | someone/somebody<br>anyone/anybody | something<br>anything | somewhere<br>anywhere |
| **Interrogative** | any | anyone/anybody | anything | anywhere |
| **Negative** | no/not any | no one/not anyone<br>nobody/not anybody | nothing<br>not anything | nowhere<br>not anywhere |
| **Positive/Interrogative/Negative** | every | everybody (all the people)<br>everyone | everything<br>(all the things) | everywhere<br>(in all the places) |

- **Some** is normally used in a positive sentence before uncountable nouns or plural countable nouns. *There's **some** cheese left.* **Some** is also used in questions when we want to make an offer, a request or when we expect a positive answer. *Would you like **some** hot chocolate? Could I have **some** cake, please? Did you buy **some** oranges? (I expect you bought some oranges.)*

- **Any** is normally used before uncountable nouns or plural countable nouns in questions. *Are there **any** more apples?* **Any** and its compounds can be used after **if** in a positive sentence. *I doubt if **anyone** can help her.* **Any** can also be used in positive sentences meaning *it doesn't matter when/which/who/where*. *You can come **any** day you want. You can go **anywhere** you want.*

- **No/not any** are used before plural countable nouns or uncountable nouns in negations. *There's **no** cheese left.* or *There isn't **any** cheese left.* **Any** is always used after negative words (hardly, never, without, seldom, rarely). *There's **hardly any** food left.* (not: ~~There's hardly no food left.~~)

- **Every** is used before singular countable nouns. **Every** and its compounds take a verb in the singular. ***Every** student **has** to obey school regulations.* (= all the students) ***Everything is** ready for the wedding.* (= all the things)

- The above rules apply to the compounds of **some – any – no – every**. *There's **someone** in the office.*

**305** Underline the correct item.

1. There's **someone**/**anyone** in my room.
2. There's **any**/**some** chicken in the fridge.
3. There's **anything**/**nothing** in the freezer.
4. Can I tell you **something**/**nothing**?
5. I've got hardly **any**/**no** money left.
6. He's given me **anything**/**everything** I asked for.
7. **No one**/**Anyone** came to visit Julie at the hospital.
8. **Nobody**/**Anyone** can help me with my project.
9. Can I visit you **some**/**no** time?
10. I walk Debbie's dog **some**/**every** Sunday.

## 13. Demonstratives – Pronouns – Possessives – Quantifiers

11. I doubt if **anyone/someone** knows about it.
12. **Anybody/Somebody** knocked on the door.
13. Would you mind lending me **some/any** money?
14. **Someone/Anyone** took Bob's wallet.
15. Did you go **anywhere/nowhere** for the weekend?
16. You can't go on holiday without **any/no** money.
17. I've got **anywhere/nowhere** to sleep tonight.
18. He's never got **nothing/anything** interesting to say.
19. I've looked **somewhere/everywhere** for my keys.
20. **Anybody/Somebody** has been playing my records!
21. "Would you like **some/any** coffee?" "Yes, please."
22. **Everything/Anything** is clear now.
23. She hasn't spoken to **someone/anyone** for ages.
24. Sally has got **any/no** friends.

### Much – Many – A lot of

|  | countables | uncountables |  |
|---|---|---|---|
| Positive | a lot (of)/lots of/ many (formal) | a lot (of)/lots of/ much (formal) | There are **a lot of** trees in the park. There is **a lot of** cheese in the fridge. |
| Interrogative | many | much | Are there **many** shops in York? Did you have **much** time to do any shopping? |
| Negative | many | much | There aren't **many** oranges. I haven't got **much** money so I can't buy any. |
| Positive | a few (= some)/ (very) few (= not many, not enough) | a little (= some)/ (very) little (= not much, not enough) | There were **a few** boys in the class. **Very few** students attended the lecture. **Very little** progress has been made. |

**A lot (of)/Lots (of)** are used with countable or uncountable nouns and are normally used in positive sentences. *He's got **a lot of** work to do. **A lot of** students work on this project.* **A lot of** can be used in questions or negative sentences in informal English. *Were there **a lot of** casualties in that road accident? (informal)*

**Many** is used with countables and **much** with uncountables. They are normally used in questions or negative sentences. *Has he got **many** friends? We haven't got **much** money.* **Many** or **much** are often used in positive sentences after **too**, **so**, **how** or in formal English. *He spends **too much** money. He's got **so many** problems. **Much** effort had been made before the peace treaty was signed. (formal)*

**A few** is used with countables and **a little** with uncountables. They both have a positive meaning. **A few** means some, a small number. **A little** means some, a small amount. *There are **a few** oranges and **a little** sugar on the table.*

**Few/Little** both have a negative meaning. **Few** means not many, almost none. **Little** means not much, almost none. **Few and little** are rather formal English.
**Very few/very little** are more usual in everyday speech. It is also common to use: **only a little**, **only a few**. *She has **a few** good friends (some friends) so she's happy. He has **very few** friends (almost no friends) so he's unhappy. I've got **a little** time (some time) so I can help you. I've got **very little** time (almost no time) so I can't help you.*

**306) Fill in : a lot of, many, few, much and little.**

Darren isn't very happy in his new job. He doesn't earn 1) ....*much*..... money even though he has 2) ............ responsibilities. Very 3) ...... ............ companies he has worked for in the past have paid him so 4) ............ money for so 5) ............ hard work. He has sent 6) ............ applications to other companies, but there are very 7) ............ jobs and too 8) ............ people looking for work these days. In the current economic climate he has 9) ............ hope of finding anything better, but when things improve he'll probably find a job which pays him 10) ............ more money.

## 13. Demonstratives – Pronouns – Possessives – Quantifiers

**All – Both – Whole – Either – Neither – None – Every – Each – One – Ones**

**All** refers to more than two people or things. It has a positive meaning and takes a verb in the plural. It is the opposite of **none**.
**All** the students passed the test. **All of them** were very happy. They were **all** very happy.
**All + that clause** means "everything" and takes a singular verb. **All that** he said was lies.

**Both** refers to two people or things. It has a positive meaning and takes a verb in the plural. It is the opposite of **neither/not either**.
Ann and Kate are eighteen. **Both** Ann **and** Kate are eighteen. They are **both** eighteen. **Both of them** are eighteen. **Both** girls are eighteen.

**Whole** (= complete) is used with singular countables. We always use **a, the, this, my etc + whole + countable**.
the whole week = all the week/all week
but: all the sugar (not: the whole sugar)

**Either** (anyone of two)/**Neither** (not one and not the other) are used before singular countables. They refer to two people or things. **Neither of/Either of** take a verb either in the singular or plural.
**Neither of** them is/are poor. **Neither** man is poor. Paul and David promised to help me. I'd like **either of** them to help me.

**None** refers to more than two people or things. It has a negative meaning and isn't followed by a noun. **None of** can be used with **nouns**, **his**, **them** etc followed by a verb either in the singular or plural. It is the opposite of **all**.
Sally, Helen and Sue haven't been to Madrid. **None of** the girls/them has/have been to Madrid.
"Are there any more tickets?" "No, **none**."
**No** can be followed by a noun.
There's **no news** about the accident.

**Every** is used with singular countables. It refers to a group of people or things and means "all", "everyone", "everything" etc.
Students get a report card **every** term.

**Each** is used with singular countables. It means one by one, considered individually.
**Each** trainee should attend a three-month course. (all trainees considered individually)

**One – ones** are used to avoid repetition of a countable noun or a pronoun.
Which shirt do you want? This **one**. (this shirt)
Which shoes did you buy? The black **ones**. (the black shoes)

**307** Use both, neither, none or all and write sentences as in the example:

1. Tracy and Sarah haven't seen the film. ...... *Neither of them have/has seen the film.* ..........
2. Lions, tigers and elephants are mammals. ............................................
3. Julie, Pam and Nick don't like rainy weather. ............................................
4. Maria and Marina are good students. ............................................
5. Jim, Peter and John can't speak German. ............................................

## 13. Demonstratives – Pronouns – Possessives – Quantifiers

6. Mark, Paula and Kristi failed the exam. ...................................................
7. Phil and Georgina are very friendly. ...................................................
8. Jean and Deborah have fair hair and blue eyes. ...................................................
9. Tim, Ted and Jim went to the zoo. ...................................................

**308) Fill in: all, both, whole, none or neither.**

Joe, Nick and Alan 1) ...*all*..... live in Summerville. Nick has spent his 2) ........................ life there but 3) ............... of them were born there. 4) ............... Joe and Nick work in an office, but 5) ............... of them enjoys it very much. 6) ............... three of them play in a band but 7) ............... of them can play their instruments very well! On Saturdays they spend 8) ............... day fixing their motorbikes. Alan and Joe 9) ............... like sailing. Sometimes they go down to the nearby river. Although 10) ............... three boys love Summerville, 11) ............... of them want to stay there forever.

**309) Fill in: every or each (sometimes both are possible).**

The Miltons are all going on holiday this year. They have looked at 1) ...*every*..... brochure in the travel agent's and they've decided to go to Portugal. They went to an island last year but 2) ............... beach they went to was filthy. Tom was sick 3) ............... day and Jane was bitten by insects on 4) ............ leg. 5) ............ time the twins went swimming they nearly drowned and 6) ....................... of the others had to take turns at swimming out to save them. Mary got an infection in 7) ..................... ear when she wore the cheap earrings she bought in the market. 8) ................ time they go on holiday, they 9) ............... take their own first-aid kit, because a minor disaster seems to happen to one of them 10) .................... time.

**310) Fill in: one or ones.**

M: What colour shoes do you want, Ted?
T: Can I have the green 1) ...*ones*... please?
M: The green 2) ................ ? Why? They're a horrible colour. Don't you like these brown 3) ................ ?
T: No. The green 4) ................ will match my shirt.
M: Which shirt?
T: My new 5) ................ .
M: Green shoes with a red shirt? Ugh! I think the brown 6) ................ are better.
T: If I get the brown 7) ................ , I'll have to buy that jacket too.
M: Which 8) ................ ? You've got jackets at home!
T: But that 9) ................ we saw earlier will look great with the brown shoes.
M: I don't know which 10) ....................... you are talking about. We'll buy the brown shoes, but you're not having a new jacket.

**311) Substitute the underlined words with: some, any, every or their compounds.**

"I've been looking 1) <u>all over</u> for my friend, Jim. Have you seen 2) <u>a man</u> waiting around here?" "Yes, I saw 3) <u>a man</u> here about ten minutes ago, asking 4) <u>all the people</u> that passed by how to get to Covent Garden. Finally, 5) <u>a woman</u> gave him 6) <u>a few</u> directions." "Oh well, I'll see him another time, but it's a pity because I had 7) <u>a book</u> to give him. – Oh, I know! I've got to go 8) <u>to school</u> this afternoon, but then I may go to Jim's tonight to have 9) <u>a bit of</u> dinner, so I can give it to him then."

1. ...*everywhere*...    2. ................    3. ................    4. ................    5. ................
6. ................    7. ................    8. ................    9. ................

## 13. Demonstratives – Pronouns – Possessives – Quantifiers

**312** Fill in : a few, few, a little or little.

Dear Dad,
Just 1) ...*a few*... words to tell you about my new restaurant. I'm a bit worried about it as very 2) ............ people are coming to eat here. 3) ............ came in last night, but they ordered very 4) ............ food - just 5) ............ sandwiches and 6) ............ coffee. It seems that very 7) ............ people can afford to eat out these days because they've got very 8) ............ money to spare. I don't think business will be very good for 9) ............ years. Perhaps you could lend me 10) ............ money to keep me going for a while?
Love,
Patricia

**313** Fill in : a lot (of), much, few or (a) little.

These days more people are learning how to use computers. 1) ....*A lot of*... them have to because of their work, some just want to play games, 2) ............ are actually interested in computing. These days you don't need 3) ............ money to buy a computer and 4) ............ knowledge of computing is required to use one. There are 5) ............ of different uses for them, such as letter writing and keeping accounts.

### Oral Activity 28

Students in teams read the text and spot the mistakes. The more mistakes they can find and correct, the more points they get.

Graham is in love with a girl called Patricia. He wants hers to marry he, and he has asked her few times, but she has always refused. He gave her a diamond ring which he had made herself and cost much money to make. But this wasn't good enough for her. She said there weren't much diamonds in it. Then he offered to buy her a big house where they could live by ourselves for the rest of theirs lives. This idea didn't have many success either. She said that she couldn't imagine itself living with him for so lots of years. "This would be too boring," she said. Finally, Graham told her that all he had were hers if only she would marry his. "This is not enough for me," she said. "You haven't really got very many".

1. *her*   2. ........   3. ........   4. ........   5. ........   6. ........   7. ........   8. ........   9. ........
10. ........   11. ........   12. ........   13. ........   14. ........   15. ........   16. ........   17. ........   18. ........

### Oral Activity 29

Students in teams look at the pictures and the list of words to make up as many sentences as possible using both - neither - all - none. Each correct answer gets 1 point. **List of words :** short/long/straight/curly/ dark/fair hair/hats/glasses/suits/dresses/thin/fat/poor/rich/happy/unhappy /young/middle-aged

Team A S1: Both men are middle-aged. Neither of them is young.
Team B S1: All the women are young. None of them is middle-aged.
Team A S2: Both men wear hats. Neither of them wear glasses.
Team B S2: Neither man is thin. Both of them are fat.

## 13. Demonstratives - Pronouns - Possessives - Quantifiers

Look at the following notes then write the statement a witness gave to the police. Use both - neither - all - none.

**look out of window - see two men - stand outside - tall - dark hair - no beard or moustache - old man come out of building - men get behind him - force him ground - he try defend himself - not able to stop them - people in street - not stop for help - walk quickly past - time old man scream - they kick him again - two men run away - police arrive**

*When I looked out of the window at about 9 o'clock I saw two men standing outside. They were both tall and had dark hair ...*

### Tense Review

**314** Fill in a suitable word or phrase to complete the sentences.

1. I wish I ............ *hadn't spoken to her* ............ like that yesterday - now she's upset.
2. Sally ............ housework before she left for work.
3. If you keep arriving late, ............ job.
4. I don't believe that story! He ............ lying.
5. OK. I ............ the last piece of cake.
6. Stop being horrible to me. I don't like ............ like that.
7. When I first went to England I had ............ driving on the left.
8. I ............ met him before, but I'm not certain.
9. By next month she ............ this novel for four months.
10. I didn't realise I had got on the wrong train ............ it reached its destination.
11. I ............ the road when I tripped and fell over.
12. He was exhausted because ............ night.
13. Don't forget ............ the meeting this afternoon.
14. Don't phone me at 7 o'clock because I ............ homework then.
15. My teeth are so bad that I ............ three times already this year.
16. You ............ you were ill. I'd have brought you some medicine.
17. All that he said ............ . Don't believe him.
18. My family ............ five members.

### In Other Words

| | |
|---|---|
| Mary didn't go out. Sally didn't go out either.<br>Neither of them went out. | Nothing can stop him.<br>There isn't anything that can stop him. |
| Ann is tall. Pam is tall, too.<br>Both of them are tall. | Ted, John and Jim don't like peanuts.<br>None of them like/likes peanuts. |
| There isn't anybody in the office.<br>There's nobody in the office. | Sue, Helen and Marge have cars.<br>All of them have cars. |

**315** Rewrite the following sentences keeping the meaning the same.

1. Paul, George and Chris are all football players. ...... *All of them are football players.* ......
2. Sam has the flu. Jim has the flu too. ............
3. Jude, Peter and Sally did not pass their exams. ............
4. Kate didn't eat dessert. Simone didn't eat dessert either. ............
5. There wasn't anybody on the sinking ship. ............
6. Nothing can make him happy. ............

## 13. Demonstratives - Pronouns - Possessives - Quantifiers

**316** Fill in the gaps using some, any, no and their compounds.

The school trip is tomorrow and I want to remind everyone of a few things. I don't want 1) ..*anyone*.. to miss the bus. Last year 2) ........................ students were left behind because they arrived late. There are hardly 3) .............. seats left on the coach, so remember to put your bags and coats in the boot before you get on. 4) .............. will be allowed to smoke on the coach. I hope you will all bring 5) ................ warm clothes. The castle is 6) ...................... to the north of the town. It's a 15-minute walk, so wear 7) ...................... comfortable on your feet. Once inside, I don't want to hear 8) ...................... shouting or swearing. If there is 9) ...................... you want to know about the castle and its history, there will be 10) ...................... at the castle gates to show us around and answer 11) ...................... questions. There will be 12) ...................... talking on the museum tour afterwards. The town is small, and so there is 13) ...................... large enough to accommodate us all for lunch. I suggest we stop for fish and chips on the journey home - I doubt if 14) ...................... will object! Does 15) ...................... have 16) ...................... questions? Good. If you remember what I've said, there will be 17) ...................... problems.

| Phrasal Verbs 12 | |
|---|---|
| **take after sb :** | look or act like a relative |
| **take away :** | remove |
| **take down :** | write down |
| **take off :** | 1) remove clothes (**opp:** put on) 2) (of aeroplanes) leave the ground |
| **take sb out :** | take sb to a restaurant etc |
| **take over :** | take control of sth |
| **take up :** | begin a hobby, sport, job etc. |

**317** Fill in the correct preposition or adverb.

1. That company has recently been taken ..*over*.... .
2. The boss asked his secretary to take .............. some notes.
3. My boyfriend is taking me .................. tonight to celebrate St Valentine's Day.
4. Jack is going to take ................ squash to get some exercise.
5. Sandra really takes .................... her mother, doesn't she?
6. The plane will be taking .......... in a few minutes.
7. The patient had to take ................ his shirt for the doctor to examine him.
8. The waiter took .................... the plates at the end of the meal.

**318** Look at Appendix 1 and fill in the correct preposition.

1. I'm hungry. Let's go out ...*for*.... lunch.
2. I found this ring quite ................ chance.
3. Can I pay ........................ cheque, please?
4. We went to the USA ........................ plane.
5. I met him quite ................ accident.
6. You must be back home by 11.00 pm .............. the latest.
7. I'm going to the shops ........................ bicycle.
8. What shall we have ........................ dinner?
9. That car is ................ sale. It's very cheap.

| Idioms 12 | |
|---|---|
| **in cold blood :** | without any feeling of remorse |
| **make one's blood boil :** | make sb angry |
| **ring a bell :** | sound familiar |
| **work a miracle :** | make sth that seems impossible happen |
| **in black and white :** | in writing |
| **against all odds :** | despite the difficulties |

**319** Fill in the correct idiom.

1. ......*Against all odds,*.......... he managed to win the race.
2. I want everything ........................ before I sign anything.
3. The decorators ........................ when they transformed our attic into a luxury bedroom.
4. The murderer killed his victim ........................ .
5. Her name ........................, but I couldn't remember where I'd heard it.
6. My brother ........................ when he told me he had crashed my car.

# 14. Prepositions

## Prepositions of Place/Movement

**320** Match the words with the pictures :

off, between, down, on top of, over, in/inside, above, in front of, past, up, among, next to/by/beside, from ... to, on, through, under, below, behind, along, opposite, at, round/around, near, outside, against, onto, out of, across, to/towards/in the direction of, into

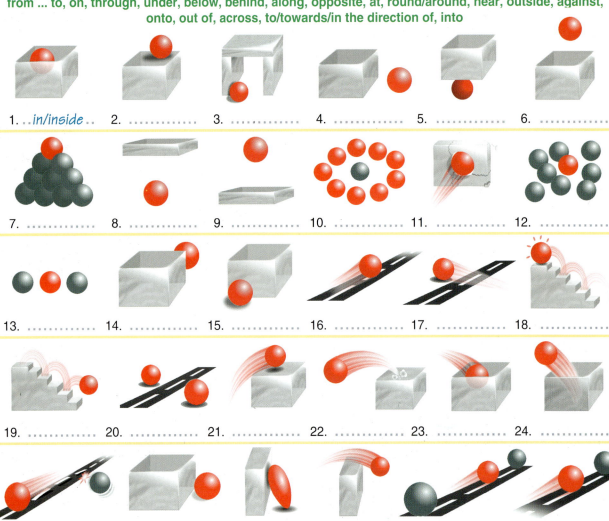

1. ...in/inside..  2. ............  3. ............  4. ............  5. ............  6. ............
7. ............  8. ............  9. ............  10. ............  11. ............  12. ............
13. ............  14. ............  15. ............  16. ............  17. ............  18. ............
19. ............  20. ............  21. ............  22. ............  23. ............  24. ............
25. ............  26. ............  27. ............  28. ............  29. ............  30. ............

## 14. Prepositions

**321** Fill in the gaps with the correct preposition.

This is Sunnyside Farm. Farmer Smith is standing 1) ..*among*.. his sheep. His children are playing 2) ............ the haystack. One of them is jumping 3) ............ it, 4) ........................ some more hay 5) ............ . There's a ladder leaning 6) ........................ the farmhouse and a man is climbing 7) ........................ it. Mrs Smith is standing 8) ........................ the farmhouse with a shawl 9) ........................ her shoulders. Her son Jim is standing 10) ........................ her. There's another man walking 11) ........................ the haystack 12) ........................ Farmer Smith.

**322** Fill in the gaps with the correct preposition.

This is the Sheriff's Office in Mexico City. The Sheriff is sitting 1) ....*at*.... his desk. There are lots of papers and books 2) ............ his desk. There are some photographs of "wanted" men all 3) ............ the office 4) ............ the walls. 5) ........................ the Sheriff's head there is a clock. A prisoner is looking 6) ............ the bars of the cell. A bunch of keys is hanging 7) ............ the cell 8) ............ the wall. 9) ........................ the Sheriff's desk there is a filing cabinet with a coat stand 10) ........................ it.

**323** Fill in the gaps with the correct preposition.

This is Burger House. 1) ...*Behind*.. the counter is a waitress. 2) ............ the counter there are some people. A young woman is standing 3) ............ her children. The boy 4) ............ her is waiting to be served. The young lady 5) ............ her is listening to her personal stereo. The waitress is putting a burger and a cup of cola 6) ............ a tray. A man has just come 7) ............ the door and he's walking 8) ............ the queue.

**324** Fill in the gaps with the correct preposition.

This is Newton High Street. There are people walking 1) .....*up*.... and 2) ................ the street. An old man is walking 3) ........................ the road at the zebra crossing. A young couple are walking 4) ............ ............ the pavement 5) ................ the post office. A boy is walking 6) ............ "Thompson's Sports" shop. He's holding a bag 7) ................ his arms. 8) ................ the bus-stop there is a bus. Some people are getting 9) ................ it while some others are getting 10) ............ it. The bus goes 11) ............ the centre of town 12) ........ the outskirts.

153

## 14. Prepositions

**in** + cities/towns/the streets/the suburbs/an armchair/danger/the middle of/a queue/prison/hospital/a book/ a newspaper/the country/the sky/a line/a row/a hotel/the centre of/the park
**Idioms with in:** cash, pen, ink, pencil, writing, one's opinion, a way (=in a manner), the end
**at** + house number (at 23 Oxford St)/home/school/university/work/the bus stop/the door/the crossroads/ the match/the station/the airport/the seaside/the bottom of/a hotel/table/desk/the top of (but: on top of)
**on** + the floor/the outskirts/a platform/foot/holiday/the River Seine/the border/this street/a farm/the screen/ an island/a beach/the coast/the right/the left/the pavement/a trip/the way/the streets
**Idioms with on:** holiday, business, a journey, a trip, TV, the radio, the phone, the market (= available to the public), purpose, the way (= as I was going)
**by** + bus/taxi/car/helicopter/plane/train/coach/ship/boat/air/sea BUT we say: **on a/the** bus/plane/train/coach/ ship/boat - **in a** taxi/car/helicopter/plane
**Idioms with by:** mistake, accident, chance

**Compare** : Tom is sitting **in the café**. (He's inside the place). He's **at the café**. (He's drinking something-event)

**325** Fill in the gaps with the correct preposition.

Last year my family went 1) ...*on*..... holiday to Thailand. We went 2) ..................... air; it was a very long journey but we were very well looked after 3) ..................... the plane by all the stewardesses. When we arrived 4) ..................... the airport we went directly to our hotel 5) ............. taxi. There was a lot of traffic 6) ............. the streets of the city and there were many people walking 7) .... ..................... the pavements. We stayed 8) ..................... a large hotel 9) ..................... the outskirts of Bangkok. We were given a wonderful suite 10) ................. the top floor of the hotel. The most enjoyable day I had was when we went 11) ................. a trip 12) ..................... boat, down the river to the crocodile farm. We had a wonderful holiday.

**326** Fill in the gaps with the correct preposition.

Last year I went 1) ...*on*... a trip which was an absolute disaster. I was going to Berlin 2) ............. business when, 3) ............. accident, I got 4) ................. the wrong train. We were 5) ................... the way to Brussels before I realised my mistake. When I got to Brussels I had more problems because all my money was 6) ............. German Marks and I didn't have my credit card with me. 7) ............. chance, I found a helpful policeman, who was soon 8) ................... the phone to my company. Thanks to his help I was able to arrange for some money to be sent to a nearby bank. I spent that night in a hotel and paid my bill 9) ............... cash before leaving. 10) ................ the end I got to Berlin twenty-four hours later than I had expected. Everyone thought my trip was a big joke, especially when I told them I had seen Brussels 11) ............... the way.

### Oral Activity 30

The teacher reads nouns from the table at the top of the page. Students in teams take turns to give the appropriate preposition and then make up a sentence. Students may have their books open to begin with, then play the game again with books closed. Each correct answer gets 1 point.

Teacher: suburbs
Team A S1: **in** the suburbs. He bought a small house in the suburbs.

Teacher: the 8 o'clock plane
Team B S1: **on** the 8 o'clock plane. He's arriving on the 8 o'clock plane.

## 14. Prepositions

### Prepositions of Time

| AT | IN | ON |
|---|---|---|
| at 10.30<br>at Christmas/Easter<br>at noon/night/midnight<br>at lunch/dinner/breakfast (time)<br>at that time<br>at the moment<br>at the weekend (on the weekend: Am. English) | in the morning/evening/afternoon/night<br>in the Easter/Christmas holiday(s)<br>in January (months)<br>in (the) winter (seasons)<br>in 1992 (years)<br>in the 19th century<br>in two hours (two hours from now) | on Monday<br>on Easter Sunday etc<br>on Christmas Day<br>on Friday night<br>on July 30th<br>on a summer afternoon<br>on that day |

We never use **at**, **in** or **on** before **yesterday**, **tomorrow**, **next**, **this**, **last**, **every**. *He's leaving **next** Sunday.*

 **327** Fill in: in, on or at.

A footballer's life starts 1) ..*at*.. the weekend. Most people go out 2) .... Friday night, but I have to be in bed 3) ... 10 o'clock. 4) ... Saturday I get up 5) .... 8 o'clock 6) ... the morning and drive to the stadium 7) ...... noon. 8) ..... lunchtime our manager talks about the team we are playing. We play most of our games 9) ...... the winter and sometimes it can be hard to play 10) .... a cold Saturday afternoon, especially 11) .... January. It isn't much fun 12) .... Christmas either. We play a lot of games 13) .... the Christmas holiday. Although we don't play 14) ..... Christmas Day, we do play 15) ........ December 26th, so I can't eat or drink too much! It would be nice to spend more time with my family 16) .... that day, but I can't.

 **328** Fill in: at, in or on.

I go to school every day 1) ..*at*.. 9 o'clock. Lessons start 2) ...... 9.15 am 3) ..... Mondays and Tuesdays. 4) ...... Wednesdays, Thursdays and Fridays they start 5) ...... 9.30 6) ...... the morning. School finishes 7) ..... 3.30 8) ........ the afternoon. 9) ...... Saturdays and Sundays I don't go to school. We have a month off 10) ....... the summer, two weeks' holiday 11) ....... Christmas, and two weeks off 12) ....... Easter.

### Oral Activity 31

The teacher says words from the box at the top of the page without their prepositions. The students in teams give sentences using the appropriate preposition. Each correct answer gets 1 point.

Teacher: January  
Team A S1: He goes skiing **in January**.

Teacher: 1993  
Team B S1: He left school **in 1993**. etc

### Time Words

**for** : is used to express a period of time. *She has been here **for** two weeks.*
**since** : is used with Present Perfect to express a starting point. *He has been here **since** Monday.*

**329** Fill in : for or since.

John Barnes has been in the police force 1) ..*since*.. 1980. Before that he worked in a supermarket 2) ............ two years, but he found it very boring. He has had lots of adventures 3) ............ he became a policeman. He was a constable 4) ............ three years, then he was promoted to sergeant. He has had to work a lot harder 5) ............ then, but he loves his job.

## 14. Prepositions

**ago:** back in time from now (used with Past Simple). *She met Steve a week **ago**.* (a week back in time from now)
**before:** back in time from then. *She sent me a letter last week. I had written to her a month **before**.* (not a month back in time from now but a month before last week when she sent me her letter.)

**330** Fill in : ago or before.

I met my penfriend, Bill, four days 1) ...*ago*.... I had never met him 2) ............ . The day 3) ............ I saw him I was a bit nervous because I didn't know what he would be like. He comes from America and, although I went there two years 4) ............ , we didn't meet then. When I met him, I discovered that his grandparents used to live near my village 100 years 5) ............ , so he might even be a distant relation.

**yet :** by this time (normally used with Present Perfect in questions and negations in end position).
*Have you seen Ann **yet**? I haven't seen her **yet**.*
**already :** before now (used in mid position or at the end with Present Perfect in statements or questions).
*I've **already** posted the invitations to the wedding. Have you **already** finished your homework?*
*I've cooked dinner **already**.* (used to put emphasis on the completion of an action)
**still :** emphasises continuity (used with present forms to show duration; placed before the main verb or after an auxiliary). *He's **still** typing those letters you gave him. I **still** care about him, even though he left me.*

**331** Fill in : yet, still or already.

Gerry : Have you been to the bank 1) ..*yet*...?
June : No. I've 2) ................ told you, I'm 3) ................ waiting for that cheque from my accountant.
Gerry : Hasn't he sent you it 4) ................ ? Why don't you phone him?
June : I've 5) ................ phoned him. He says he hasn't finished working out my tax 6) ................ .

**during (prep) + noun :** throughout. *I stayed in Paris **during** the Christmas holiday.*
**while (conj) + clause :** when, during the time that. ***While** she was on holiday, she wrote me a letter.*

**332** Fill in : during or while.

We went to a few tropical islands 1) ........*during*...... the summer holiday last year. My parents spent most of their time in the hotel 2) ................ I was sunbathing on the beach. 3) ................ a boat journey from one island to another there was a terrible storm. My mother was seasick 4) ................ the trip, 5) ............ my father and I were trying to help her.

**on time :** at the right time. *The train left **on time**.* (not earlier or later than the stated time)
**in time :** early enough, not late. *He was **in time** for the 5 o'clock train.* (some time before 5.00)

**333** Fill in : on time or in time.

Mr Savage was driving very fast last night because he wanted to be home 1) ...*in time*... for the late film. He knew it probably wouldn't start 2) ............ but he didn't want to take any chances. Suddenly, a boy on a bicycle appeared in front of his car and Mr Savage just managed to stop 3) ............ to avoid hitting him. He was so frightened by this that he drove the rest of the way home very slowly. Unfortunately, the film had started 4) ............ and he missed the first half hour of it.

# 14. Prepositions

**by** (prep) : any time before and not later than. *You must be back **by** 12.00. (not later than 12.00)*
**by the time** : before. *They had finished packing **by the time** the taxi came. (before the taxi came)*
**until/till** (conj) : up to the time when. *She was at work **until/till** 3.30. (up to 3.30, not later than 3.30)*
**Till/until** can be used in the negative with verbs that show a point in time *(eg. leave, finish, start ...).*
**Compare:** *He won't start working **until** Friday. (on Friday, not before that). He won't have started working **by** Friday. (He won't begin till after Friday.)*
**at** : exactly at a stated time. *She'll be back **at** 9.00. (9.00 sharp)*

**334** Fill in with : by, by the time, until/till or at.

When I went out last Saturday I told my father I'd be back 1) ...by.... 1 o'clock at the latest. However, I was having such a good time that I didn't even look at my watch 2) ............. 2:30! 3) ............. I found a taxi to take me home it had gone 3 o'clock, and I finally arrived home 4) ............. 3:30. My father was furious and told me I'd have to be home 5) ............. 7 o'clock every night of the week 6) ............. the end of the month!

**within** (prep) : before the end of. *You must finish this project **within** a week. (in a week's time)*
**after** (prep/conj) : following sth in time. *You can watch TV **after** you've tidied your room.*
**afterwards** (adv) : then, after that. *He went for a walk **afterwards**.*
**from ... to/till/until** : *The restaurant serves customers **from** 12.00 **to** 8.00 pm.*

**335** Fill in with: within, after, afterwards or from ... to/until/till.

I'm in trouble with my history teacher. He gave us a project to finish 1) ..within.... a week, and I haven't even started it yet. I was going to do it 2) ............. dinner on Thursday, but my friend phoned and invited me out to the cinema. He didn't tell me we were going to a party 3) ............. ! We stayed at the party 4) ............. 11 o'clock 5) ............. 3.00 in the morning. Now it's Friday and the History class starts at 2 pm. If I don't finish the project 6) ............. the next two hours, my teacher will probably make me stay behind 7) ......... school.

**at the beginning (of)** : at the point/time sth starts. *There's usually a preface **at the beginning of** a book.*
**in the beginning** : at first, originally. *I found computer programming difficult **in the beginning**.*
**at the end (of)** : at the point/time sth finishes. *There's usually an index **at the end of** a book.*
**in the end** : at last, finally. ***In the end** I got used to programming computers.*

**336** Fill in with : at the beginning, at the end, in the beginning or in the end.

I started a new job as a telephone operator 1) ...at the beginning......... of this year. I found the job rather complicated 2) ..........................., but I got used to it 3) ........................... . I'm quite good at it now, and I'm getting a pay-rise 4) ........................... of this month. I've got a month's holiday soon, starting 5) ........................... of July and finishing 6) ........................... of September. I couldn't decide where to go at first, but I decided on Malta 7) ........................... .

**337** Fill in with: after, afterwards, from ... to, before, by the time, within, or in the end.

I began English six months 1) ...ago.... I had studied English 2) ............. at school, but 3) ............. leaving, I began to forget a lot of the English I had learnt. Initially I attended classes several times a week and would sometimes study in the library 4) ............. 5) ............. a few weeks of beginning classes my English improved considerably, so I decided 6) ............. four months to attend fewer classes and now attend one class a week. 7) ............. I think I made the right decision; my English is continuing to improve and I have more time to spend with my family. 8) ............. now 9) ............. the end of June I will be revising for my exams.

# 15. Questions and Short Answers

## Yes/No Questions

**To form questions** we put the auxiliary or modal (can, be, will, have etc) before the subject. We use **do/does** to form questions in Present Simple and **did** to form questions in Past Simple. *He is ready.* ➡ **Is he** ready? *She likes reading.* ➡ **Does she like** reading? (not: *Does she likes reading?*) *Ann went out yesterday.* ➡ **Did Ann go** out yesterday? (not: *Did Ann went out yesterday?*)

## Wh-questions

Wh- questions begin with a question word (**who, what, where, why, when, whose, which, how** etc). **Whose** cat is this? It's Ted's. **Where** did you stay? At the Park Hotel. When there is a preposition, it usually goes at the end of the question, though in formal English it can be put before the question word. **Who** does this car belong **to**? **To whom** does this car belong? (formal)

We use questions to ask for **information** or **permission**. We also use questions to make **suggestions**, **requests**, **offers** or **invitations**.

| | |
|---|---|
| Asking for information: | **Where** did you meet her? At a party. |
| Asking for permission: | **Could I** borrow your pen? Yes, you can. |
| Making suggestions: | **Shall we** go out? Yes, alright. |
| Making requests: | **Could you** help me, please? Yes, of course. |
| Making offers: | **Would you like** some cake? No, thanks. |
| Making invitations: | **Would you like to** come to my wedding? Yes, I'd love to. |

**(338)** Write the speech situation for each question: asking for information/ permission, or making suggestions/requests/offers/invitations.

1. May I borrow your shampoo? ......*asking for permission*......
2. What time does the match start?
3. Could you help me with this, please?
4. Would you like to come to Barbados with me?
5. Shall we go for a walk?
6. Can I do anything for you?
7. Can I leave early today?
8. Would you take this back to the library for me?
9. Would you like something to eat?
10. Can you visit Australia without a visa?
11. Could you carry this box for me, please?
12. Shall we have a party this weekend?
13. Where did you stay while in Madrid?

## 15. Questions and Short Answers

We normally use the following question words to ask about:

| people | things/animals/actions | place | time | quantity | manner | reason |
|---|---|---|---|---|---|---|
| Who<br>Whose<br>Which<br>What | What<br>Which | Where | When<br>How long<br>What time<br>How often | How much<br>How many | How | Why |

- **Who** is used without a noun to ask about people. *Who told you the truth?*
- **Whose** is used to express possession. *Whose pen is this? It's his.*
- **Which** is used for people, animals or things before **nouns**, **one/ones**, **of** or alone. *Which car is yours? There are two newspapers here. Which one would you like to read? Which of the students will come on the school trip? Which is your bag?*
  **Which** is normally used when there is a **limited choice**. *Which is your favourite writer - Charles Dickens or Mark Twain?* (there are only two writers to choose from - limited choice)
  **Which** can also be used with the **comparative** and **superlative**. *Which is faster, a Porsche or a Fiat? Which is the best composition of all?*
- **What** is used before a noun or alone to ask about things. *What day is it today? What did he say? What's this?* **What** is also used for people, animals and things when there is an **unlimited choice**. *What books do you prefer reading?* (there are many books to choose from - unlimited choice) **What** can also be used in these patterns: **What ... like?, What ... for?, What colour?, What size?, What time?, What is he like?, What is it used for?** etc. *What's the weather like today?*
- **What** and **which** are sometimes both possible. *What/Which day did he leave?*

**339** Fill in: who, whose, what, which, where, when, how long, how often, what time, why, how much or how many.

1. ...*How much*... does this book cost? £5.
2. ................ does your mother go to work? 9 am.
3. ................ is your school? Near my house.
4. ................ do you go to the beach? Rarely.
5. ................ is this coat? It's Jack's.
6. ................ is your bag? The big blue one.
7. ................ did you get for Christmas? A shirt.
8. ................ is that? It's Peter.
9. ................ have you been married? One year.
10. ................ are you crying? Because I am sad.
11. ................ did you start school? In September.
12. ................ country is bigger, England or Spain?
13. ................ pence are there in a pound? 100.
14. ................ colour is a kiwi fruit? It's green.

**340** Fill in: which or what.

Tom: 1) ...*What*.... did you do on holiday, Julie?
Julie: I went to Egypt.
Tom: Oh really? 2) ................ places did you see?
Julie: Cairo, the Pyramids, Aswan and some others.
Tom: 3) ................ one did you like the best?
Julie: I'm not sure. They were all fascinating.
Tom: 4) ................ did you think of Cairo?
Julie: It's very big, and there are a lot of tourists.
Tom: 5) ................ hotel did you stay in?
Julie: I don't remember its name. It was lovely, though.
Tom: 6) ................ did you buy there?
Julie: I bought some nice rugs. Actually, I bought one for you. Look! 7) ................ one would you like?
Tom: They're all beautiful. 8) ................ of them do you prefer?
Julie: I don't mind. And look at these! 9) ................ of these vases do you think your mother would like?
Tom: She'd be happy with either of them. 10) ................ are you going to do with the other one?

## 15. Questions and Short Answers

### Subject/Object Questions

If **who**, **which** or **what** are the subject of the question, the word order is the same as in statements. If they are the object of the question, the verb is in question form.

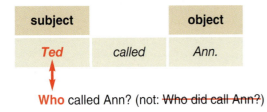

Who called Ann? (not: ~~Who did call Ann?~~)

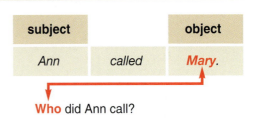

Who did Ann call?

**341** Write questions to which the bold type words are the answers.

1. **Tom** lives in Paris. ......*Who lives in Paris?*......
2. Chris saved **Mark**. ......................
3. Clare likes **John**. ......................
4. Jenny likes **fish**. ......................
5. **Jim** shouted at Pam. ......................
6. Jane saw **Kitty**. ......................
7. He wrote **a book**. ......................
8. **Susan** likes James. ......................
9. Steven had dinner with **Mary**. ......................
10. **Jackie** loves Michael. ......................
11. **James** hit Trevor. ......................
12. Tom went out with **June**. ......................
13. Terry drove **an old car**. ......................
14. **Steve** hates Janet. ......................
15. Walter stole **a wallet**. ......................
16. Colin met **Pam**. ......................

**342** Write questions to which the bold type words are the answers.

Somebody stole **a frozen chicken**. It was stolen from **Astra Supermarket**. This happened **yesterday**. A **man** did it. He was wearing **a large hat**. He **fainted** when he was walking home. He was taken to **hospital**. When he got there the doctors found **the chicken**. It was **under his hat**. He had fainted **from the cold**. **The police** came to the hospital. They took him to **the police station**.

1. ...*What did somebody steal*............ ?
2. ......................................... ?
3. ......................................... ?
4. ......................................... ?
5. ......................................... ?
6. ......................................... ?
7. ......................................... ?
8. ......................................... ?
9. ......................................... ?
10. ........................................ ?
11. ........................................ ?
12. ........................................ ?

### Indirect Questions

- **Indirect questions** are used when we ask for information politely. They are introduced with **Do you know...?, Can/Could you tell me ...?, Have you any idea ...? + question word/ if** or **whether**. **Do you know where** Peter is? **Could you tell me how much** these trousers cost? **Have you any idea what time** Sue will be back? **Do you know if/whether** she's coming to the party?
- The **word order** of Indirect questions is the same as in **statements** (subject + verb). *Can you tell me **where you bought** it? (not: ~~Can you tell me where did you buy it?~~) Can you tell me **what time it is**? (not: ~~Can you tell me what time is it?~~)*
- The auxiliary verb **do** is not used in Indirect questions : *How long **does** the journey take?* ➡ *Do you know **how long the journey takes**? What time **did** he leave?* ➡ *Can you tell me **what time he left**?*

160

## 15. Questions and Short Answers

**343** Turn the following into Indirect questions.

1. Who wrote this book? Can ......*you tell me who wrote this book?*..........
2. Where's the post office? Do ..................................................
3. How much is a ticket for the football match? Have ..................................................
4. Did it rain last week? Do ..................................................
5. What's the date today? Could ..................................................
6. Why is the train late? Could ..................................................
7. Are the buses on strike tomorrow? Have ..................................................
8. Did he leave his last job? Could ..................................................
9. How can he afford such an expensive car? Have ..................................................

### Question Tags

- Question tags are short questions which we add at the end of a statement. We use them to ask for confirmation of, or agreement with, our statement. *It's hot today,* **isn't it**?
- Question tags are formed with an auxiliary verb and an appropriate pronoun. They take the same auxiliary verb as in the statement if there is one, otherwise they take **do/does** (Present Simple) or **did** (Past Simple). *She* **was** *at home,* **wasn't she**? *He* **left** *late,* **didn't he**?
- A positive statement is followed by a negative question tag, whereas a negative statement is followed by a positive question tag. *She plays tennis well,* **doesn't she**? *He hasn't come yet,* **has he**? *He's always late,* **isn't he**? *She is never late,* **is she**?
- Everyone/someone/anyone/no one form their question tags with an auxiliary verb + they. *Somebody should help her,* **shouldn't they**?
- Question tags can be said with a rising intonation (when we are not sure and we expect an answer) or a falling intonation (when we don't expect an answer).
  *He works in a bank,* **doesn't he?** (not sure)    *He looks horrible,* **doesn't he?** (sure)

### Study the following question tags.

| | | |
|---|---|---|
| 1. "I am" | "aren't I?" | I am older than you, **aren't I**? |
| 2. "I used to" | "didn't I?" | They used to work here, **didn't they**? |
| 3. Imperative | "will you/won't you/ can you/could you?" | Please help me, **will you/won't you/ can you/could you**? |
| 4. "Let's" | "shall we?" | Let's play tennis, **shall we**? |
| 5. "Let me/him" etc | "will/won't you?" | Let him buy it, **will you/won't you**? |
| 6. "Don't" | "will you?" | Don't do that again, **will you**? |
| 7. "I have" (= possess) | "haven't I?" | She has your book, **hasn't she**? |
| 8. "I have" (used idiomatically) | "don't I?" | She had an operation yesterday, **didn't she**? |
| 9. "There is/are" | "isn't/aren't there?" | There are some seats left, **aren't there**? |
| 10. "This/That is" | "isn't it?" | That pen is Mary's, **isn't it**? |

**344** Belinda's mum is angry with Belinda. Fill in the question tags.

You know why I'm angry, 1) ...*don't you*...?
It's because I haven't cleaned my room, 2) .................. ?
You didn't say you'd clean it, 3) .................. ? And you're late, 4) .................. ?
Well, I missed my bus, 5) .................. ?
You're not very responsible, 6) .......... ?
Let's talk about it tomorrow, 7) .................. ?

# 15. Questions and Short Answers

**345** Add the question tags then read them with a rising or falling intonation.

| sure | not sure | | |
|---|---|---|---|
| ✓ | | 1. She's late today, ...*isn't she*... | ? |
| | ✓ | 2. He's an actor, .................... | ? |
| | ✓ | 3. You stayed in last night, .................... | ? |
| | ✓ | 4. You don't enjoy opera, .................... | ? |
| ✓ | | 5. I'm a bit clumsy, .................... | ? |
| | ✓ | 6. You know where the supermarket is, .................... | ? |
| | ✓ | 7. Let's go for a walk, .................... | ? |
| ✓ | | 8. The boys went out with you, .................... | ? |
| ✓ | | 9. Paul should apologise, .................... | ? |
| ✓ | | 10. You will help me, .................... | ? |
| | ✓ | 11. Everyone remembers her, .................... | ? |
| ✓ | | 12. This is your wife, .................... | ? |
| | ✓ | 13. Let me go out, .................... | ? |
| ✓ | | 14. He won't tell anyone, .................... | ? |
| ✓ | | 15. There's a later flight, .................... | ? |

## Oral Activity 32

The students in teams look at the picture and make statements with question tags. Each correct sentence gets 1 point. The team with the most points is the winner.

Mary   Mark   Pam   Tim          the bride's parents

Team A S1: Mark says to Mary, "Let's dance, shall we?"
Team B S1: Mary doesn't want to dance, does she?
Team A S2: Mark will be disappointed, won't he?
Team B S2: Mary has got blonde hair, hasn't she? etc

## Short Answers

**Short answers** are used to avoid repetition of the question asked before. Positive short answers are formed with **Yes + personal pronoun + auxiliary verb** (do, can, will, have, may etc). *Will she call us? Yes, she will.* Negative short answers are formed with **No + personal pronoun + auxiliary verb** (in negative). *Did he give you anything?* **No, he didn't.**

**346** Complete the dialogue using short answers.

A: Have you seen Peter's new play?
B: 1) Yes, ...*I have*.... . I saw it last week.
A: Did you like it?
B: 2) No, .................... . I was really disappointed.
A: Was the acting all right?
B: 3) Yes, ...................., but the dialogue was boring.
A: Are you going to tell Peter what you thought?
B: 4) No, .................... . I don't want to offend him.
A: Did you go alone?
B: 5) No, .................... . Lou and Pam came with me.
A: Had they seen Peter's other play?

B: 6) Yes, .................... .
A: Were they bored as well?
B: 7) No, .................... . They found it interesting.
A: I'd like to see it. Can you get me a ticket?
B: 8) Yes, .................... . Do you want more than one?
A: 9) No, .................... . I prefer seeing plays alone.
B: Fine. Will you be at home tomorrow evening?
A: 10) Yes, ...................., after 7 o'clock.
B: Okay. I'll bring you the ticket then.

## 15. Questions and Short Answers

### So-Not

**So** and **not** can be used after: think, hope, expect, suppose, I'm afraid, guess, it seems, say, tell sb, it appears, believe or imagine in short answers.

| | |
|---|---|
| I think so – I don't think so/I think not | It seems so – It doesn't seem so/It seems not |
| I hope so – I hope not | He said so – He didn't say so |
| I expect so – I don't expect so/I expect not | He told me so – He didn't tell me so |
| I suppose so – I don't suppose so/I suppose not | I guess so – I guess not |
| I'm afraid so – I'm afraid not | I believe so – I don't believe so/I believe not |
| It appears so – It doesn't appear so/It appears not | I imagine so – I don't imagine so/I imagine not |

Will he come? **I think so.**    Can you do the crossword? **I'm afraid not.**

**347** Fill in the blanks with phrases using the verbs given and so or not.

1. A: Did you pass the exam? (hope)
   B: Well, ..*I hope so*..... . I studied very hard.
2. A: Is the bank open? (think)
   B: ........................... . It's 6 o'clock.
3. A: Can you lend me £10? (afraid)
   B: ........................... . I don't have any money.
4. A: Shall we watch TV? (guess)
   B: ........................... . There's nothing else to do.
5. A: Are they twins? (imagine)
   B: ........................... . They look alike.
6. A: Is John at work? (suppose)
   B: ........................... . He's not at home.
7. A: How do you know he moved house? (tell me)
   B: ........................... when I spoke to him yesterday.
8. A: Is Sarah upset about something? (say)
   B: ........................... , but she does look unhappy.
9. A: Is it going to rain? (appear)
   B: ........................... . It's very cloudy.
10. A: Will he come to the party? (seem)
    B: ........................... . He's too busy.
11. A: Is Irene going to lose her job? (believe)
    B: ........................... . She'll find another one, though.
12. A: Is everyone coming? (expect)
    B: ........................... . We were all told to come.

### So-Neither/Nor-But

| | |
|---|---|
| **So** + auxiliary verb + personal pronoun or noun (agreement with a positive sentence) | She lives in Venice. **So do I.** (I live in Venice too.) Tim saw that film. **So did Ann.** (Ann saw it too.) |
| **Neither/Nor** + auxiliary verb + personal pronoun or noun (agreement with a negative sentence) | He doesn't enjoy horror films. **Neither/Nor do I.** (I don't enjoy horror films either.) not: ~~So don't I.~~ |
| **But** + noun/pronoun + positive auxiliary verb (positive addition to negative statement) | Ann hasn't got a car, **but I have.** Sue doesn't play tennis well, **but Bill does.** |
| **But** + noun/pronoun + negative auxiliary verb (negative addition to positive statement) | Jim drives carefully, **but his brother doesn't.** She works hard, **but I don't.** |

**348** Look at the table and write sentences as in the example:

| | Eve | Jo | Bill | Sue |
|---|---|---|---|---|
| live in London | ✔ | | ✔ | |
| speak Italian | | ✔ | ✔ | |
| drive a car | | ✔ | | ✔ |
| play the violin | ✔ | | | ✔ |

1. Eve lives in London. ...*So does Bill, but Jo and Sue don't*... .
2. Jo doesn't play the violin. ........................... .
3. Eve can't speak Italian. ........................... .
4. Eve can't drive a car. ........................... .
5. Jo speaks Italian. ........................... .
6. Sue doesn't live in London. ........................... .
7. Eve can play the violin. ........................... .
8. Jo drives a car. ........................... .

# 15. Questions and Short Answers

| Asking for permission / Making requests | Giving permission / Answering requests |
|---|---|
| **Can I / Could I** stay here? <br> **May I / Might I** use your car? | Yes, you can. / Yes, of course (you can). / No, you can't. <br> Yes, you may. / Yes, of course (you may). / No, you may not. / I'd rather you didn't. / I'm afraid not. etc |

| Making suggestions / invitations | Answering suggestions / invitations |
|---|---|
| **Will you / Would you / Would you like to** have dinner with me? <br> **Shall we** have dinner together? | I'd like to. / I'd love to. / Yes, all right. / I'm afraid I can't. / I'd love to but I can't. / I'm sorry I can't. |

| Making offers | Answering offers |
|---|---|
| **Shall I / we, Can I / we, Would you like me to do** the washing-up? | Yes, please. / No, thank you. / No, thanks. |

**349) Answer the questions.**

1. A: Shall I help you with the washing-up?
   B: ..*No, thank you*... . I'll do it myself.
2. A: Can I help you with your homework?
   B: ........................, I'm finding it very difficult.
3. A: Would you like to go fishing with me?
   B: ........................ . I've made other plans.
4. A: Could I borrow some money from you?
   B: ........................ . I'm broke.
5. A: Shall I telephone the doctor?
   B: ........................, the pain's getting worse.
6. A: May I use your book for a minute?
   B: ........................, but don't write in it.
7. A: Would you like me to make you a cup of tea?
   B: ........................, I only drink coffee.
8. A: Shall we go to see the new film?
   B: ........................ . I'm visiting my parents.
9. A: Shall I buy you a cola?
   B: ........................ . I'm thirsty.
10. A: Would you like to come out with me?
    B: Yes, ........................ .

**350) Write questions and short answers.**

1. ...*Would you like*... some coffee? ...*Yes, please*......
2. "........................ have some eggs please?" "........................"
3. "........................ have the jam please?" "........................"
4. "........................ pass me the butter please?" "........................"
5. "........................ me to pass you the bread?" "........................ I've had enough."
6. "........................ help me in the garden after breakfast?" "........................ I am late for work."
7. "........................ go to the cinema tonight?" "........................ but I have to work late."

**351) Add question tags and short answers to the statements below.**

1. "You're not afraid of flying, ........*are you*........?" "Yes, ........*I am*........."
2. "You haven't been abroad before, ........................?" "Yes, ........................."
3. "You went to Paris by train last year, ........................?" "Yes, ........................."
4. "You prefer travelling by car, ........................?" "Yes, ........................."
5. "You don't really want to go to New York, ........................?" "No, ........................."
6. "You're going to stay in New York for a while, ........................?" "No, ........................."
7. "You're staying in the same hotel as last year, ........................?" "Yes, ........................."

## 15. Questions and Short Answers

**352** Write the questions the interviewer asked Rosie Down.

I: 1) ..*How do you feel now that you've won an Oscar?*..
R: I feel wonderful.
I: 2) ............................................ in 1973?
R: No, I started acting in 1983.
I: 3) ............................................
R: Yes, I've made a lot of money from acting.
I: 4) ............................................
R: I'm not telling you how much I earn.
I: 5) ............................................ Hollywood?
R: I found life in Hollywood very exciting.
I: 6) ............................................ your new film?
R: I'm going to make my new film very soon.
I: 7) ............................................
R: Samantha Moore stars with me in it.
I: 8) ............................................
R: I'm making my new film in South America.
I: 9) ............................................
R: I chose the cinema rather than the theatre because it pays more money.

**353** Fill in the blanks with responses using *so* or *neither*.

D: Hi, I'm Dave. I arrived yesterday.
S: 1) ...*So did I*............ . The university looks like a nice place. I like it very much.
D: 2) .................... . I don't know many people here though.
S: 3) .................... . Actually, I haven't spoken to many people.
D: 4) .................... . What are you studying? I'm going to study History.
S: 5) .................... ! I loved it at school.
D: 6) .................... . I wouldn't like to teach it, though.
S: 7) .................... . I want to be an archaeologist.
D: 8) .................... . I think it's a fascinating subject.
S: 9) .................... . I can't imagine spending three years studying Computer Science.
D: 10) .................... . We seem to agree about everything, don't we?

### Oral Activity 33

The students in teams read the following text then ask questions and answer them in turn.

**There is a fish pond in Radcliffe Park. Fishing is not allowed there. Two students were arrested last week and charged with stealing fish. They entered the park at 2 o'clock in the morning, carrying nets. They caught two Japanese fish worth over £100 each. A policeman stopped them as they were walking home. He was suspicious because he saw fish tails sticking out of the students' shirts. The students, both aged 20, were fined £70 each.**

Team A S1: What is there in Radcliffe Park?
Team B S1: A fish pond.

Team B S2: Who was arrested?
Team A S2: Two students. etc

**354** Use the prepositions in brackets and write questions to match the statements.

1. Jim is very angry. Who ............*is he angry with*............................................? (with)
2. Tina is annoyed. What ............................................................? (about)
3. Shirley got engaged. Who ............................................................? (to)
4. Bob is furious. What ............................................................? (about)
5. A prisoner escaped last night. Where ............................................................? (from)
6. The children are laughing. What ............................................................? (at)
7. I think you should apologise. What ............................................................? (for)
8. My parrot died last week. What ............................................................? (of)

# 15. Questions and Short Answers

9. He's just taken a photograph. Who .................................................................................? (of)
10. I forgot to remind you. What .........................................................................................? (about)

## Tense Review

**355** Put the verbs in brackets into the correct form.

1. Martha usually ......... *visits* ......... (visit) her grandfather every weekend.
2. His eyes are hurting because he ........................... (forget) to put on his sunglasses.
3. I'm exhausted; I think I ........................... (go) to bed.
4. It was kind of you ........................... (invite) me to dinner.
5. She's really looking forward to ........................... (meet) you.
6. I've been looking for Sue for hours, but I ........................... (not/be able to) find her yet.
7. When I was in Africa, I ........................... (bite) by a poisonous spider.
8. If you ........................... (remember) to bring your cheque book, you would have been able to pay for your meal.
9. She ........................... (play) that computer game since 7 o'clock this morning!
10. I ........................... (talk) to my mother on the phone when I heard the scream.
11. Do you think you ........................... (finish) that book by tomorrow?
12. Tom suggested ........................... (go) for a picnic, but I didn't feel like it.
13. He allowed me ........................... (borrow) his motorbike.
14. She had to cycle to work while her car ........................... (repair).
15. Your father will be disappointed with you if you ........................... (not/pass) the test.

| Phrasal Verbs 13 | |
|---|---|
| **turn sb down** : | refuse an offer |
| **turn sth down** : | reduce the volume, heat, noise etc |
| **turn on** : | switch on (lights, radio etc) (opp: turn off) |
| **turn to sb** : | go to sb for help |
| **turn up** : | 1) (of an opportunity) arise  2) arrive |
| **turn sth up** : | increase the volume |
| **turn sth out** : | produce sth |

**356** Fill in the correct preposition or adverb.

1. I wish you'd turn the radio ...*down*...; it's too loud!
2. That factory turns ................. 150 typewriters a day.
3. We offered them £260,000 for the house, but they turned us ................. .
4. You can always turn ................. me if you're in trouble.
5. John said he was coming at 6.00, but he didn't turn ................. until 8.00.
6. If you've finished, please turn the light ................. .
7. I can't hear the TV. Could you turn it ................. ?
8. It was getting dark so I turned ................. the lights.
9. When a better job turned ................. , he decided to accept it.

 **357** Look at Appendix 1 and fill in the correct preposition.

1. He explained his plans to us ...*in*... detail.
2. Call the fire brigade! The house is ................. fire!
3. This office is ......... a mess! We need to tidy it up.
4. He dislikes using credit cards, so he always pays ................. cash.
5. I've been ................. touch ......... the manager about the problem.
6. Do you believe ................. ghosts?
7. Colin congratulated me ................. winning the competition.
8. What's the difference ......... butter and margarine?
9. I'll discuss this matter ................. my lawyer.
10. The post office is shut because the workers are ................. strike.
11. ................. my opinion, that was an excellent film.
12. My parents took me ................. a tour of Italy.
13. Mr Jones can't speak to you - he's ......... the phone.
14. She loves the countryside because she was brought up ................. a farm.
15. She'll never forgive you ................. lying to her.
16. Tom is really fed up ................. his job.
17. The robber was sentenced ..... two years in prison.
18. Why are you so anxious? There's nothing to worry ................. .

# Revision Exercises IV

### Phrasal Verbs 14

| | |
|---|---|
| fall behind : | fail to keep up with |
| fall for : | 1) be cheated<br>2) become suddenly attracted to |
| fall in with : | agree |
| fall on : | attack eagerly |
| fall out (with) : | quarrel |

**358** Fill in the correct preposition or adverb.

1. Because I've been ill and away from school, I've fallen ...*behind*... with my work.
2. He was such a handsome and interesting man that she fell ................. him at once.
3. She fell ..................... with her flatmate about whose turn it was to clean the bathroom.
4. Not having eaten for days, the dogs fell ............. the meat greedily.
5. The old couple fell ..................... the man's lies and lost £2,000.
6. After discussing it for hours, Jim eventually fell ...... .................. the idea of moving to the country.

## Revision Exercises IV

**359** Choose the correct answer.

1. I need a break. I think I'll go to the seaside ..C.. Easter.
   A) in   B) on   C) at   D) from

2. She performed brilliantly that evening, ........... ?
   A) hasn't she   B) didn't she
   C) hadn't she   D) did she

3. "Why are you upset?"
   "........ time Pete rings me he asks for money!"
   A) Every   B) Both
   C) All   D) Some

4. "Where's Judy?"
   "She won't be here ............... 8 o'clock."
   A) after   B) until
   C) on   D) by the time

5. If I ............... the job, I'll give a party.
   A) will get   B) am getting
   C) am going to get   D) get

6. "Is that Jane and Mary's house?"
   "No, ............... is the one across the road."
   A) theirs   B) hers
   C) their   D) there

7. I'm taking an umbrella. It ............... rain.
   A) must   B) may
   C) has to   D) should

8. This is ............... book I've ever read.
   A) more brilliant   B) most brilliant
   C) the most brilliant   D) the brilliant

9. I've been working ............... all day and I'm exhausted.
   A) hardly   B) the hardest
   C) harder   D) hard

10. Paul is ......... experienced he'll get the job.
    A) such   B) so
    C) much   D) too

11. "Someone's taken my cassette recorder."
    "I don't know ....... would do a thing like that."
    A) who   B) that
    C) what   D) which

12. This is the house ........... Charles Dickens died.
    A) which   B) where
    C) that   D) when

13. Is there ............... in the office?
    A) anywhere   B) anybody
    C) somewhere   D) everywhere

14. The ship's crew ......... all given two days' leave.
    A) were   B) had
    C) was   D) is

15. ............... a difficult exam that was!
    A) How   B) So
    C) What   D) Such

16. ........... he is nearly eighty, he is still very active.
    A) Despite   B) However
    C) Even   D) Although

## Revision Exercises IV

**360** Turn from Active into Passive.

At 5 o'clock on Sunday morning a strange noise woke Jim up. He looked out of the window and saw somebody driving his car away! He ran towards the stairs, and halfway down his dog tripped him up. Fortunately he didn't break anything, but by the time he got outside they had driven his car out of sight. When he went back to the house, he discovered that somebody had locked him out. As he was climbing in through the kitchen window, a policeman saw him and thought he was a burglar. The policeman arrested him and took him to the police station. They phoned his wife and told her to come. When she told them who he was, they allowed him to go home, but they never found his car!

..................................................................................
..................................................................................
..................................................................................
..................................................................................
..................................................................................
..................................................................................

**361** Turn from Direct to Reported speech using an appropriate introductory verb.

1. "How about going to the beach?" Paul said. ...*Paul suggested going to the beach.*...
2. "I'm sorry I didn't ring you yesterday," Julia said to me. ..................................
3. "That's why I didn't speak to him," she said. ..................................
4. "What a lovely meal that was!" she said. ..................................
5. "Don't forget our appointment tomorrow," he said to me. ..................................
6. "Be quiet," she said to the children. ..................................
7. "I won't do your homework for you!" Pam said to Jim. ..................................
8. "You stole the money!" he said to Julie. ..................................
9. "Yes, it might be a good plan," she said. ..................................
10. "I didn't break the window," said Bob. ..................................

**362** Rewrite the sentences in the Causative.

1. You should hire someone to clean up the garden. ...*You should have the garden cleaned up.*...
2. A famous artist has painted his portrait. ..................................
3. The hairdresser permed my hair yesterday. ..................................
4. Twelve people's houses were burnt down in the fire. ..................................
5. A well-known surgeon will operate on the footballer's leg. ..................................
6. Gary arranged for his luggage to be flown home. ..................................

**363** Fill in "the" where necessary.

1. Sean was brought up in ...*the*... Republic of Ireland, not in ...—... Scotland.
2. I've never been to ............... Tahiti but I've been to ............... Hawaiian Islands.
3. He's travelled all over ............... British Isles, ............... France and ............... Netherlands.
4. Let's go to ............... Red Rose - it's better than ............... Dick's.
5. They lived in ............... north of Canada for two years and then moved to ............... Washington D.C.
6. I'd rather do some shopping at ............... Selfridges than go to ............... Tate Gallery.
7. Does ............... Lloyds Bank have a branch near ............... Edinburgh Castle?
8. I prefer reading ............... Time Magazine to reading ............... Washington Post.
9. All ............... injured were taken to ............... hospital by ............... helicopter.
10. Does ............... Great Wall of ............... China run through ............... middle of ............... country?
11. ............... Ambassador is going to ............... Philippines on ............... Royal Yacht.
12. ............... Yangtze Kiang river flows through ............... China to ............... East China Sea.

# Revision Exercises IV

## 364 Correct the mistakes.

Lorna Steel possibly is the most talented actress the world has ever seen. Her excited career covers sixty years. She usually made at least five films the year. She will probably be remembered like the most popular actress of our time. Deeply the film industry was shocked by the time she announced her retirement last year. She had been going to the studios by a huge black luxurious limousine every day in the past 40 years. No one quite could believe her presence would any longer brighten up our cinema screens. She now is retired and lives in an extremely large beach house near the Mexican border. Those days she makes very rarely any public appearances. She is beautiful still, but now prefers to devote her valuable time in looking through old, stray dogs.

## 365 Fill in the correct preposition or adverb.

1. The police are ..*on*.. the trail of the robbers.
2. They're friends, although they have little ................ common.
3. The baby takes ................ his father.
4. My colleague was ill, so I stood ................ her at the office.
5. The nurses went ................ strike for higher wages.
6. John and Bill fell ................ and so they are no longer speaking.
7. Half the students turned ................ late for class.
8. The boss is away ................ business.
9. The lawyer investigated the case ................ detail.
10. Mercedes Benz has just taken ................ British Leyland.
11. Sandra arrived ................ Tokyo last week.
12. I've put on a lot of weight. I'd better go ................ a diet.
13. She flew ................ Paris ................ Milan because it would have taken too long to go ................ road.
14. There's a beautiful house ................ sale just outside the city.
15. When I was in the Navy, I used to spend a lot of time ................ sea.
16. You have to learn to stand ................ people who are nasty to you.
17. We set ................ on our journey at 6 o'clock in the morning.
18. Sam fell ................ with his studies and failed his exams.
19. If you want to get fit, why don't you take ................ a sport.
20. I wanted to join the police force but they turned me ................ because I was too short.

## 366 Put the verbs in brackets into the correct tense.

When Francis Lee was a boy, he 1) ......*wanted*.... (want) to be an astronaut. He 2) ........................ (watch) TV one day in 1969 when he 3) ................ (see) Neil Armstrong walk on the moon. Since then he 4) ........................................ (always/dream) of doing the same. Every night when there is a full moon, he 5) ........................ (stare) up at it for hours and 6) ................ (imagine) himself walking around on it. At the moment, however, he 7) ........................ (work) as a night-watchman at a meat factory. He 8) ........................ (do) the same job since he left school fifteen years ago, but he still hopes that one day his dream 9) ........................ (come) true. He 10) ........................ (hear) that in the 21st century they 11) ................ (sell) tickets to fly to the moon. For this reason he 12) ........................ (save) half of his wages every month for the past two years.

## Revision Exercises IV

**367** Put the verbs in brackets into the correct tense.

Tom Wilson 1) ..is.. (be) an explorer. He 2) .............. (be) to nearly every country in the world, but the most exciting time he 3) ........................ (ever/have) was when he 4) ............ (go) to the Congo jungle. A magazine 5) .............. (ask) him to retrace the route of a famous explorer who 6) .............. (disappear) in the 1920's. As he 7) .............. (follow) a small river, he got separated from his guides. He 8) .............. (go on) alone, hoping he 9) ........................ (find) them, but instead he 10) ...................... (encounter) a group of natives. He 11) ................... (stay) with them for several days and 12) ........................ (find out) that a very old woman 13) ........................ (actually/meet) the famous explorer. She 14) .............. (know) how he 15) .................. (die). Tom 16) .............. (become) very friendly with the natives and now he 17) ................ (plan) to go back and see them again. He is sure they 18) ................ (welcome) him back.

**368** Fill in a suitable word or phrase.

1. It was the first time she ......*had been to/had seen/had read*.............. a play by Shakespeare.
2. She ..................................... him several times on the phone before she met him.
3. When she discovered that her car ................................. she phoned the police.
4. The windows are dirty - we need to have ............................................. .
5. By the end of the year she ............................................. here for five years.
6. Every day he ............................................................................. by train.
7. She was tired because ............................................................. hard all day.
8. He ................................................... a bicycle for his birthday by his parents.
9. I don't ........................................................ pass the test - he's hardly studied.
10. The news ................................ until 6 o'clock, so we have time to go to the shop.
11. At least four people ............................................................... the accident.
12. If you leave now, you ..................................................................... the bus.
13. I ........................................................ what to do if you hadn't told me.
14. James ....................................... a friend's house until he finds a flat.
15. To join the club, ................................................................ a £5 membership fee.
16. I ............................... the project until 8 o'clock - can you wait till then?
17. Your hair ............................................................. - it's much too long.
18. We .......................... serviced because the engine was making a strange noise.
19. It ................................................. we woke up, so we decided to stay at home.

**369** Put the verbs in brackets into an infinitive or -ing form.

Last month, my friend John invited me 1) ..*to stay*... (stay) with him in his house in the country. I decided 2) .............. (go) by car because I hate 3) .............. (travel) on public transport. As I was driving through the country, a sheep ran into the road and I had to swerve to avoid 4) ............ (hit) it. I was driving too fast 5) .............. (control) the car and I crashed into a tree. It was no good 6) .............. (try) to start the car again so I got out and tried 7) .............. (get) a lift from someone. Eventually a lorry stopped 8) .............. (pick) me up, but the driver was very boring and never stopped 9) .............. (talk) about his problems. Two hours later I arrived in the village near my friend's house, very happy 10) .............. (walk) the rest of the way. But I'm sorry 11) ............ (say) I got lost and didn't arrive at my friend's house until 3 o'clock in the morning. I really regret not 12) .............. (take) the train.

# Summary of Tenses

**370** Rephrase the following sentences as in the example:

1. It wasn't necessary for us to have booked a table. We needn't ... *have booked a table.*
2. It's possible that she has already told him. She ..................
3. It was wrong of her to punish that child. She ..................
4. Let's go for a pizza. Shall ..................
5. It isn't possible for me to see you this evening. I ..................
6. She is obliged to be at work at 6 o'clock every morning. She ..................
7. It would be a good idea for you to write to her. You ..................
8. I'm sure he isn't Spanish. He ..................
9. I'm certain that he stole my pen. He ..................
10. My friends all like rock music. All ..................
11. Pam has a dog. Don has a dog too. They ..................
12. There isn't anything in the fridge. There is ..................
13. He has never played polo before. It's the first time ..................
14. When did they move to Rome? How long is it ..................
15. Could you help me with this? Do you mind ..................
16. They will send you the contract tomorrow. You will have ..................
17. I wish I hadn't said that to her. If ..................
18. The weather is too bad for camping. The weather is not ..................
19. I advise you to see a lawyer. You ..................
20. That's the office I work in. That's the office ..................
21. I'm sure he didn't say that. He ..................
22. If you don't invite them, they won't come. Unless ..................

## SUMMARY OF TENSES

### Present Simple

| Affirmative | Negative |
|---|---|
| I work | I **don't** work |
| You work | You don't work |
| He work**s** | He **doesn't** work etc |
| She work**s** | **Interrogative** |
| It work**s** | Do I work? |
| We work | Do you work? |
| You work | **Does** he work? etc |
| They work | |

### Present Continuous

| Affirmative | Negative |
|---|---|
| I **am** work**ing** | I'm not working |
| You are working | You aren't working |
| He is working | He isn't working etc |
| She is working | **Interrogative** |
| It is working | Am I working? |
| We are working | Are you working? |
| You are working | Is he working? etc |
| They are working | |

### Future Simple

| Affirmative | Negative |
|---|---|
| I **will** work | I **won't** work |
| You will work | You won't work |
| He will work | He won't work etc |
| She will work | **Interrogative** |
| It will work | **Shall/Will** I work? |
| We will work | Will you work? |
| You will work | Will he work? etc |
| They will work | |

### Future Continuous

| Affirmative | Negative |
|---|---|
| I **will be** work**ing** | I **won't** be working |
| You will be working | You won't be working |
| He will be working | He won't be working etc |
| She will be working | **Interrogative** |
| It will be working | Will I be working? |
| We will be working | Will you be working? |
| You will be working | Will he be working? etc |
| They will be working | |

### Future Perfect

| Affirmative | Negative |
|---|---|
| I **will have** work**ed** | I **won't** have worked |
| You will have worked | You won't have worked |
| He will have worked | He won't have worked etc |
| She will have worked | **Interrogative** |
| It will have worked | Will I have worked? |
| We will have worked | Will you have worked? |
| You will have worked | Will he have worked? etc |
| They will have worked | |

## Summary of Tenses

### Future Perfect Continuous

**Affirmative**
I will have been working
You will have been working
He will have been working
She will have been working
It will have been working
We will have been working
You will have been working
They will have been working

**Negative**
I won't have been working
You won't have been working
He won't have been working etc

**Interrogative**
Will I have been working?
Will you have been working?
Will he have been working? etc

---

### Present Perfect

**Affirmative**
I have worked
You have worked
He has worked
She has worked
It has worked
We have worked
You have worked
They have worked

**Negative**
I haven't worked
You haven't worked
He hasn't worked etc

**Interrogative**
Have I worked?
Have you worked?
Has he worked? etc

---

### Present Perfect Continuous

**Affirmative**
I have been working
You have been working
He has been working
She has been working
It has been working
We have been working
You have been working
They have been working

**Negative**
I haven't been working
You haven't been working
He hasn't been working etc

**Interrogative**
Have I been working?
Have you been working?
Has he been working? etc

---

### Past Simple

**Affirmative**
I worked
You worked
He worked
She worked
It worked
We worked
You worked
They worked

**Negative**
I didn't work
You didn't work
He didn't work etc

**Interrogative**
Did I work?
Did you work?
Did he work? etc

---

### Past Continuous

**Affirmative**
I was working
You were working
He was working
She was working
It was working
We were working
You were working
They were working

**Negative**
I wasn't working
You weren't working
He wasn't working etc

**Interrogative**
Was I working?
Were you working?
Was he working? etc

---

### Past Perfect

**Affirmative**
I had worked
You had worked
He had worked
She had worked
It had worked
We had worked
You had worked
They had worked

**Negative**
I hadn't worked
You hadn't worked
He hadn't worked etc

**Interrogative**
Had I worked?
Had you worked?
Had he worked? etc

---

### Past Perfect Continuous

**Affirmative**
I had been working
You had been working
He had been working
She had been working
It had been working
We had been working
You had been working
They had been working

**Negative**
I hadn't been working
You hadn't been working
He hadn't been working etc

**Interrogative**
Had I been working?
Had you been working?
Had he been working? etc

# Irregular Verbs

| Infinitive | Past | Past Participle | Infinitive | Past | Past Participle |
|---|---|---|---|---|---|
| be | was | been | lie | lay | lain |
| bear | bore | born(e) | light | lit | lit |
| beat | beat | beaten | lose | lost | lost |
| become | became | become | make | made | made |
| begin | began | begun | mean | meant | meant |
| bite | bit | bitten | meet | met | met |
| blow | blew | blown | pay | paid | paid |
| break | broke | broken | put | put | put |
| bring | brought | brought | read | read | read |
| build | built | built | ride | rode | ridden |
| burn | burnt | burnt | ring | rang | rung |
| burst | burst | burst | rise | rose | risen |
| buy | bought | bought | run | ran | run |
| can | could | (been able to) | say | said | said |
| catch | caught | caught | see | saw | seen |
| choose | chose | chosen | seek | sought | sought |
| come | came | come | sell | sold | sold |
| cost | cost | cost | send | sent | sent |
| cut | cut | cut | set | set | set |
| deal | dealt | dealt | sew | sewed | sewn |
| dig | dug | dug | shake | shook | shaken |
| do | did | done | shine | shone | shone |
| draw | drew | drawn | shoot | shot | shot |
| dream | dreamt (dreamed) | dreamt (dreamed) | show | showed | shown |
| drink | drank | drunk | shut | shut | shut |
| drive | drove | driven | sing | sang | sung |
| eat | ate | eaten | sit | sat | sat |
| fall | fell | fallen | sleep | slept | slept |
| feed | fed | fed | smell | smelt (smelled) | smelt (smelled) |
| feel | felt | felt | speak | spoke | spoken |
| fight | fought | fought | spell | spelt (spelled) | spelt (spelled) |
| find | found | found | spend | spent | spent |
| fly | flew | flown | spill | spilt (spilled) | spilt (spilled) |
| forbid | forbad(e) | forbidden | split | split | split |
| forget | forgot | forgotten | spoil | spoilt (spoiled) | spoilt (spoiled) |
| forgive | forgave | forgiven | spread | spread | spread |
| freeze | froze | frozen | spring | sprang | sprung |
| get | got | got | stand | stood | stood |
| give | gave | given | steal | stole | stolen |
| go | went | gone | stick | stuck | stuck |
| grow | grew | grown | sting | stung | stung |
| hang | hung | hung | strike | struck | struck |
| have | had | had | swear | swore | sworn |
| hear | heard | heard | sweep | swept | swept |
| hide | hid | hidden | swim | swam | swum |
| hit | hit | hit | take | took | taken |
| hold | held | held | teach | taught | taught |
| hurt | hurt | hurt | tear | tore | torn |
| keep | kept | kept | tell | told | told |
| know | knew | known | think | thought | thought |
| lay | laid | laid | throw | threw | thrown |
| lead | led | led | understand | understood | understood |
| learn | learnt (learned) | learnt (learned) | wake | woke | woken |
| leave | left | left | wear | wore | worn |
| lend | lent | lent | win | won | won |
| let | let | let | write | wrote | written |

# Appendix 1: Verbs, Adjectives, Nouns with Prepositions

**A**
- accuse sb of (doing) sth (v)
- advantage of (n)
- afraid of sb/sth (adj)
- aim at sb/sth (v)
- amazed at/by sth (adj)
- angry at/with sb for doing sth (adj)
- annoyed about sth (adj)
- annoyed with sb for doing sth (adj)
- apologise to sb for sth (v)
- apply to sb for sth (v)
- arrive at (a small place) (but: arrive home) (v)
- arrive in (a big place) (v)
- ashamed of sb/sth (adj)
- ask sb for sth (but: ask sb a question) (v)
- associate with sb (v)
- astonished at/by sth (adj)
- attitude towards/to (n)
- aware of sth (adj)

**B**
- bad at sth (adj)
- believe in sth (v)
- belong to sb (v)
- blame sb/sth for sth (v)
- (put the) blame on sb/sth (n)
- bored with sth (adj)
- borrow sth from sb (v)
- brilliant at sth (adj)
- bump into sb/sth (v)

**C**
- (in)capable of sth (adj)
- care about sb/sth (v)
- care for sb/sth (= look after/like) (v)
- take care of (exp)
- cause of (n)
- change sth for sth (= exchange one thing for another) (v)
- charge sb for (= ask sb to pay) (v)
- charge sb with (= accuse sb of) (v)
- cheque for (n)
- clever at sth (but: clever of sb to do sth) (adj)
- come from (v)
- compare sth/sb to sth/sb else (= show the likeness between) (v)
- compare sth/sb with sth/sb else (= examine people or things to find similarities and differences) (v)
- (nothing can) compare with sth (= nothing is as good as) (v)
- complain to sb about sth/sb (v)
- concentrate on sth (v)
- congratulate sb on (doing) sth (v)
- (in) connection with sb/sth
- a connection between two things) (n)
- conscious of sth (adj)
- consist of sth (v)
- contact with sb/sth (but: contact between two things) (n)
- convert into (v)
- crash into sb/sth (v)
- crowded with (people etc) (adj)
- cruel to sb (adj)
- cruelty towards/to (n)
- take care of sb/sth (= look after) (v)

**D**
- damage to (n)
- deal with (v)
- decide on (v)
- delighted with sth (adj)
- demand for (n)
- depend on sb/sth (v)
- die of (an illness) (v)
- difference between two things (n)
- different from/to sb/sth (adj)
- disadvantage of (n)
- disappointed with sth (adj)
- discuss sth with sb (v)
- dissatisfied with (adj)
- divide sth into (v)
- dream about sb/sth (v)
- dream of being/doing sth (= imagine) (v)
- drive into sb/sth (v)

**E**
- engaged to sb (adj)
- escape from (v)
- excellent at sth (adj)
- excited about (adj)
- explain sth to sb (v)

**F**
- fail in (v)
- famous for sth (adj)
- fed up with sth (adj)
- fond of sb/sth (adj)
- forgive sb for sth (v)
- (un)friendly to sb (adj)
- frightened of sb/sth (adj)
- full of sth (adj)
- furious about sth (adj)
- furious with sb for doing sth (adj)

**G**
- generous to sb (but: generous of sb to do sth) (adj)
- good at sth (adj)
- good to sb (but: good of sb to do sth) (adj)
- grateful to sb for sth (adj)

**H**
- happen to sb/sth (v)
- head for (v)
- hear about (= be told) (v)
- hear from (= receive a letter) (v)
- hear of sb/sth (= know that sb/sth exists) (v)
- hope for sth (v)
- (no) hope of (n)
- hopeless at sth (adj)

**I**
- impatient with (adj)
- impressed by/with sb/sth (adj)
- increase in (n)
- insist on (v)
- interested in sth (adj)
- introduce sb to sb (v)
- invitation to (n)
- invite sb to (v)

## Appendix 1: Verbs, Adjectives, Nouns with Prepositions

| | | | |
|---|---|---|---|
| **J** | jealous of sb/sth (adj) | | |
| **K** | keen on sth (adj) | (be) kind to sb (but: kind of sb to do sth) (adj) | know of/about (v) |
| **L** | laugh at sb (= mock)/sth (v)<br>listen to sb/sth (v) | live on (money/food) (v) | look at sb/sth (v) |
| **M** | (be) married to sb (v) | mean to sb<br>(but: mean of sb to do sth) (adj) | |
| **N** | need for (n) | (be) nice to sb (but: nice of sb to do sth) (adj) | |
| **O** | occur to sb (v) | | |
| **P** | patient with (adj)<br>pay sb for sth (v)<br>photograph of (n)<br>picture of (n)<br>(un)pleasant to sb (adj)<br>(un)pleasant of sb to do sth (adj) | pleased with sth (adj)<br>point at sb/sth (v)<br>(im)polite to sb (but: (im)polite of sb to do sth) (adj)<br>prefer sb/sth to sb/sth else (v) | prevent from (v)<br>proof of (n)<br>protect sb/sth from/against sb/sth (v)<br>proud of sb/sth (adj)<br>provide sb with sth (v) |
| **R** | react to (v)<br>reaction to (n)<br>reason for (n)<br>regard sb/sth as (v)<br>relationship with sb/sth (but: a relationship between two things) (n) | rely on sb/sth (v)<br>remind sb about sth (= tell sb not to forget) (v)<br>remind sb of sb/sth (= cause to remember) (v)<br>reply to (n)/(v) | responsible for sth (adj)<br>rise in (n)<br>rude to sb (but: rude of sb to do sth) (adj) |
| **S** | (feel) sorry for sb (adj)<br>satisfied with sth (adj)<br>save from (v)<br>scared of sb/sth (adj)<br>search for sb/sth (v)<br>sensible of sb to do sth (adj)<br>sentence sb to (prison) (v)<br>shocked at/by sth (adj) | short of sth (adj)<br>shout at sb (= reprimand) (v)<br>shout to sb (so as to be heard) (v)<br>similar to sth (adj)<br>smile at sb/sth (v)<br>solution to (n)<br>sorry about sth (adj)<br>sorry for doing sth (adj) | (be/feel) sorry for sb (v)<br>speak to sb about (v)<br>spend money on (v)<br>spend time in/on doing sth (v)<br>stupid of sb to do sth (adj)<br>suffer from (an illness) (v)<br>surprised at/by sth (adj)<br>suspicious of sb/sth (adj) |
| **T** | talk to sb about sth (v)<br>tease sb about sth (v)<br>terrified of sb/sth (adj)<br>think about sb/sth (=consider) (v) | think of sb (= remember sb) (v)<br>think of sth = (have an idea) (v)<br>tired of sth (adj)<br>throw at (in order to hit) (v) | throw to (in order to be caught) (v)<br>translate into (v) |
| **U** | unconscious of (adj)<br>unpleasant to (adj) | unreasonable of sb to do sth (adj)<br>upset about sth (adj) | use of sth (n) |
| **V** | valid for (adj) | | |
| **W** | wait for sb/sth (v)<br>warn sb of/against sb/sth (v) | waste of (n)<br>weak in (adj) | worried about (adj)<br>write to sb (v) |

Note: **discuss** sth (v), **enter** a place (= go into a place) (v), **reach** a place (v)

# Appendix 2: Spelling Rules / Pronunciation

## Prepositions with Word Phrases

| | |
|---|---|
| **At** | **at** home/work/school/university/a station/an airport/the seaside, a hotel, **at** sea (= on a voyage), **at the beginning** (= when sth started), **at the end** (= when sth finished), **at the latest** |
| **By** | **by** accident, **by** car/train/plane/boat/ship/bus/bicycle, **by** chance, **by** cheque, **by** mistake, **by** road/rail/air/sea/tube |
| **For** | (have sth) **for** breakfast/lunch/dinner, (go) **for** a drink, (go) **for** a walk/swim, **for sale** (= sold by the owner) |
| **In** | **in** a mess, **in** bed, **in** case, **in** cash (also pay cash), **in** common, **in** connection with, **in** contact with, **in** detail, **in** hospital, (fall/be) **in** love (with), **in** my opinion, **in** one's car, **in** prison, **in the beginning** (= originally), **in the end** (= finally), **in time** (= soon enough), **in touch** |
| **On** | **on** a diet, **on** a farm, **on** a ship, **on** a trip/excursion/cruise/tour/expedition, **on** holiday (but: go somewhere for a holiday), **on** business, **on** fire, **on** my bicycle, **on** my own, **on** strike, **on** the bus, **on** the phone, **on** the radio/TV, **on** the trail, **on time** (= exactly), **on foot**, **on sale** (= sold at a reduced price) |

## Appendix 2: Spelling Rules

| | |
|---|---|
| **1. -(e)s ending**<br>a. words ending in -s, -ss, -ch, -x, -sh, -z, -o * add -es | bus - bus**es**, miss - miss**es**, church - church**es**, box - box**es**, wash - wash**es**, fizz - fizz**es**, do - do**es** |
| b. nouns ending in vowel + o, double o, short forms/ musical instruments/proper nouns ending in -o add -s | radio - radio**s**, zoo - zoo**s**, photo - photo**s**, piano - piano**s**, Eskimo - Eskimo**s** |
| **2. -f/-fe ending**<br>nouns ending in -f/-fe drop -f/-fe and add -ves | thie**f** - thie**ves**, wi**fe** - wi**ves** (but : chiefs, roofs etc) |
| **3. -y ending**<br>a. words ending in consonant + y drop -y and add -ies, -ied, -ier, -iest, -ily | stud**y** - stud**ies** - stud**ied**, prett**y** - prett**ier** - prett**iest**, prett**y** - prett**ily** |
| b. words ending in consonant + y add -ing | stud**y** - study**ing** |
| c. words ending in vowel + y add -s, -ed, -ing, -er, -est | play - play**s** - play**ed**, play**ing** (but: paid, said, laid) grey - grey**er** - grey**est** |
| **4. -ie ending**<br>words ending in -ie change -ie to -y before -ing | d**ie** - d**ying** |
| **5. dropping -e**<br>a. words ending in -e drop -e and add -ing, -ed, -er, -est | liv**e** - liv**ing** - liv**ed** (but: be - being), lat**e** - lat**er** - lat**est** |
| b. adjectives ending in -e add -ly to form their adverbs | mer**e** - mer**ely**, rar**e** - rar**ely** (but : true - truly) |
| c. adjectives ending in -le change -le to -ly to form their adverbs | horrib**le** - horrib**ly** (but : whole - wholly) |
| d. verbs ending in -ee add -ing | see - see**ing** |

## Pronunciation

**Pronunciation of -(e)s ending** (noun plurals and the 3rd person singular of verbs in the Present Simple)

| /s/ after /f/,/t/,/p/,/k/ | /ɪz/ after /z/, /dʒ/, /tʃ/, /s/, /ʃ/ | /z/ after /b/, /g/, /m/, /d/, /l/, /n/, /v/ or any vowel sound |
|---|---|---|
| laughs, repeats, stops, knocks | chooses, manages, catches, kisses, bushes | robs, digs, screams, adds, falls, runs, dives, waters, plays |

**Pronunciation of -ed ending**

| /ɪd/ after /t/,/d/ | /t/ after /k/, /tʃ/, /f/, /s/, /ʃ/, /p/ | /d/ after /b/, /dʒ/, /m/, /v/, /g/, /l/, /n/, /z/, vowel + /r/ |
|---|---|---|
| posted, ended | worked, touched, laughed, danced, washed, hoped | rubbed, damaged, screamed, loved, hugged, filled, listened, seized, stirred |

# Pre-Test 1 (Units 1 - 4)

## A  Choose the correct item.

1. Jim was cooking dinner in the kitchen while Jo .............. the dog.
   - A is feeding
   - B has been feeding
   - C was feeding
   - D had been feeding

2. It was nice of Tom .............. me these flowers!
   - A to buy
   - B buy
   - C buying
   - D is buying

3. I .............. dinner with James tomorrow.
   - A am having
   - B have been having
   - C have had
   - D had had

4. It was lovely .............. Ted again!
   - A see
   - B to see
   - C saw
   - D to seeing

5. You can't leave the table until you .............. your dinner.
   - A finished
   - B finish
   - C are going to finish
   - D will finish

6. Dave .............. in Manchester for several years before he decided to move to London.
   - A will have worked
   - B has worked
   - C had been working
   - D works

7. Don't phone me tonight. I ............ for my French exam.
   - A will study
   - B will be studying
   - C study
   - D will have studied

8. Those cakes .............. delicious! Can I have one more?
   - A tastes
   - B are tasting
   - C tasting
   - D taste

9. They .............. Paris twice this month.
   - A have gone in
   - B had gone to
   - C have been to
   - D had been in

10. Harry was sunburnt because he .............. on the beach for six hours.
    - A had been sitting
    - B has sat
    - C has been sitting
    - D is sitting

11. Mary is a good girl. She .............. her mother with the housework.
    - A is helping
    - B always helps
    - C had always helped
    - D always helped

12. Pete .............. as a waiter for ten years, then he opened his own restaurant.
    - A works
    - B has worked
    - C worked
    - D has been working

13. John .............. questions! He's so boring.
    - A has always been asking
    - B always asked
    - C is always asking
    - D asks always

14. Sarah ........... a bike to work, but now she drives.
    - A used to ride
    - B would ride
    - C had ridden
    - D used to riding

15. It .............. . The garden's all white.
    - A has been snowing
    - B snows
    - C had snowed
    - D was snowing

16. He's a famous singer. He .......... a lot of concerts so far.
    - A is giving
    - B has given
    - C gives
    - D had been giving

17. By the time we arrive home, she .......... cooking.
    - A will have finished
    - B is going to finish
    - C will have been finishing
    - D will finish

18. Before he knew what was happening, the car .............. into a tree.
    - A has crashed
    - B was crashing
    - C has been crashing
    - D had crashed

19. While Paul ........... the carpets the doorbell rang.
    - A hoovers
    - B was hoovering
    - C has been hoovering
    - D had hoovered

20. Stephen won't phone us until he ..... some news.
    - A had
    - B is having
    - C will have
    - D has

177

# Pre-Test 1 (Units 1 - 4)

**21** ....... to the bank later? If you are, can you deposit this cheque for me?
  A  Will you be going   C  Do you go
  B  Have you gone       D  Did you go

**22** The guards wouldn't let anyone ............. the building.
  A  leave      C  to leave
  B  leaving    D  to leaving

**23** It's no use ............. her — she won't tell you.
  A  to ask     C  asking
  B  ask        D  to asking

**24** The students were made ............. their essays.
  A  rewriting   C  rewrite
  B  to rewrite  D  to rewriting

### B Fill in the correct preposition or adverb.

**25** When our car broke .................., we had to walk to the nearest garage.
**26** Somebody tried to break .................. our house, but our neighbour saw him so he ran away.
**27** The prisoner got .................. while the guard was sleeping.
**28** I should have got .................. the bus. That was my stop!
**29** Thomas speaks French and English well because he was brought ............... by English parents in France.
**30** Denise was determined to carry .................. the task she'd been given, no matter how long it took.
**31** "Ms Laurence is on another line. Could you hold .................. for a moment, please?"
**32** He's a very cheerful person who gets .................. with everyone he meets.
**33** Schools break .................. for Easter a week before Easter Sunday.
**34** I tried to ring him, but I couldn't get .................. .

### C Fill in the correct preposition.

**35** You always blame me .................. things that are not my fault.
**36** Mr Nichols accused his secretary .................. stealing money from the till.
**37** Jim is very fond .................. his parents.
**38** The man was arrested and charged .................. murder.
**39** That comedian is famous .................. his brilliant impersonations of politicians.
**40** I am depending .................. you to help me organise the wedding reception.
**41** I wasn't aware .................. the fact that he had retired.
**42** We congratulated Shirley .................. the success of her first book.
**43** Many people believe .................. life after death.
**44** What's the difference .................. a chimpanzee and a monkey?

### D Fill in yet, already, for, since or how long.

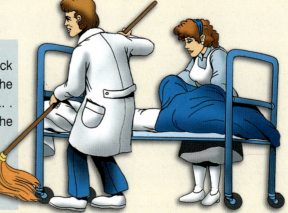

Paul starts work at the hospital very early. It's only 8 o'clock and he has **45)** .................. made the beds and cleaned the floors, but he hasn't cleaned the staff room **46)** ................ . He has worked here **47)** .......................... ten years, and he quite likes it. He knows exactly **48)** ....................... each job takes and **49)** .......................... last month, when they hired a helper for him, the job has been better than ever.

# Pre-Test 1 (Units 1 - 4)

**E** Complete the sentences using an appropriate word or phrase.

50 Don't forget ..................................................................... John and Ann an invitation to dinner.
51 They ..................................................................... the house for a long time. It's very dirty!
52 I must ..................................................................... my book at school. I can't find it anywhere.
53 Jane admitted ..................................................................... me lies.
54 Gill is upset because she ..................................................................... her job.
55 Tom must ..................................................................... in the garden. He looks tired.
56 Paul suggested ..................................................................... to the theatre, but I'd already seen the play.
57 I ..................................................................... to the supermarket for a week. There's nothing in the fridge.
58 Tom refused ..................................................................... his sister with her homework.
59 She's moving to Madrid this summer because they ..................................................................... a job in the embassy there.

**F** Rephrase the following sentences.

60 The last time he went to Rome was two years ago.
   He hasn't .....................................................................
61 When was the last time you went to a museum?
   How long ago .....................................................................
62 He was too ill to go to work.
   He wasn't .....................................................................
63 The film was boring.
   I was .....................................................................
64 It's a long time since he heard from his brother.
   He hasn't .....................................................................
65 I've never ridden a camel before.
   It's the .....................................................................
66 Walking for miles is tiring.
   It's .....................................................................
67 It's too hard for them to climb up the mountain.
   It isn't .....................................................................
68 This is the silliest story I've ever read.
   I've never .....................................................................
69 Could you lend me your gloves, please?
   Would you mind .....................................................................

**G** Put the verbs in brackets into the correct tense.

When Sam and Laura **70)** .................. **(move)** into their new house last month everything was in a mess. Someone **71)** ........................ **(break)** several windows and the roof **72)** ................................ **(leak)**, leaving stains on the ceiling. Now they **73)** ........................ **(work)** on the house in their free time. They **74)** ................................ ........................ **(already/ repair)** the roof, and they **75)** ................... ........................ **(paint)** the rooms, though they **76)** ....................... ........................ **(not/finish)** yet. When they have enough money, they **77)** ........................ **(buy)** some new furniture. They hope they **78)** ........................ **(finish)** by summer so they **79)** ........................ **(be able)** to invite some friends for a visit.

179

# Pre-Test 1 (Units 1 - 4)

   **Put the verbs in brackets into the correct tense.**

Last week police 80) ........................... (arrest) Paul Dawson. They 81) .......................... (suspect) him of being the leader of a gang of robbers who 82) ...................... (steal) art treasures from museums and homes since last January. Prior to his arrest, Dawson 83) ................................ (spend) two years in prison for theft. They 84) ..................................... (release) him only 16 months ago. The police 85) ............................................. (try) to find the gang's hideout for months. They feel sure they 86) ................................ (arrest) the rest of the gang by the end of the month. This 87) ........................ (be) the biggest art theft operation to be uncovered since 1974 when police 88) ..................................... (catch) a gang which 89) ................................. (steal) over a million pounds worth of paintings from galleries all over the country.

   **Put the verbs in brackets into the infinitive or -ing form.**

Paul and Simon decided 90) ......................... (go) on an expedition in the mountains. They considered 91) .................... (tour) Scotland, but then decided to go to Wales instead. Although Paul is accustomed to 92) ..................... (walk) in the hills and mountains, Simon had never been before. He normally objected to 93) .................... (do) anything dangerous, but he agreed 94) ......................... (take) part this time. They remembered 95) .................... (take) a lot of equipment with them to avoid 96) ...................................... (get) into trouble but, unfortunately, during their trip there was a terrible storm. On their journey a professional mountaineer spotted them and they were made 97) ................................ (stop) their expedition temporarily. They agreed that it was no use 98) ............................ (try) to continue in such bad weather conditions so they ended up 99) ................................ (set up) camp in the mountains. Eventually the storm stopped and although they were cold, wet and starving, they couldn't resist 100) ............................ (finish) their climb. They thought it would make a good story to tell their friends.

# Pre-Test 2 (Units 5 - 8)

**A** Choose the correct item.

1. You .............. buy any sugar. There's plenty.
   A should  C mustn't
   B needn't  D couldn't

2. He claimed .............. the Loch Ness monster when he was in Scotland.
   A to see  C seeing
   B to be seen  D to have seen

3. Tina suggested .............. to the concert.
   A going  C to have gone
   B have gone  D to go

4. There's .............. a lot of food! I can't eat it all.
   A very  B such  C so  D how

5. .............. hot day it is today!
   A How  B What  C What a  D Such

6. .............. strong your brother is!
   A What  B How  C What a  D What an

7. .............. working very hard, he didn't get a promotion.
   A Despite the fact  C Although
   B In spite of  D Whereas

8. Peter, .............. father is a politician, works for *The Times*.
   A who  B who's  C which  D whose

9. .............. ridiculous question!
   A What a  B How  C Such  D What

10. He put on his raincoat .............. he wouldn't get wet.
    A in case  C so as not
    B so that  D just as

11. The film was .............. long that I fell asleep before the end.
    A such  B very  C enough  D so

12. He wrote her phone number down .............. forget it.
    A in case  C so as not to
    B so that  D not to

13. You .............. forget Monday's meeting.
    A needn't  B haven't  C mustn't  D might not

14. I've no idea when she .............. here.
    A will get  C would get
    B has got  D had got

15. .............. nice of you to remember my birthday!
    A How  B That  C What  D What a

16. I'm sorry .............. you didn't get the job.
    A saying  C to say
    B to saying  D for saying

17. I brought her some medicine in case she .............. any.
    A wouldn't have  C hadn't
    B didn't have  D doesn't have

18. He regrets .............. everyone his plans.
    A telling  B to tell  C told  D will tell

19. There's the man .............. stole Ted's bicycle!
    A who  B whom  C what  D which

20. You .............. made such a big cake. There's lots left over.
    A mustn't have  C didn't need
    B may have  D needn't have

 **B** Fill in the correct preposition or adverb.

21. She was advised to give .................. eating chocolate.
22. Can you give me my book .................. when you've finished it?
23. They went .................. talking for hours.
24. My neighbour looks .................. my cat when I'm away.
25. When the police surrounded the criminal he gave himself .................. .

# Pre-Test 2 (Units 5 - 8)

26  There aren't enough biscuits to go .................. . Would anyone like some cake instead?
27  They called .................. the meeting because the chairperson couldn't come.
28  Can you help me look .................. my keys? I can't find them.
29  Although they had had a fight at the start of the evening, they had made ............. before the night was over.
30  Can you make .................. what it says on that sign over there?

## C  Fill in the correct preposition.

31  Sue loves squash, but she isn't keen .................. tennis.
32  You can't rely .................. Jim to get here on time.
33  Mrs Jacobs was very proud .................. her daughter for winning the race.
34  Our boss insists .................. everyone being very smartly dressed.
35  He wore sunglasses to protect his eyes .................. the sun.
36  I'm hopeless .................. bowling, but I like billiards.
37  That man reminds me .................. my uncle Norman.
38  Bad weather prevented the ship .................. departing.
39  All the boys were jealous .................. Tim because he had such a nice bicycle.
40  Paul's family mean a lot .................. him. He couldn't live without them.

## D  Rephrase the following sentences using the words in bold type.

41  How clever that boy is!                                              **WHAT**
    ...................................................................................................................
42  Could you help me with the dishes please?                            **MIND**
    ...................................................................................................................
43  She put on a coat so that she wouldn't be cold.                      **SO AS NOT TO**
    ...................................................................................................................
44  This cola is quite cheap, but it's good.                             **ALTHOUGH**
    ...................................................................................................................
45  Is this the first time you've been to a ballet?                      **EVER**
    ...................................................................................................................
46  People say she's the best athlete in the country.                    **SAID**
    ...................................................................................................................
47  He's too young to be driving a car.                                  **ENOUGH**
    ...................................................................................................................
48  She locked the windows because she didn't want to be burgled.        **SO THAT**
    ...................................................................................................................
49  People believe there's life on other planets.                        **BELIEVED**
    ...................................................................................................................
50  If you don't have his number, you can't phone him.                   **UNLESS**
    ...................................................................................................................

## E  Rephrase the following using the appropriate modal verb.

51  I advise you to go to hospital.
    ...................................................................................................................
52  I don't think he's rich. He always wears shabby clothes.
    ...................................................................................................................

# Pre-Test 2 (Units 5 - 8)

**53** It wasn't necessary for him to leave so soon.

..................................................................................................................................................

**54** You are not allowed to smoke here.

..................................................................................................................................................

**55** It's possible the letter will arrive tomorrow.

..................................................................................................................................................

**F** Put the verbs in brackets into the correct tense.

Ken: What 56) .................................. (you/do) this evening, Carol?
Carol: I 57) ............................... (go) to the circus. Do you want to come?
Ken: No, thanks. I 58) ..................................... (already/be) there.
Carol: Did you enjoy it?
Ken: I 59) ................................. (enjoy) it more if my little sister hadn't been with me.
Carol: Why?
Ken: The circus was good, but while the clowns 60) ................................ (perform), I suddenly realised that my sister 61) ........................................ (disappear).
Carol: Oh, dear!
Ken: I couldn't find her anywhere. I 62) .................................... (look) for her for about ten minutes when a policeman came up to me and told me they had found a little girl.
Carol: Where was she?
Ken: When they found her, she 63) .............................. (try) to climb into the lion's cage!
Carol: Oh, no! I'm sure you 64) .......................................... (be) happy when she starts school.
Ken: Yes I will. She 65) .................................. (start) next year, and I can't wait.

**G** Put the verbs in brackets into the correct tense.

Steve: What are you doing this August, Mary?
Mary: It looks like I 66) ......................................... (stay) here and working. What about you?
Steve: Well, hopefully I 67) ..................................... (finish) all my work by then, so I 68) ............................ (be able) to go to Holland for a while.
Mary: Great! I 69) ................................ (go) there last year. 70) .......................... (you/ever/be) to Holland before?
Steve: Well, we drove through it while we 71) ................................. (travel) to Germany but we 72) ............................................ (not/stop).
Mary: I didn't know you 73) ....................................... (be) to Germany.
Steve: Yes. My cousin 74) .......................................... (live) there for the last six years and I visit him every summer.
Mary: What does he do?
Steve: He 75) .......................................... (work) in a café.

183

# Pre-Test 2 (Units 5 - 8)

**H** **Rewrite the following passage in the passive.**

**76)** Heavy rains burst Whitton Dam two days ago. **77)** Floodwater has damaged many houses. **78)** People are still evacuating flooded houses. **79)** The council will repair the dam when the rains stop. **80)** They have to take new measures to prevent more flooding.

76 .................................................................................................................................................................
77 .................................................................................................................................................................
78 .................................................................................................................................................................
79 .................................................................................................................................................................
80 .................................................................................................................................................................

**I** **Rewrite the following passage in the passive.**

**81)** The doctors have treated three young children for burns at the city hospital. **82)** Firemen rescued the boys from their burning house yesterday. **83)** The fire started when one of the boys dropped a match into the litter bin. **84)** They are transferring the children to a special burns unit today. **85)** They will keep the children there for at least two weeks.

81 .................................................................................................................................................................
82 .................................................................................................................................................................
83 .................................................................................................................................................................
84 .................................................................................................................................................................
85 .................................................................................................................................................................

**J** **Use Sam's thoughts to write wishes and conditionals as in the example:**

- I didn't bring my compass with me. I got lost.
- 86 It is snowing. I feel cold.
- 87 There's no wood. I can't light a fire.
- 88 I didn't bring my radio with me. I can't listen to the weather forecast.
- 89 There's no telephone here. I can't call for help.
- 90 I wasn't told how difficult this would be. I decided to try it.

*e.g. I wish I had brought my compass with me. If I had brought my compass with me, I wouldn't have got lost.*

86 .................................................................................................................................................................
87 .................................................................................................................................................................
88 .................................................................................................................................................................
89 .................................................................................................................................................................
90 .................................................................................................................................................................

# Pre-Test 2 (Units 5 - 8)

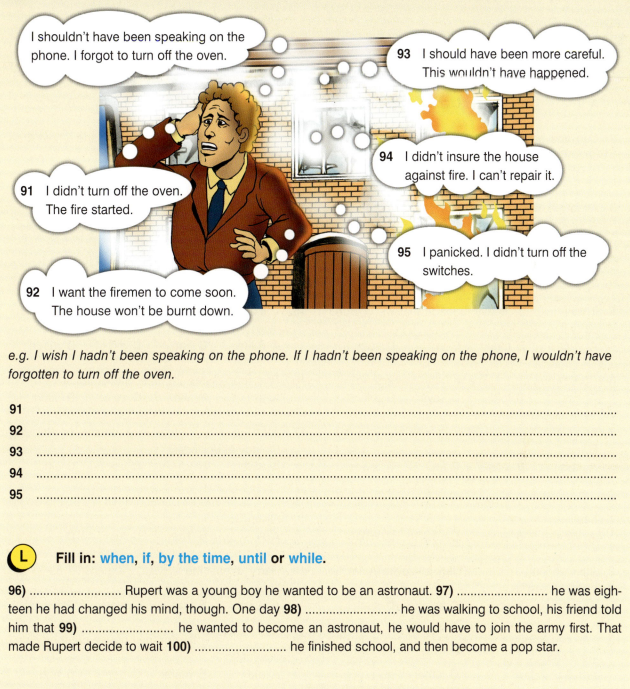

**K** Use John's thoughts to write wishes and conditionals as in the example:

e.g. I wish I hadn't been speaking on the phone. If I hadn't been speaking on the phone, I wouldn't have forgotten to turn off the oven.

91 ................................................................................................................................................
92 ................................................................................................................................................
93 ................................................................................................................................................
94 ................................................................................................................................................
95 ................................................................................................................................................

**L** Fill in: **when, if, by the time, until** or **while**.

96) ........................ Rupert was a young boy he wanted to be an astronaut. 97) ........................ he was eighteen he had changed his mind, though. One day 98) ........................ he was walking to school, his friend told him that 99) ........................ he wanted to become an astronaut, he would have to join the army first. That made Rupert decide to wait 100) ........................ he finished school, and then become a pop star.

185

# Pre-Test 3 (Units 9 - 12)

**A** Choose the correct item.

1. The prisoner was taken to .............. court to stand trial.
   A a    B —    C the    D one

2. Can you pass me the book .............. is on the chair?
   A what    B who    C whose    D which

3. Although he is my neighbour, I .......... know him.
   A nearly    B hard    C bare    D hardly

4. She is the .............. talented pianist I've ever met.
   A most    B much    C more    D very

5. It was .............. heavy luggage that we couldn't carry it.
   A such    B much    C so    D such a

6. Could you .............. me who this belongs to?
   A say    B told    C says    D tell

7. Ann's got .............. patience with children than Eve.
   A less    B least    C few    D fewer

8. .............. is the fastest of the two; a cheetah or a tiger?
   A Where    B Who    C Which    D What

9. After working .............. a clerk for seven years, he became a writer.
   A like    B so    C as    D such

10. You can borrow my ................... camera for the weekend.
    A father-in-law    C father-in-law's
    B father's-in-law    D fathers-in-law

11. Your money ................. safer in the bank than at home.
    A are    B were    C be    D is

12. She had .............. free time after she retired than previously.
    A much    B more    C most    D many

13. He wants .............. sugar in his tea.
    A a few    B few    C little    D a little

14. She .............. she wanted to be a musician.
    A told    B said    C say    D tells

15. The athlete .............. his best and came first in the race.
    A done    B had    C did    D made

16. This soup tastes .............. chicken soup.
    A as    B like    C so    D such

17. John, .............. father is a doctor, is studying Biology at university.
    A which    B whom    C whose    D who

18. .............. Panama Canal divides North and South America.
    A A    B The    C An    D —

19. Harry chose the .............. expensive tie in the shop.
    A least    B less    C fewer    D fewest

20. I .............. an offer for their house but they didn't accept it.
    A did    B made    C done    D had

 **B** Fill in the correct preposition or adverb.

21. If you come to London, I can put you .................. for as long as you want.
22. I hadn't seen my friend Lenny for weeks, then I ran .................. him in the post office.
23. The letters B. A. stand .................. British Airways.
24. Tom set .................. a painting and decorating business with his uncle.
25. We will have to put .................. the party as David is ill.

# Pre-Test 3 (Units 9 - 12)

26 If they set .................. at 9 o'clock, they should be here soon.
27 Always put .................. your campfire before leaving the campsite.
28 "Mrs Jones can speak to you now. I'll put you .................. ."
29 When I ran .................. of coffee, my neighbour gave me some.
30 The receptionist was ill so Jane stood .................. for her.

## C  Fill in the correct preposition.

31 Kevin complained to the manager because he wasn't satisfied .................. his pay rise.
32 Don't shout .................. me! It wasn't my fault.
33 Don travels by train because he's terrified .................. flying.
34 "What did you think .................. the film?" "I liked it."
35 I've been suffering .................. toothache for days.
36 I took the wrong suitcase from the airport .................. mistake.
37 She was so worried .................. the test that she couldn't sleep.
38 Leaving all the lights on is a waste .................. electricity.
39 It was only .................. chance that I found my lost earring.
40 The detective was suspicious .................. the man with the dark glasses in the corner.

## D  Rephrase the following sentences using the words in bold.

41 Jo's motorbike is faster than Roy's.  **AS**
.................................................................................................................................
42 This is the first time we have been to the circus.  **BEFORE**
.................................................................................................................................
43 It wasn't necessary for us to hurry.  **NEEDN'T**
.................................................................................................................................
44 Pluto is the furthest planet of all from the Earth.  **OTHER**
.................................................................................................................................
45 Sandra has more friends than Carol.  **DOESN'T**
.................................................................................................................................

## E  Rephrase the following using an appropriate word or phrase.

46 The bank robbers ............................................................................ by the police yesterday.
47 This dress is ............................................................................ that I can't buy it.
48 If we ............................................................................ a map, we wouldn't have got lost.
49 ............................................................................ it was July, the weather was bad.
50 They bought plenty of food ............................................................................ run out.

## F  Put the verbs in brackets into the correct form.

Brian wishes he **51)** ........................ **(be)** fitter. When he ran in a race last week, he **52)** ................................
**(beat)** by everyone. If he **53)** ................................ **(run)** faster, he would have been able to win the race. He
**54)** ................................ **(advise)** many times by his doctor to stop smoking because if he doesn't, he
**55)** ................................ **(make)** himself very ill.

187

# Pre-Test 3 (Units 9 - 12)

**G** Put the verbs in brackets into the correct form.

Paula wishes she **56)** ................................. (**live**) in France. She **57)** ................................. (**invite**) to Paris last month, but she didn't go. If she **58)** ................................. (**have**) more money, she would have gone. She **59)** ................................. (**offer**) a job in Marseilles which starts next year. If she takes the job, she **60)** ................................. (**have to**) leave England for several years.

**H** Turn the following sentences into the causative form.

61  Wendy asked an artist to paint her husband's portrait.
................................................................................................................................
62  A tailor makes Mr Bond's suits.
................................................................................................................................
63  A gardener is cutting my grass at the moment.
................................................................................................................................
64  We might ask the engineer to check the machine.
................................................................................................................................
65  He will ask the plumber to repair the broken pipes.
................................................................................................................................
66  He asked the nurse to examine his leg.
................................................................................................................................
67  We will ask the secretary to type the letters.
................................................................................................................................
68  The cleaner is tidying my room at the moment.
................................................................................................................................
69  He may ask someone to fix the fence.
................................................................................................................................
70  My wife always makes breakfast for me.
................................................................................................................................

**I** Rewrite the sentences putting the words in the correct order.

71  home / they / arrived / late / last night
................................................................................................................................
72  look at that / sheepdog / beautiful / black
................................................................................................................................
73  we / old / bought / a(n) / wooden / valuable / table
................................................................................................................................
74  the children / all day / in the fields / happily / played
................................................................................................................................
75  I'll / large / have / a / chocolate / sponge / fresh / cake / please
................................................................................................................................
76  he / fast / rather / drives / often
................................................................................................................................
77  usually / first / the / person / she / is / to arrive
................................................................................................................................
78  probably / to work / won't / go / I / tomorrow
................................................................................................................................

188

# Pre-Test 3 (Units 9 - 12)

79 he / deeply / is / sleeping / still / very
................................................................................

80 I / meet / this afternoon / you / will / definitely
................................................................................

81 of / bought / a(n) / bottle / he / expensive / French / perfume / her
................................................................................

82 sometimes / on Friday / late / at the office / I / stay
................................................................................

83 listen to / rock / loud / that / terrible / music
................................................................................

84 all afternoon / worked / in the barn / the farmer / hard
................................................................................

85 I bought / a(n) / red / sports / cheap / old / car
................................................................................

86 talk / must / you / slowly / more
................................................................................

87 at 5 o'clock / afternoon / set out / they / yesterday
................................................................................

88 she is / for school / on time / always / almost
................................................................................

89 at 10:30 / always / phones / he / me / at night
................................................................................

90 the film / entertaining / thought / he / quite / was
................................................................................

**J** Rewrite the following in reported speech using appropriate introductory verbs.

91 "I'm sorry that I lost your ticket," he said.
................................................................................

92 "The weather is so cold," she said. "And I haven't got a jacket."
................................................................................

93 "Let's try that new Italian restaurant," he said.
................................................................................

94 "Come with me!" the policeman said to them.
................................................................................

95 "No, I didn't read your diary," she said.
................................................................................

96 "All right, I'll post the parcel for you," she said.
................................................................................

97 "Why are you smiling?" he asked. "Because I've won £100," she said.
................................................................................

98 "It wasn't me who took your glasses," he said.
................................................................................

99 "I'm sorry for making you angry yesterday," he said.
................................................................................

100 "Why don't we go camping this summer?" he said.
................................................................................

# Pre-Test 4 (Units 13 - 15)

## A  Choose the correct item.

1 We're going to drive to the country .............. Easter Sunday.
   A at    B in    C on    D over

2 I'm sorry, but I haven't got .............. advice to give you.
   A some    B any    C no    D an

3 Derrick got scratches on .............. hand playing with the cat.
   A each    B all    C every    D both

4 "Who is speaking?" ".............. Linda Thomas."
   A This is    C That is
   B Those are    D These are

5 Ann had to use my ruler because she had left .............. at home.
   A her    B she    C herself    D hers

6 When Diane won the lottery, she bought .............. a new car.
   A herself    B her    C hers    D she

7 Not .............. people know what the capital of Bolivia is.
   A much    B a lot of    C more    D many

8 Jane and Marie played well in the concert because .............. of them had practised a lot.
   A either    B neither    C both    D all

9 Neil spent the .............. night revising for his exam.
   A all    B most    C whole    D much

10 He's done the shopping, but he hasn't started cooking .............. .
   A still    B yet    C already    D now

11 She started work here five years .............. .
   A before    B then    C ago    D from

12 Has she .............. left? I wanted to speak to her.
   A already    B still    C yet    D again

13 The two cyclists blamed .............. for causing the accident.
   A itself    C each other
   B them    D himself

14 He got to the office just .............. for the meeting.
   A for time    C on time
   B in time    D the time

15 You must finish this .............. 7 o'clock or it will be too late to send it.
   A until    B on    C by    D during

16 .............. the beginning of the film there is a huge storm.
   A In    B To    C On    D At

17 Susan wasn't sure about taking the job, but .............. the end she accepted it.
   A at    B to    C on    D in

18 Cathy doesn't like thrillers. .............. .
   A So do I    C Nor do I
   B So don't I    D Nor I do

19 My .............. garden is really beautiful.
   A sister's-in-law    C sister-in-laws
   B sister-in-law's    D sisters-in-law

20 You must finish this project .............. the next two hours.
   A within    B until    C during    D for

21 I've got several pens — you can use one of .............. .
   A my    B me    C myself    D mine

22 There is .............. chance of him getting his money back. She's spent it all.
   A little    B a little    C few    D a few

23 Betty taught English .............. she was in Turkey.
   A during    B while    C at    D until

24 I can lend you .............. money if you need it.
   A some    B much    C any    D little

# Pre-Test 4 (Units 13 - 15)

25. Could you ............. how much this costs?
 A say me  B say to me  C tell me  D tell

26. There were so ............. different flavours of ice-cream that I couldn't choose.
 A much  B many  C a lot of  D lots of

27. ............. of the students failed the test. They all passed.
 A None  B Some  C Not every  D All

28. "Which of the two records did you buy?"
 "I didn't buy ............. of them."
 A any  B both  C one  D either

29. "Which books are yours?"
 "The ............. on the table."
 A one  B those  C ones  D mine

30. I'd prefer to watch a film rather than ............. to music.
 A to listen  B listen  C listening  D listened

31. I love going to the mountains ............. the winter.
 A in  B at  C on  D from

32. A lawnmower is a machine ............. is used for cutting grass.
 A what  B which  C who  D whom

33. He used to be a footballer, ............. ?
 A he did  C would he
 B didn't he  D isn't he

34. The faster you are, the ........ work you'll get done.
 A most  B much  C more  D many

35. His uncle is a guard at ......... prison outside town.
 A the  B some  C an  D —

36. Sheila works ............. an accountant in a large company.
 A like  B as  C so  D to

37. If he ............. the music so loud, the neighbours wouldn't have called the police.
 A has played  C was playing
 B didn't play  D hadn't played

38. It was ............ good music that I couldn't stop dancing.
 A so  B such  C such a  D too

39. It took me ............. day to find the answer to your question.
 A whole  B all  C most  D the most

40. I'd like three ............. of jam, please.
 A cartons  B bottles  C slices  D jars

## B  Fill in the correct preposition or adverb.

41. Lydia takes .......................... her mother — she has the same eyes.
42. He took .......................... his jumper because it was so warm in the room.
43. She decided to take .......................... knitting as a relaxing pastime.
44. Could you turn .......................... the light? I can't see.
45. We offered him £200 for the painting, but he turned us .......................... .
46. The party started at 9:00, but most of the guests didn't turn .......................... till much later.
47. If you turn .......................... the TV we'll all be able to hear it.
48. If I don't study this weekend, I'm afraid I'll fall .......................... at school.
49. Luke fell ..................... with his brother over some money and they haven't spoken to each other since then.
50. Debbie fell .......................... Martin as soon as she met him because he was so handsome.

## C  Fill in the correct preposition.

51. This house has been ................... sale for months.
52. I rang him ................... accident — I was trying to ring my mother.
53. I haven't got enough cash. Can I pay ................... cheque?

191

# Pre-Test 4 (Units 13 - 15)

54 He described the plan to me .................. detail.
55 "Mr Smith is .................. the phone — he'll be with you in a minute."
56 I met Mary .................. chance while I was shopping in town.
57 I won't have any dessert — I'm .................. a diet.
58 We don't take credit cards — you must pay .................. cash.
59 The bus drivers are .................. strike. We'll have to take a taxi.
60 We've been friends for years because we have a lot .................. common.

**D   Rephrase the following sentences.**

61 She gave him a furious look.
   She looked ..................................................................................................
62 If you eat less, you'll lose more weight.
   The ........................................................................................................
63 I'm sure he took my wallet.
   He ..........................................................................................................
64 How much does the ticket cost?
   Could ......................................................................................................
65 They had never been to such an enjoyable concert.
   It ............................................................................................................

**E   Put the verbs in brackets into the correct tense.**

Dear Daria,
This 66) .................................. (probably/come) as a surprise to you, but I 67) .................................. (decide) to move to London! I 68) .................................. (think) about it for a long time, but it was only last week that I 69) .................................. (make up) my mind. I 70) .................................. (already/find) a flat to live in, and I 71) .................................. (go) tomorrow to make arrangements about moving my furniture. I was lucky to get a flat so quickly — I 72) .................................. (only/look) for a couple of days before I found it. Hopefully, I 73) .................................. (settle) in by the end of the month. I 74) .................................. (originally/ think) about staying with my sister, but her house 75) .................................. (be) so small that I changed my mind.

                                                              Love,
                                                              Melinda

**F   Complete the sentences using a suitable word or phrase.**

76 If you've finished your homework, you ............................................................ out.
77 I wish I .................................................................. my purse - now I haven't got any money.
78 By December we .................................................................. in this flat for five years.
79 In .................................. having booked in advance, the hotel didn't have a room for them.
80 Tom .................................................................................................. repaired last week.

# Pre-Test 4 (Units 13 - 15)

**G** Fill in the blanks with the correct preposition.

There are some people lying 81) .......................... the pool today. A boy is jumping 82) .......................... the water. A young girl is swimming in the pool. A man is coming 83) .......................... of the water climbing 84) .......................... the steps. There's a little dog lying 85) .......................... one of the sunbeds.

**H** Write questions to which the words in bold type are the answers.

86) The National Bank was robbed **yesterday**. 87) The robbery happened **at 10 o'clock in the morning**. 88) The robbers took **Í10,000** and ran into the street. 89) **A passer-by** called the police but the robbers escaped in Queen Street. 90) The police are looking for **two men aged about 30 with scars on their faces**.

86 ..........................................................................................................................................................
87 ..........................................................................................................................................................
88 ..........................................................................................................................................................
89 ..........................................................................................................................................................
90 ..........................................................................................................................................................

**I** Rewrite the following passage in the passive.

91) Lord Simon Slope is holding a party at his country manor. 92) Many major celebrities have always attended his parties. 93) George Blackheart will accompany Mary Fisher. 94) Everyone expects the party will be a glamorous event. 95) Lord Slope is going to give all the money he raises to charity.

91 ..........................................................................................................................................................
92 ..........................................................................................................................................................
93 ..........................................................................................................................................................
94 ..........................................................................................................................................................
95 ..........................................................................................................................................................

**J** Turn the following into reported speech using appropriate introductory verbs.

96  "What a lovely performance!" she said.
    ..........................................................................................................................................................

97  "Don't move or I'll shoot!" the robber said to the man.
    ..........................................................................................................................................................

98  "Have you done the shopping?" she said. "No, but I promise I'll do it in the afternoon," he said.
    ..........................................................................................................................................................

99  "It was you who poisoned my dog," he said to me.
    ..........................................................................................................................................................

100 "This is a nice car," he said. "How much did you pay for it?"
    ..........................................................................................................................................................

# Progress Test 1 (Units 1 - 2)

NAME: ..................................................  DATE: ..............................

CLASS: ................................................  MARK: ..............................

(Time: 30 minutes)

**A** Choose the correct item.

1  My brother .............. for a large company.
   A  is working    B  works    C  has worked

2  I .............. my wallet. I can't find it anywhere.
   A  have lost    B  have been losing
   C  am losing

3  You're late. I .............. for half an hour.
   A  am waiting    B  have waited
   C  have been waiting

4  I love this house. I .............. here all my life.
   A  am living    B  have been living
   C  have lived

5  They .............. with friends at the moment.
   A  are staying    B  have been staying
   C  stay

6  We usually .............. out on Saturday evenings.
   A  are going    B  go
   C  have been going

7  This shampoo .............. of roses.
   A  smells    B  is smelling
   C  has been smelling

8  John .............. very polite to people these days.
   A  has been    B  is being
   C  has been being

9  .............. the film?
   A  Do you enjoy    B  Have you enjoyed
   C  Are you enjoying

10  Paul .............. the bank. He hasn't come back yet.
    A  has been to    B  has gone to
    C  has been in

11  She .............. poor, but now she is rich.
    A  used to be    B  would be    C  has been

12  He .............. a new suit yesterday.
    A  was buying    B  bought    C  had bought

13  She realised that she .............. to lock the door.
    A  forgot    B  had been forgetting
    C  had forgotten

14  He .............. at five o'clock yesterday evening.
    A  worked    B  was working
    C  had been working

15  It was a lovely day, so we ........... to go for a walk.
    A  decided    B  had decided
    C  have decided

16  The plane ........... when I reached the airport.
    A  already left    B  had already left
    C  had already been leaving

17  There was no money left because we .......... it all.
    A  spent    B  had spent
    C  had been spending

18  My parents .............. in a big house in the country.
    A  used to live    B  would live    C  living

19  ............. your homework, yet?
    A  Had you done    B  Did you do
    C  Have you done

20  Where ............. your holiday last year?
    A  have you spent    B  did you spend
    C  had you spent

## Progress Test 1 (Units 1 - 2)

**B** Choose the correct item.

21  My little sister believes .............. fairies.
    A on          B of          C in

22  When he told the joke, his friends broke .............. laughter.
    A out         B into        C up

23  Claire blamed John .............. the accident.
    A on          B for         C in

24  He was accused .............. stealing the money.
    A for         B with        C of

25  She doesn't associate .............. her neighbours.
    A with        B of          C for

26  Joanne is very clever .............. telling stories.
    A in          B on          C at

27  She lost contact .............. her friends when she moved away.
    A of          B with        C about

28  The new boss brought .............. many changes in the company.
    A about       B round       C out

29  The bus was crowded .............. passengers and there was nowhere to sit.
    A of          B with        C for

30  My favourite author brought .............. a new book last month.
    A out         B up          C about

# Progress Test 2 (Units 3 - 4)

NAME: ..................................................  DATE: ..............................

CLASS: ..................................................  MARK: ..............................

(Time: 30 minutes)

### A  Choose the correct item.

1  She .............. work by six o'clock.
   A  will finish     B  will have finished
   C  is going to finish

2  Now that I've got a job, I .............. a car.
   A  will buy        B  am buying
   C  am going to buy

3  The train .............. Manchester at nine o'clock.
   A  leaves          B  is leaving      C  will leave

4  Look out! You ..............!
   A  are falling     B  are going to fall
   C  will fall

5  I promise I .............. home in time for the party.
   A  will be         B  will have been
   C  am going to be

6  By the end of the day, she .............. for ten hours.
   A  will be working    B  will have worked
   C  will have been working

7  He .............. the doctor this afternoon.
   A  is seeing       B  sees
   C  will have seen

8  I .............. James tonight, so I'll tell him the news.
   A  will see        B  will be seeing
   C  will have been seeing

9  This time next week, we .............. on the beach.
   A  will lie        B  will have been lying
   C  will be lying

10 I think I .............. some sandwiches. Do you want some?
   A  am making       B  will make
   C  am going to make

11 Remember .............. some milk. We've run out.
   A  buying          B  buy            C  to buy

12 This dress is .............. for me to wear.
   A  too short       B  short enough
   C  short too

13 Amy is a very .............. person.
   A  interest        B  interesting    C  interested

14 Paul left without .............. goodbye this morning.
   A  say             B  to say         C  saying

15 We go .............. once a week to keep fit.
   A  swim            B  swimming       C  to swim

16 I heard Mr Brown .............. on the phone.
   A  talk            B  talking        C  to talk

17 The coffee wasn't .............. for me to drink.
   A  cool enough     B  enough cool    C  cool too

18 She was very .............. by the story he told.
   A  amuse           B  amusing        C  amused

19 Martin suggested .............. to the cinema.
   A  go              B  going          C  to go

20 The horror film we watched was .............. .
   A  terrify         B  terrifying     C  terrified

196

# Progress Test 2 (Units 3 - 4)

 **Choose the correct item.**

21 "Carry .............. your work until I get back," said the teacher.
   A out    B up    C on with

22 He couldn't decide .............. what to wear to the party.
   A on    B with    C for

23 Mrs Jones couldn't deal ......... all the housework, so she hired a cleaner.
   A of    B with    C on

24 Small children depend .............. their parents for survival.
   A with    B to    C on

25 Could you hold .............., please. I'm busy at the moment.
   A up    B back    C on

26 The teacher explained the question .............. the students.
   A of    B to    C at

27 I am fed .............. taking the bus to work.
   A up with    B for    C on with

28 We got .............. the train and found our seats.
   A on    B through    C on with

29 I couldn't get .............. to the office. The line was busy.
   A away    B through    C on

30 Tom was furious .............. Sue for forgetting their anniversary.
   A with    B of    C for

197

# Progress Test 3 (Units 5 - 6)

NAME: .................................................... DATE: ...........................

CLASS: .................................................... MARK: ...........................

(Time: 30 minutes)

## A  Choose the correct item.

1  'Great Expectations' ............ by Charles Dickens.
   A  is written      B  was written
   C  has been written

2  ............ that he was a great athlete when he was young.
   A  It is said      B  He is said
   C  He was said

3  He ............ be rich. He never has any money.
   A  must           B  could           C  can't

4  Where's Mary? She ............ be here by now.
   A  could          B  might           C  ought to

5  I couldn't take my car. It ............ .
   A  was repaired   B  was being repaired
   C  has been repaired

6  ............ help you with the shopping, Dad?
   A  Will I         B  Would I         C  Shall I

7  ............ I speak to Mr Shaw, please.
   A  Might          B  May             C  Must

8  I didn't know about the meeting because I ............ .
   A  haven't been told    B  hadn't been told
   C  had been told

9  We ............ go to the theatre if you like.
   A  may            B  can             C  shall

10 The boss ............ to be retiring soon.
   A  is reported    B  is being reported
   C  is reporting

11 You ............ go home soon. It's getting late.
   A  can            B  had better      C  mustn't

12 Our new furniture ............ yet.
   A  isn't delivered  B  hasn't been delivered
   C  wasn't delivered

13 You ............ rude to your teacher.
   A  shouldn't have been   B  mustn't have been
   C  should have been

14 He ............ any bread. We already had a lot.
   A  needn't buy    B  needn't have bought
   C  didn't need to buy

15 My bag ............ yesterday.
   A  stole          B  is stolen       C  was stolen

16 I ............ stay in tonight. My mother says so.
   A  've got to     B  had to          C  need to

17 The children .................... to wait quietly for their teacher.
   A  are told       B  were told       C  was told

18 ............ you lend me some money, please?
   A  Shall          B  Could           C  Must

19 The building ............ by an earthquake.
   A  was destroyed  B  is destroyed
   C  destroyed

20 You ............ walk on the grass.
   A  should         B  can't           C  mustn't

198

# Progress Test 3 (Units 5 - 6)

 **Choose the correct item.**

21  I couldn't sleep last night. There was a party going ............. next door.
    A on          B round        C away

22  The secretary introduced me ............. my new boss.
    A for         B in           C to

23  Alice was jealous ............. her sister because she was very pretty.
    A about       B of           C for

24  This job calls ............. skill and patience.
    A for         B off          C out

25  I haven't heard ............. Peter since he moved away.
    A about       B of           C from

26  John gave ............. smoking because it was bad for his health.
    A up          B out          C off

27  Tony isn't keen ............. chocolate, but he loves crisps.
    A with        B on           C for

28  It never occured ............. her to ask her parents for help.
    A to          B of           C on

29  I gave ............. Sarah's book when I had finished reading it.
    A up          B out          C back

30  It was mean ............. him not to send you a birthday card.
    A to          B of           C for

199

# Progress Test 4 (Units 7 - 8)

NAME: ..................................................  DATE: ..........................

CLASS: ..................................................  MARK: ..........................

(Time: 30 minutes)

**A  Choose the correct item.**

1  If I had locked up my bike, it .............. have been stolen.
   A couldn't     B wouldn't     C would

2  If you .............. hungry, have a sandwich.
   A be          B were         C are

3  Mum will be angry if she .............. you doing that.
   A sees        B saw          C had seen

4  I'll phone you .............. I get to the station.
   A if          B when         C until

5  I had fallen asleep .............. he got home.
   A by the time B when         C until

6  I .............. you if I had known your number.
   A would call  B will call
   C would have called

7  I put on the heating .............. the house would be warm.
   A in order to B so that      C in case

8  I wish I .............. more for the exam.
   A have studied B had studied C will study

9  I'll take my umbrella .............. it rains.
   A so that    B in order to  C in case

10  I wish he .............. so rude to people.
    A wouldn't be B won't be   C would be

11  It was .............. interesting book that I couldn't stop reading it.
    A so          B such        C such an

12  I wish I .............. to buy a new dress for the party.
    A can afford  B could afford
    C would afford

13  .............. the bad weather, we had a wonderful holiday.
    A Despite     B Although    C Whereas

14  .............. an amazing view!
    A How         B So          C What

15  If you .............. your dinner, you can watch TV.
    A had finished B have finished
    C would finish

16  .............. you're tired, I'll make the dinner.
    A Since       B Because     C For

17  If I .............. you, I would see a doctor.
    A am          B will be     C were

18  The bag was .............. heavy that I couldn't carry it.
    A such        B so          C such a

19  .............. you wear warm clothes, you will catch a cold.
    A Unless      B If          C Providing

20  This is the car .............. I repaired last week.
    A who         B which       C where

# Progress Test 4 (Units 7 - 8)

**B) Choose the correct item.**

21 He had been looking .............. a job for months before he found one.
  A forward to    B for    C up

22 Mark did not reply .............. Sue's letter.
  A for    B at    C to

23 It was very impolite .............. you to ignore me.
  A with    B of    C for

24 Why didn't you remind me .............. the meeting this morning?
  A about    B for    C to

25 The police are looking .............. the case of the stolen painting.
  A into    B for    C through

26 Mr Jones is always unpleasant .............. his secretary.
  A to    B for    C with

27 The staff are provided .............. uniforms to work in.
  A of    B for    C with

28 Josie made .............. an excuse to explain her lateness.
  A out    B up    C for

29 Andrea has a good relationship .............. her parents.
  A to    B between    C with

30 I couldn't make .............. the name at the end of the letter.
  A out    B up    C for

# Progress Test 5 (Units 9 - 10)

NAME: ..................................................  DATE: ...........................

CLASS: ..................................................  MARK: ...........................

(Time: 30 minutes)

**A** Choose the correct item.

1 Paula ........... going to the beach at the weekend.
   A promised   B suggested   C warned

2 She gave me ............. very useful advice.
   A a   B any   C some

3 Sally bought a ........... of milk at the supermarket.
   A carton   B glass   C block

4 John is very honest. He always ............. the truth.
   A told   B tells   C says

5 My father plays ............. piano very well.
   A a   B an   C the

6 He said he ............. her the following day.
   A will call   B had called   C would call

7 Carl is at ............. school. He will be home soon.
   A a   B –   C the

8 Steve ............. to give me a lift to work.
   A denied   B agreed   C admitted

9 Mark has had a lot of ............. working with cars.
   A experienced   B experiences
   C experience

10 Tom's mum ............. him not to touch the iron.
   A warned   B invited   C offered

11 She ............. that it was a beautiful necklace.
   A threatened   B exclaimed   C promised

12 Those trousers ............. far too big for you.
   A are   B is   C was

13 She ............. to paint the fence for me.
   A invited   B offered   C complained

14 He ate three ............. of toast for breakfast.
   A bars   B loaves   C slices

15 Simon said that he ............. a great time at the party.
   A had had   B has had   C is having

16 We have never been to ............. Italy before.
   A a   B –   C the

17 Alison was ............. first person to arrive at the party.
   A a   B –   C the

18 Neil ............. his mother that he felt ill.
   A told   B said   C told to

19 The police ............. investigating the crime.
   A is   B was   C are

20 He ............. me where I had been all day.
   A asks   B asked   C said

# Progress Test 5 (Units 9 - 10)

**B** Choose the correct item.

21. Carrie was satisfied ............. her school report.
    A of   B about   C with

22. Martin translated the poem ............. Italian for his teacher.
    A into   B of   C from

23. I can't think ............ anything to wear to the party.
    A about   B of   C on

24. My teacher always shouts ............. children who are late.
    A at   B to   C for

25. The secretary put me ............. to the manager.
    A up   B through   C down

26. My little brother is terrified ............. the dark.
    A about   B for   C of

27. Put ............. your coat before you go outside.
    A out   B on   C off

28. We put ................ the meeting because the manager was ill.
    A out   B on   C off

29. James said he was sorry ............. forgetting my birthday.
    A for   B from   C of

30. The thief was sentenced ............ a year in prison.
    A on   B with   C to

# Progress Test 6 (Units 11 - 12)

NAME: .................................................. DATE: ...........................

CLASS: .................................................. MARK: ...........................

(Time: 30 minutes)

**A** Choose the correct item.

1  Jane .............. her hair cut at the moment.
   A  is having    B  has    C  was having

2  Tony had a .............. dream last night.
   A  worse    B  badly    C  bad

3  Colin .............. his wallet stolen twice this year.
   A  will have had    B  had had    C  has had

4  We .............. our house decorated last month.
   A  are having    B  had    C  will have

5  Jodie smiled .................. as she opened her presents.
   A  happy    B  happier    C  happily

6  She gave me a .............. ring for my birthday.
   A  pretty gold little    B  little pretty gold
   C  pretty little gold

7  He .............. his teeth checked twice a year.
   A  has    B  has had
   C  will have had

8  Martin is the .............. boy in the basketball team.
   A  tall    B  taller    C  tallest

9  Kate likes .............. her clothes made for her.
   A  is having    B  having    C  have

10  This box is .............. than the other one.
    A  heavy    B  heavier    C  heaviest

11  Laura is in hospital. She .............. her tonsils taken out.
    A  is having    B  was having    C  has

12  James did very .............. in his exams.
    A  good    B  well    C  better

13  Amy ran .............. up the stairs to her bedroom.
    A  quick    B  quicker    C  quickly

14  I bought a .............. bag at the market.
    A  old leather lovely    B  old lovely leather
    C  lovely old leather

15  We must .............. our car repaired immediately.
    A  have had    B  have    C  be having

16  Paul .............. his windows smashed by a falling tree.
    A  had    B  will have    C  is having

17  The blue dress is .............. the black one.
    A  least expensive of    B  less expensive
    C  less expensive than

18  Diane .............. a dress made for her.
    A  having    B  has    C  has had

19  He found a .............. box in the attic.
    A  black small wooden    B  wooden black small
    C  small black wooden

20  I would prefer .............. at home than go to the theatre.
    A  stay    B  to stay    C  staying

# Progress Test 6 (Units 11 - 12)

 **Choose the correct item.**

21  Mr Brown wants to set ............ his own business.
   **A** up    **B** off    **C** out

22  It was raining, so we stayed ............ home all afternoon.
   **A** in    **B** at    **C** on

23  I ran ............ some old records while I was tidying the attic.
   **A** into    **B** across    **C** after

24  He's been waiting ............ the bus for half an hour.
   **A** of    **B** about    **C** for

25  Everyone stood ............ when the teacher entered the room.
   **A** up to    **B** up    **C** for

26  Mum told me to keep an eye ............ my little sister.
   **A** at    **B** on    **C** in

27  I ran ............ sugar, so I sent Paul to the shops.
   **A** out of    **B** down    **C** after

28  I'm a bit short ............ time; can we talk later?
   **A** on    **B** of    **C** in

29  I got on the wrong bus ............ mistake.
   **A** at    **B** for    **C** by

30  She is very upset ............ losing her job.
   **A** for    **B** about    **C** at

205

# Progress Test 7 (Units 13 - 14)

NAME: ..................................................  DATE: ...........................

CLASS: .................................................  MARK: ...........................

(Time: 30 minutes)

**A** Choose the correct item.

1  We are going to the beach ............. the weekend.
   A in   B on   C at

2  My wallet is in ............. bag over there.
   A this   B that   C those

3  Mary is in hospital. I am going to visit ............. tomorrow.
   A hers   B she   C her

4  I'm going to Paris ............. weekend.
   A this   B that   C these

5  'Which shoes do you like?' 'The black ............. .'
   A one   B ones   C those

6  '............. did you go last night?' 'To a restaurant.'
   A What   B When   C Where

7  My birthday is on a Saturday ............. year.
   A this   B that   C those

8  ............. CDs did you buy yesterday?
   A How much   B How many   C How long

9  Where did you go ............. holiday last year?
   A in   B on   C at

10 '............. jumper is this?' 'It's Tony's.'
   A Which   B Whose   C Who

11 The teacher told us a story ............. the end of the lesson.
   A in   B on   C at

12 I am taller than you, .............?
   A aren't you   B aren't I   C am I

13 There's ............. cheese in the fridge.
   A some   B any   C every

14 Jenny and I haven't seen ............. since we left school.
   A ourselves   B each other   C themselves

15 David left school two years ............. .
   A before   B ago   C while

16 He would love to have a house ............. .
   A himself   B his own   C of his own

17 The children behaved ............. very well at the party.
   A each other   B ourselves   C themselves

18 I have hardly ............. free time these days.
   A some   B any   C no

19 Don't go near the water, .............?
   A won't you   B did you   C will you

20 I've ............. finished my homework.
   A already   B yet   C still

# Progress Test 7 (Units 13 - 14)

 **Choose the correct item.**

21  We congratulated Sam ............ passing his driving test.
    A on    B for    C about

22  Can you be quiet, please. I'm ............ the phone.
    A at    B with    C on

23  Mrs Smith isn't here. She has gone out ............ lunch.
    A at    B for    C with

24  Paul takes ............ his mother. They look very similar.
    A after    B down    C over

25  She turned ............ the light and looked around the room.
    A off    B up    C on

26  We must be home by ten o'clock ............ the latest.
    A in    B on    C at

27  Can I pay for these CDs ............ cheque, please?
    A with    B for    C by

28  Mike turned ............ half an hour late for the meeting.
    A out    B down    C up

29  There are no trains today because the drivers are ............ strike.
    A in    B on    C at

30  I can't forgive her ............ ruining my favourite dress.
    A about    B of    C for

207

# Progress Test 8 (Units 1 - 15)

NAME: ..................................................  DATE: ............................

CLASS: ..................................................  MARK: ............................

(Time: 30 minutes)

**A** Choose the correct item.

1  If I won the lottery, I ............. on an exotic holiday.
   A  will go        B  would go       C  went

2  The TV will have ............. .
   A  to be repaired   B  to have been repaired
   C  being repaired

3  ............. we reached the station, the train had left.
   A  As soon as    B  Until         C  By the time

4  Jason ............. TV at the moment.
   A  watches       B  is watching
   C  was watching

5  It was kind of him ............. me repair the car.
   A  help          B  helping       C  to help

6  He ............. to help me with my homework.
   A  refused       B  denied        C  complained

7  My sister's hair ............. very long.
   A  are           B  is            C  were

8  Claire ............. dinner when the telephone rang.
   A  was eating    B  ate           C  has eaten

9  He ............. be tired. He has been working all day.
   A  must          B  mustn't       C  can't

10  She bought a ............. coat yesterday.
    A  brown lovely leather   B  lovely brown leather
    C  lovely leather brown

11  Janet ............. her house decorated last week.
    A  had          B  has had
    C  will have had

12  She enjoys going to ............. cinema.
    A  a            B  —             C  the

13  ............. jacket over there is Daniel's.
    A  This         B  That          C  Those

14  ............. I borrow your pen, please?
    A  Will         B  Shall         C  Can

15  Tom spent the afternoon .......... on his computer.
    A  play         B  playing       C  to play

16  James' car ............. last night.
    A  is stolen    B  will be stolen
    C  was stolen

17  Paul ............. work by seven o'clock this evening.
    A  has finished    B  will finish
    C  will have finished

18  ............. did you wake up this morning?
    A  What time    B  How long      C  How much

19  Pam ............. her hair cut every six weeks.
    A  has          B  has had       C  will have

20  Sarah hurt ............. when she fell down the stairs.
    A  yourself     B  himself       C  herself

21  The longer he waited, the ............. he felt.
    A  nervous      B  more nervous
    C  most nervous

22  He hasn't finished cleaning the house ............. .
    A  already      B  still         C  yet